THE FIRST STEP

Tait entered the world of outlaw motorcycle gangs in late February 1982.

A brother talked to Tait inside a bar where he bounced. "Come on outside," the biker said.

He walked toward a pickup truck and pointed to a rigid-frame chopper strapped to the bed. "What do you think?"

"It's pretty nice. It's a Harley."

"If you want it, it's yours for $2,500."

"I don't have that kind of money now."

"That's all right. You can pay us when you get it. If you want to pay a buck a week or ten bucks a week. Just take the bike. There's a stipulation. You have to start hanging around."

Tait took the bike.

"[Lavigne is] the journalistic equivalent of Batman."
—*The Globe and Mail*

Hells Angels:
INTO THE ABYSS

Yves Lavigne

HarperCollins*Publishers*Limited

http://www.harpercollins.com/canada

First published in hardcover by HarperCollins Publishers Ltd: 1996
First HarperCollins Publishers Ltd mass market edition: 1997

Canadian Cataloguing in Publication Data

Lavigne, Yves, 1953-
    Hells Angels : into the abyss

ISBN 0-00-638570-2

1. Tait, Anthony.   2. Hell's Angels.   3. Motorcycle gangs -
North America.   4. Organized crime - North America.
5. Undercover operations - North America.   I. Title.

HV6453.N7L38 1996   364.1'06'07   C-95-932445-3

---

    01 02 03 04 /❖ OP/ 10

Printed and bound in the United States

*To those who fight against the
tyranny and terror of crime*

"He who fights with monsters should look to it that he himself does not become a monster. And when you gaze long into an abyss, the abyss also gazes into you."

Friedrich Nietzsche,
Beyond Good and Evil

"Men may be without restraints upon their liberty; they may pass to and fro at pleasure; but if their steps are tracked by spies and informers, their words noted down for crimination, their associates watched as conspirators—who should say that they are free?"

Sir Thomas May,
19th-century British
constitutional scholar

Introduction

THE DARKNESS OF CRIME lies not in its villainy or horror but in the souls of those who choose to live their lives in the abyss. A man who toils from youth to old age to violate the line that divides civilization from wilderness; who proclaims he is not of society but an outsider sworn to break its laws and rules, yet who readily seeks refuge in its lenient legal system, embraces its judicial paternalism and gains sustenance from its moral weakness; whose very existence as an outlaw is defined by society's being, is but a shadow of the real world, bereft of freedom and doomed to tag along in society's wake.

Such is the plight of the Hells Angels, who impudently claim to be the last free men, though shackled by their narrow vision of life to a violent ride on a dead-end road of their own making.

The Hells Angels Motorcycle Club was formed on March 17, 1948, and incorporated in 1966 as a club "dedicated to the promotion and advancement of motorcycle riding, motorcycle clubs, motorcycle highway safety and all phases of motorcycling and motorcycle driving." Club leader Sonny Barger, who spent 13 years in jail, spouted one phrase repeatedly over five decades:

"The Hells Angels are not involved in anything but motorcycling."

On paper, the Hells Angels Motorcycle Club is harmless. On asphalt, the club harbors insidious crime syndicates that bribe, corrupt and kill to expand their drug-financed underworld empires. The club consists of a large number of seasoned criminals who use the fear and intimidation fostered by its reputation for taking care of business, as well as its vast network of associates, to further their criminal ends. The Hells Angels Motorcycle Club shelters first-rate criminal gangs wealthy enough to shield their operations with the best lawyers and public relations consultants drug money can buy.

Drug businesses prosper while members are jailed. The club even has a prison newsletter for its many jailed members: *H.A.M.C. World B.H.C. Newsletter*. (That stands for Hells Angels Motorcycle Club World Big House Crew.) The Big House Crew tattoo has the name printed on a curled banner beneath the winged Death's Head that is the centerpiece of the club's colors. San Diego Hells Angel David (OB Dave) Harbridge edits the monthly newsletter, which named 102 Hells Angels behind bars on April 11, 1988, in one of its first issues.

The newsletter includes updates on who's incarcerated where, the status of conviction appeals by Hells Angels, letters from imprisoned Angels around the world and newspaper clippings of members' arrests, trials and convictions. Hells Angels trade information on how to appeal convictions and non-association clauses in their paroles that prohibit them from hanging out with other Angels.

Hells Angels: Taking Care of Business, my first account of the Hells Angels in 1987, was a venture into fear. *Hells Angels: Into the Abyss* tells a similar tale of evil. It exposes the souls of men who seek not the light without but embrace the darkness within. Men in whose desolate hearts the seeds of evil sprout at the behest of wicked minds.

The book charts the life of Hells Angel Anthony Tait, a Federal Bureau of Investigation informant made into a walking microphone-transmitter that became the proverbial fly on the wall and broadcast intimate and secret conversations to hidden tape recorders.

It recounts the story of the FBI's most successful operation against the Hells Angels, and details Tait's rise through the club ranks until he became one of its most powerful officers.

Being a Hells Angel is a lifestyle. This book goes inside that lifestyle and charts a cast of liars, thieves, killers, hookers and drug dealers entwined in skeins of evil, lust, violence and fear—a netherworld where often more affection is given to animals than to people.

It listens to members plot murders and watches them deal drugs. It eavesdrops on self-described American legend Sonny Barger as he talks about everything from dogs to death, as he expresses his fear of the Internal Revenue Service, the FBI and the oversexed, underaged women that members bring to the clubhouse.

It peers behind the façade of brotherly love and respect the Hells Angels present to a naive world and shows them use violence against their own and rat on each other to save their hides.

It documents how they steal from each other, mistrust and spy on one another, casually trade in drugs and death and boast of the hard-earned abilities to manufacture in clandestine laboratories methamphetamine, the white-trash drug of choice.

It peers over their shoulders as they stuff crates of drug dollars into counting machines and fudge computer spreadsheets to cheat partners, bury millions of drug dollars in their yards, then pettily bicker at club meetings about the right of poorer Hells Angels to sell T-shirts, bumper stickers, key tags and mugs to make ends meet.

It records the bitter rivalry between East Coast and West Coast Hells Angels as the arrogance of the Oakland chapter runs rampant over the club and the oldest and richest Hells Angels impose their callous will and yuppie ideals on less powerful members.

The FBI's Operation CACUS centered on an informant who allowed law enforcement to penetrate the darkest recesses of the world's most publicized and mythologized outlaw motorcycle gang. While I was on a research trip to California in 1990 for my second book, *Good Guy, Bad Guy*, my friend Bert Sousa, a Sacramento Police Department officer who investigated the Hells Angels when he wasn't flying attack helicopters for the military, suggested I meet Anthony Tait and write a book about Operation CACUS.

I met Tait in 1991 by the side of FBI Special Agent Tim McKinley's pool in the Bay Area and got sunburned as we talked through the afternoon. Tait said he would talk for 50 percent of the book's profits. Tait had optioned the rights to his story to a Los Angeles writer for one year, and I would not deal with Tait until rights reverted to him. Bert Sousa persisted in his attempts to persuade me to write the story. In September of 1992, after a year of talks and preliminary research to assure myself the tale was worth telling, Tait signed the rights to his story over to me.

Tait and I had spent two weeks together that spring as I drove a convertible Chrysler LeBaron through scenic California on a tour that started on the Pacific Coast highway, cruised through Los Angeles and gobbled up roads in the arid central valley. He packed a bag full of guns in the trunk, including a Ruger Mini-14 .223-caliber rifle with folding stock and an assortment of handguns.

The first night, we stopped in Santa Maria and shared a motel room. Tait pulled out his Browning Hi-Power 9-mm pistol, his favorite gun, and put it on the bedside table. I awoke on East Coast time—middle of the night in California—with a desperate need to pee. Tait's bed lay between me and the bathroom. I didn't know how edgy Tait was and worried that he'd shoot a shadow at the foot of his bed. It was a miserable night. I established a ground rule the next morning: ask before you shoot.

The next night, we cruised motel parking lots in San Bernardino in search of potential Hells Angels cars before we settled on a place for the night. Tait handed me a five-shot .38-caliber revolver with a shrouded hammer to keep by the bed. If shit happened, I had to fend for myself. Fair enough. He also took the bed farthest from the door, with me in between. I told him where I would dive if something happened. I didn't want bullets from two directions.

At the end of the first week, we headed north on I-5 to the San Francisco area. I pulled in at a rest stop so Tait could relieve himself. I watched him in the rearview mirror as he walked away. He wore a T-shirt and god-awful shorts that would have scared a gator off a Florida golf course. How could someone who looked like a salesman from Dubuque, Iowa, have infiltrated the Hells Angels and risen so high in the club's ranks? I realized then that I would have to get further into Anthony Tait's head than anyone had been to understand the drives that propelled him into the underworld and then into the arms of law enforcement to sell out his fellow bikers.

Tait was a curious mix of contradictions. He told tales of violence and sex and relished both. Yet he claimed to be profoundly shocked by the language in my first book, which was praised even by octogenarians for its gritty realism.

Tait provided whatever information he could remember during taped interviews in California and over the telephone. He left a lengthy paper trail that I assembled over the next four years to verify every anecdote. Information on Tait's less-than-honorable discharge from the army and his misadventures in Alaska were obtained from court records. In 1993 the military upgraded the discharge to a general discharge. I sought incidents to illuminate Tait's attitude toward life to help readers understand the man and his "accomplishments."

The bulk of the story was obtained from court

records filed by the FBI and through interviews with Operation CACUS agents, the Bureau of Alcohol, Tobacco and Firearms, the California Bureau of Narcotic Enforcement and the Western States Information Network. I made copious use of my own files accumulated over 18 years of investigating outlaw motorcycle gangs.

Except for Tait, no persons interviewed for this book were paid. They offered their time, expertise and comments on a purely professional basis to further public understanding of the menace posed to society by the members of the Hells Angels Motorcycle Club who are active criminals.

The Hells Angels organization has changed considerably since its postwar formation by footloose servicemen, but the values and morals of its members have remained consistent. The Hells Angels don't know who drafted their club emblem, the Death's Head. They do know it was ripped off from the military, as was their name. The Death's Head is a skull with a pilot's helmet and pilot's wings. A skull with wings is a longstanding air force emblem.

The name Hells Angels was taken from several bomber squadrons in World War I. Howard Hughes's 1930 movie *Hell's Angels* with Jean Harlow brought the name to public attention. The fabled Flying Tigers in China under Gen. Claire Chennault named one of its three squadrons of fighters Hell's Angels. The 188th Airborne Division in Korea also called itself Hell's Angels.

Despite this bold appropriation of name and image from the public domain, the Hells Angels brazenly use their club colors to intimidate society and mark themselves as outlaws.

They have for the past decade filed discrimination suits against bars that won't serve bikers who wear club colors. The suits illustrate how the Hells Angels, despite their claim that they are outlaws who wish to live outside society's laws and norms, are double-dealing social wannabes. The Hells Angels use courts and laws at every opportunity to justify and legitimize their existence. They beg and bully society to recognize them. They contrive situations that allow them to fight in court for public recognition. They choose the rights they want to be theirs. If society didn't exist, they'd invent it out of need.

The Hells Angels are like the coward who hides behind a woman's skirt. The skirt in which they cloak their crimes is that of justice. They bury their two-sided faces in its folds and cry injustice at every attempt to foil their criminal enterprises. Like many other predatory minority groups in North America today, they hope to intimidate a bureaucracy-laden justice system into giving them carte blanche to elevate their rights above those of their victims.

The Hells Angels no longer deserve the label "outlaw." They were once rebels. They are now middle-aged snivelers. The more they whine, the more the winged Death's Head grows to resemble Bozo the Clown on drugs.

The rival Outlaws Motorcycle Club has a saying: "All Hells Angels Must Die." The Hells Angels died a long time ago. All that remains is the trademark skeletal, grinning Death's Head that sucks on society's teat.

Wean the little bastard.

One

SONNY BARGER WAS PRIMED to kick ass. Some Hells Angels had breached his order—a decree from the world's most powerful Hells Angel—and they were going to suffer the consequences big time.

Members of the motorcycle club's Oakland chapter had met at their 4019 Foothill Boulevard clubhouse shortly before 7:00 that Wednesday night. Hungry for blood, they mounted their Harleys and pulled away, two abreast, to form a daunting procession designed to show force. Thunder rolled through Oakland streets, over the Bay Bridge to gaily colored San Francisco and along Freeway 280. The grinning Death's Heads that adorned the Angels' backs were to have another reason to smile that day.

Hells Angels representatives from western U.S. and Canadian chapters filed into the San Francisco club-house at 1199 Tennessee Street, milled around the large second floor and waited for a scheduled West Coast Officers' Meeting to start. The Hells Angels Motorcycle Club is a highly structured organization whose chapters hold weekly meetings called church to discuss problems

and plan activities. Chapter representatives in turn meet
monthly to share information from around the country
and troubleshoot. Hells Angels in the western United
States and Canada do so at WesCOMs; eastern U.S. and
Canadian chapters air their beefs at East Coast Officers'
Meetings, or ECOMs.

George (Gus) Christie, president of both the
Ventura chapter and the West Coast Officers, prepared
to call the meeting to order.

Anthony Tait, sergeant-at-arms for the Anchorage
chapter—Barger would soon make him West Coast
sergeant-at-arms—complained about the donuts. Tait
hated stale donuts.

Tait wore many hats, all of them linked to the violent side of the Hells Angels. As Anchorage sergeant-at-
arms, he kept order in meetings and provided clubhouse
security. As Anchorage security officer, he monitored
police radio frequencies on runs, provided security and
set up watch lists for clubhouse and campsite guard
duty. As intelligence officer, he compiled data on known
police informants, club enemies and outlaw motorcycle
gangs. He was also the Alaska trademark officer, keeping
tabs on anyone the club felt violated its name and
Death's Head logo.

Tait put his donut and coffee on the table and sat
across from Vallejo chapter president Derrick Wayne
(Kanack) Kualapai. Some members of Kualapai's chapter
weren't popular with the club because they remained
friends and drug-dealing partners of former Oakland
Angel Terrence Damien (Terry) Dalton, who had been
expelled from the club in April for stealing at least
$3,000 from a drawer in the Oakland clubhouse. Given
the opportunity to confess at an Oakland church, he had
not done so, so some Angels beat him severely, pistol-
whipped him, put a gun in his mouth and threatened to
blow his brains out. Then they painfully covered his club
tattoos, confiscated all his property and escorted him and
his family out of town with nothing but the clothes on
their backs. Finally, they warned him not to return. All

this is standard practice—if an expelled Hells Angel is allowed to live.

Tait knew of the incident because Oakland president Michael Vincent (Irish) O'Farrell had reported it at a recent WesCOM. But Hells Angels politics were the last thing on Tait's mind as he sat next to Kualapai. He just couldn't get over the fact that whoever bought donuts when San Francisco hosted the WesCOM couldn't find fresh ones.

Across the street and a few buildings over, three men huddled behind the concrete parapet on the roof of a five-storey building and listened intently to the voices that spilled from the speaker of a tape recorder in a padded briefcase that lay in the cooling gravel. FBI Special Agent Timothy McKinley, Special Agent Theodore Baltas of the Bureau of Alcohol, Tobacco and Firearms and Special Agent Dave Tresmontan of the California Bureau of Narcotic Enforcement wanted to ensure the transmitter planted on their spy was picking up the clubhouse conversation clearly.

Their operation was a historic one. For the first time ever, law enforcement was tearing the cloak of secrecy that surrounded Hells Angels meetings, listening to them and taping what they heard. McKinley and Baltas had been doing so since the spring, not only for the information they garnered but to ensure they could rush in and prevent certain death for their spy if he were discovered.

The spy had worked for the FBI since 1985. A patch-wearing Hells Angel since 1983 but associated with the club for much longer, he was the most valuable asset the law enforcement intelligence community had ever had in the biker underworld. No one had ever infiltrated the Hells Angels, let alone risen so rapidly to its top ranks. He had access to all information and was part of the group that planned and decided. He partied and politicked with the club's most notorious drug manufacturers, dealers and killers, who all accepted him as one of them. He made his mark and was known for his violence and shrewd judgment. He took care of business. He was, by all appearances, loyal to the club. But he answered to the Hells Angels' enemies. Anthony Tait was a spy in hell.

At around 7:30, a dull roar prompted Baltas to raise his head and scan the elevated Freeway 280 half a mile away. About 20 Hells Angels were coming. The roar grew louder until the motorcycles blasted down Tennessee Street past the lookout and stopped at the clubhouse.

McKinley, Baltas and Tresmontan heard the bikes before the Angels in the building did. Now the roar came from the speaker at their feet. They heard what the Angels in the meeting room heard. But Anthony Tait and his brothers had no idea who was at the door or that within minutes, all hell was going to break loose.

The Oakland Angels backed their bikes to the curb. Barger, Elliot Serrano (Cisco) Valderrama, chapter vice-president, and 375-pound Albert (Big Al) Perryman strode into the clubhouse with a television set, a VCR and a stack of videotapes. Barger didn't greet anyone, apologize or ask permission to interrupt. Although West Coast Officers carry more juice on paper than individual chapter or charter heads, not one man complained at the intrusion and show of disrespect for a group of influential Hells Angels involved in one of the club's most important meetings. Such is the power and fear wielded by Sonny Barger and the Oakland chapter, the world's premiere group of Hells Angels. The others, who called him Chief, dared not move as Barger took care of business.

Valderrama spoke first. "We have a situation here," he said. "And we'd like to get it out of the way before we go on with the meeting. We'd first like to ask anybody if there is any reason that anybody needs to see the tape that we made of Terry [Dalton] before he was kicked out. I'd like to know. If anybody has any doubt in their minds and needs to see the tape, I'd like them to raise their hand now."

No one reacted. A raised hand meant its owner

didn't accept the Oakland Angels' word that Terry Dalton had been expelled for good reason, and such a show of disrespect would merit a severe beating.

"Okay, so we're going to go ahead and show it. I'll explain it as we go along. The main reason why is that nobody raised their hand in here, but we have had questions about this fucking guy before, from people that evidently don't believe what the fuck happened.

"Now, we have a whole bunch of tapes. You guys want to see 'em all, I'll show 'em all to you. You want to just see a couple of them to show what it is, I'll just show a couple."

Now Barger put his hand over the patch that covers the hole in his throat where his cancerous larynx was replaced with an electronic voice box. "What is happening is we had money from Germany that we collected. And Krusi [Werner Sohm] had it in a drawer in our back room. And the money kept disappearing and disappearing. We put a video camera (with a fisheye lens on the fiberoptic cable) in the ceiling and we caught the guy. We left it in there 'cause we wanted to make sure that it wasn't more than one person.

"We got four or five tapes of one guy. Our problem is, and I'm glad nobody raised their hand, is that we said this guy stole money from our treasury and we threw him out of the club and we do not want him around any Hells Angels. We told him that. And we said at this meeting, we do not want any Hells Angels around him. And if we catch any around him, we're going to treat them the same way we treat him.

"Now, we are going to show you the tape of why we are gonna treat a certain charter the way we're going to treat them. And that's like we treated him: we blocked out his tattoo and we kicked his ass. And we're going to do that to at least four other Hells Angels after everybody sees this tape."

The Angels talked softly to each other as the VCR was hooked up to a television set.

"Okay," Valderrama continued. "We threw a video camera up on top to show down here because there's where the money is being taken out of. Money had been missing there for a long period. I mean a long, long period. As money kept being missing and was brought to our attention somebody's been taking the money, we didn't believe so we counted it."

"We'd be missing like 20, 40, 50, 60 dollars at a time," Irish O'Farrell said.

"Like about every week," Valderrama said. "And sometimes 100, sometimes 80, sometimes 40, sometimes 20. But remember, this happened over a period of a long time. It took us a long time just to get our shit together to get the camera in there. We even had marked money. Some of it was in our change machine."

"That's our back mailroom," Barger said as an overhead view of a room appeared on the television screen.

Talk resumed quietly around the table as the narration stopped and the video continued.

"We have six tapes here of three days each tape," Valderrama said, "after we got our shit together. Now mind you, money'd been missing a long time before that. We caught him a few times taking the money out. Every time we caught him in the room, money was then missing 'cause the money was checked every day. And then when so much money was taken out it was so conspicuous [we] couldn't let him do it. And then when we did have it on videotape we let it go ahead a week or so to make sure there wasn't anybody else at all . . .

"Still, we wanted the fucking proof. Now we have all these tapes for anybody that doesn't believe us that wants to check them out. And fuck anybody that doesn't believe us now."

"Our problem," said Irish, "is that we had a member from another charter call and tell us that he had seen Terry over at one of his member's houses. He told them he didn't feel it was right, and then he called us. He didn't tell us the names of those members that have been associating with him because he didn't want to say their names without them standing there. Which I understand but don't completely agree with it because if you're talking one Hells Angel to another, it shouldn't make any difference.

"Be that as it may, he called us and told us this, and then he went and told them to call us, to contact us. So then we got a call from Kanack. And I want to know if he'd tell us now the names of the people that are associating with him or having anything to do with him."

Kanack squirmed in his seat and admitted he had seen Dalton and his child. He was a business associate and friend of Dalton's and couldn't just sever ties.

"Kick him out of your house," Barger rasped loudly.

"This came out last night," Kanack Kualapai shot back. "My charter did not hear about a phone call, that we were supposed to call Oakland. People he's staying with heard that it was being looked on in a bad light. That's all it is."

"You don't care how we feel about you!" Barger yelled.

"No, no," Kualapai objected.

"We said it exactly like this," Valderrama said. "When we kicked Terry out, we told him and we told everybody else that anybody that associates with Terry, we're going to treat them the exact same way as we treat Terry. And that's as our enemy."

Kualapai said he hadn't been told that Oakland didn't want anyone to associate with Dalton.

"Now Terry has been kicked out of our club," Barger said. "He has been told to not hang around a Hells Angel. We're telling you to tell your club that. Anybody that is around him will be treated exactly like him. We didn't finish the job and we should have."

Kualapai tried to interject.

"Let me finish," Barger said. "If we find him in anybody's house, the person whose house he's found in will be dealt with exactly like him, whether the guy is a member or not. And I want that made plain. We, the Oakland Hells Angels, are ready to go to war with your charter or anybody else's in this room that does not like what we just said."

"We kicked the fuckin' punk out of the club. And if any Hells Angel wants to run around with a fucking punk, that's what they are. I hope I made myself clear. And I hope it gets back to every charter just . . . like . . . that."

"Do you know where he's at now?" O'Farrell asked.

"Yeah," replied Kualapai.

"Is he at a member's house now?"

"I don't know."

"Was this made plain that every member of Vallejo should be here?" O'Farrell asked.

Kanack mumbled something inaudible.

"I personally feel that if you told them they didn't have to show up, or you told them that they did and they didn't, *that* is very bad," Barger said. "And they will be treated with disrespect whether they are Hells Angels or not.

"We took our time to come over here. We want this straightened out and if it was a misunderstanding, they should have been the first ones here to try and straighten it out. If there was not a misunderstanding, they did the right thing by staying away, 'cause they knew what would happen to them."

"Beyond that, I took all the stuff out of Terry's house," Kualapai said. "I talked to you and it came up at the OM. And then I'd gotten a phone call the morning that it happened. And I really feel that I conveyed it the way I understood it, that it would be a disrespect to you people. But, as far as being dealt with the same way as Terry was, I don't remember that part coming up."

Angels around the table could see that Kualapai was fumbling, and it whetted their bloodlust.

"I remember it," yelled one. "Yeah," said another.

"I told it to you," said Valderrama. "I remember that. I remember fuckin' sayin' it."

Gerald Michael (Butch) Lester, a Vallejo member who was charged in 1995 with the brutal 1986 murder of a former Hells Angel member, realized his ass was on the line and took action to save it. He kicked back his chair and attacked Kualapai, his president, who easily thrashed him. Then an Oakland Angel lunged at

Kualapai and began to punch him viciously until Big Al
Perryman lumbered over and crushed Kualapai against
the wall with his large gut. He choked Kualapai with one
hand and punched him with the other, but the fat man
soon tired and grew short of breath. He gasped for air
and let Kualapai slide to the floor. Mark Perry, a badass
Oakland member, kicked, stomped on and punched
Kualapai and bit him in the face.

McKinley, Baltas and Tresmontan had no idea what was
going on. They had expected another relatively boring
Officers' Meeting, but now they could hear fists smacking
flesh so close to the spy's transmitter that it seemed he
must be the person being beaten. The severe beating lasted
a full minute and a half. McKinley and Baltas were prepared to rush into the clubhouse to save Tait. It would
mean blowing the best investigation the FBI had ever conducted against the Hells Angels, but bureau rules state that
the informant's safety comes ahead of everything else.

They waited for Tait to mouth the bust code, a call
for immediate help. But the words "My mother isn't
going to like this" were not uttered. Instead, they heard
Tait exclaim: "That's a pretty good asskicking." They
knew he was safe.

"That's enough," Barger said. "Now, if you know
where the motherfucker's at, we want to know."

"He's . . . out to Brentwood . . . but I don't know the
address," Kualapai replied as he gasped for breath.

"When you find it out, you call one of our —"
Barger started to say when he was interrupted by an
Angel who yelled: "Is he out there to Dexter's"—Vallejo
Angel Larry Leon Ditmar's—"farm out there in fucking
Brentwood?"

There was no answer.

"Let's get this back to order now," O'Farrell ordered.
The Oakland Hells Angels left abruptly and Kualapai and
another Vallejo member slipped away, but the meeting
went on until 11:00, business as usual.

San Francisco vice-president Stephen Jay (Big Steve or Frisco Steve) Nelson reported he had confronted a man who was wearing a fake embroidered Death's Head on his denim jacket in front of the Dudley-Perkins Harley-Davidson Motorcycle shop in San Francisco. He forced the man to remove the jacket, but did not take it from him for fear of being charged with strong-armed robbery. A few irate Angels asked what the policy was on pulling patches. One Angel had spent a year in jail for forcibly pulling a fake patch.

WesCOM policy is that a Hells Angel must take, by force if necessary, any insignia that vaguely resembles the Death's Head, O'Farrell said. If the insignia is being worn by a manufacturer, alert the trademark attorneys. Gordon Gary (Flash) Grow, WesCOM trademark officer, said the Hells Angels needed $4,000 for legal fees to perfect their trademark.

Anthony Tait forgot about his stale donut.

Anthony Tait's father taught him how to survive. Survival is a dirty art, and Gordon Tait learned it professionally. He was born in Scotland, boxed professionally and worked for a shipping line before he enlisted in the British Army during World War II and worked as an intelligence officer. After the war he served in the British Army of Occupation in Palestine. He was a captain in the Palestinian police in Haifa and hunted Menachem Begin, Moshe Dayan and Yitzhak Shamir, who were then terrorists who blew up the King David Hotel. He returned to Britain to find jobs were so scarce that colonels and majors took minor office chores. He boxed in Europe, married and moved to Alaska, where it would be difficult for the "terrorists" he had hunted to fulfill the contract they had put on his head for hanging their supporters. He changed his name from Samuel Gordon Tait to Gordon Samuel Tait. His son Anthony John was six years old when he arrived on the last frontier in 1960.

Gordon Tait taught his son the skills he thought a

man needed to make it in a violent world. He stressed
the power of observation as the most important weapon
in a man's arsenal. They stood on a corner or on a ship
and Gordon told his son to take in the scene for a
minute. He made him turn around and describe what he
saw. Tait described more and more details. Gordon made
his son count cars, differentiate makes and models,
remember what else happened in the area when the car
passed, what the driver looked like and wore. He made
him look for anything out of the norm.

Gordon showed Tait how to put a hair in a lock's
keyway and taught him to dust talcum powder so lightly
on a doorknob it could not be seen but left telltale marks
if touched. He warned that when he went into an unfa-
miliar "hot" area not to sleep in the bed because a killer
who bursts into a room shoots into the bed first. He also
suggested Tait fill a trashcan with water in case someone
threw a firebomb into the room. At age 14, Tait learned
to rock a car before he got into it in case someone had
placed a bomb with a mercury switch underneath it.

Gordon taught his son to shoot a rifle, shotgun and
handgun. He thought his son was a "piss-poor pistol
shot" but a great shotgunner. Tait learned karate and
how to box and throw knives. Tait liked to learn a little
about everything, but never dedicated himself to the
mastery of one skill.

"Martial arts are okay, but they're a lot of shit," he
would say. "It doesn't matter what kind of punch knocks
you out. If you're knocked out, you're knocked out." Tait
was aggressive and chose to take the offense rather than
a defensive stance. When Gordon owned a bakery, they
sat on stacks of 100-pound flour sacks, baited bluejays
and magpies with bread crusts thrown out a window and
shot them with a .22-caliber rifle.

Tait picked up a wanderlust from his father, a need
to move on when things got too comfortable. Tait moved
from job to job, woman to woman. "Everybody lives on
the edge" was his philosophy. "If you don't, you're not
savoring the full auspice of life. To get up in the morn-

ing, go into an office and sell insurance and come home
to look at a fat wife and a couple of snotty brat kids, and
you've got a shitty old station wagon to drive, that to me
would be as big a ball and chain as you could ever get.
That's not living. That's just eking out an existence.
You've got to enjoy yourself.

"A son can't have the same kind of relationship with
a mother that he does with a father," Tait would say.
"Especially if your interests lie in the same area. I love
my mother and I've learned a lot from her. I learned how
to dance real well from her because it's part of her
upbringing in Scotland. Her family was well off so I had
to learn how to play the piano and dance and my mother
got me interested in the violin. She tried to get me into
art, but I didn't like art. I always thought Picasso was
weird. I liked the older artists, Michelangelo, da Vinci."

Tait's military career was brief and troubled. He was not
cut out to take orders.

The recruiting office sent Tait his plane ticket
shortly after his seventeenth birthday on May 27, 1971.
He had just finished a controversial tenth grade during
which he was seen as a discipline problem. Tait enlisted
on June 15 and went through nine weeks of basic training at Fort Lewis, Washington, followed by advanced
individual training. Tait disagreed with the way the army
taught self-defense. He told them he was way out of their
league and mocked the names they gave various martial-
arts moves.

His basic infantry course covered demolition,
grenade launchers, mortars, machine guns, anti-tank
mines and light anti-tank weapon (LAWs) rockets. He
received four weeks of paratrooper school at Fort
Benning, Georgia, then went to Fort Bragg, North
Carolina, and the 82nd Airborne Division, which sent
him back to Fort Benning for the mountaineering phase
of the Ranger school. He flew to Panama for the jungle
phase of the course.

Tait re-enlisted on April 11, 1972, and asked to be posted to Alaska. He was transferred from Fort Bragg to the US Army 4th Battalion, 23rd Infantry, 172 Light Infantry Brigade at Fort Richardson, outside Anchorage. Tait's problems began when he found himself with time on his hands.

He went AWOL from Fort Richardson in July 1972 for 27 days. He knew the Uniform Code of Military Justice and made sure he reported before 30 days, after which he would have been considered a deserter. Tait was busted one grade in rank, fined and restricted to barracks for two weeks. He took the bus to the main post to do his laundry without asking permission. He was fined again.

Tait ran into his former platoon sergeant as they moved equipment lockers from one building to another on January 2, 1973.

"You see that mimeograph machine over there?" the sergeant said. "If you get me that thing, I'll wangle you some three-day passes. We'll use it in the training office."

Tait picked up the machine and put it in the same truck they used to move their equipment lockers. He never got the passes.

The sergeant approached Tait again on January 14. "There's a typewriter at the servicemen's club that's sitting on the bench. We could really use that thing."

"Okay."

"You did a great job last time. You get that thing there and I guarantee you a couple of days off. Anything else you want?"

"Yeah, I want one of those fancy Vietnam wristwatches."

"Okay. We got a bunch of them in supply."

Tait took the typewriter.

One month later, he was called to the military police investigator's office.

"I'm going to read you your rights. We have reason to believe you misappropriated a government typewriter and a government mimeograph machine."

"I didn't do anything like that. I was asked to pick

something up and I did." Tait said he did not consider taking the equipment theft because it remained on the base.

Tait gave investigators information on the theft of parachutes and protective masks. He pleaded guilty during a special court-martial. He was busted in rank from private E-2 to buck private E-1, made to forfeit his salary of $150 a month for three months and confined at the U.S. Army Retraining Brigade in Fort Riley, Kansas, for 60 to 70 days. He spent the first two weeks of his sentence—from April 27 to May 9—in stockade in Alaska awaiting the transfer.

On his release from Fort Riley, Tait was assigned to the 3rd Armored Cavalry Regiment in Fort Bliss, Texas. The commanding officer there was hard on the reconnaissance platoon. He made them run through the desert all night doing reconnaissance for tanks and armored scout vehicles. Tait didn't think that was how the job should be done; he thought the most they should do was 15 miles a night. Tait also felt he didn't get enough time off. They trained for six days and on Sundays they cleaned their gear. Monday morning came too early for Tait.

Recon units were loaded onto C-130 transport planes and flown overseas on October 6, 1973. Tait and his fellow soldiers weren't told where they were going or what for. All they knew was that they ended up somewhere hot inside a hangar large enough to house six C-130s. Soldiers were confined to the building to stay hidden from Soviet spy satellites. They couldn't cook for two weeks and ate C-rations they washed down with water delivered by water buffalo planes that sat on the hot tarmac all day.

The soldiers knew something was up. They were issued more equipment than they had ever used in training: two LAWs rockets each, four hand grenades instead of one, 1,000 rounds of .223-caliber ammunition. They did jumping jacks, squat thrusts, situps and pushups all day. They ran around the hangar. Then they were put back on the planes and flown back to Fort Bliss. They didn't know until later, when they read newspapers on their return to the United States, that they had been on standby in Iran as Israel fought the Yom Kippur War against Egyptian and Syrian invaders.

Tait was fed up with the army. "This is a sack of shit. I've had about enough of this." He teamed up with two other soldiers, one of whom had a car, and went AWOL again. They drove east for nearly a month and reported themselves AWOL at Fort George G. Meade, Maryland, after another 27 days on the lam.

The army sent them to a facility while it decided what to do with the wayward soldiers.

"We don't want to go back. We want to stay right here and do a regular assignment," Tait and his buddies said.

But they had messed up. They didn't know Fort Meade was a discharge unit. They were held for four months, until March 1974. Tait was given an "undesirable discharge." A psychiatric evaluation found no evidence of abnormality but noted that Tait had an explosive personality.

No one at Fort Bliss was notified that Tait had reported at Fort Meade. A note was put into his file: "Private E-2 Anthony Tait was dropped from the rolls as a deserter on October 16, though a letter was sent from this unit to his home he has never tried to contact this unit."

After discharge Tait worked at various jobs along the eastern seaboard, including a construction job. He approached an undercover cop who lived in his building and informed on a couple of PCP and heroin pushers on the work site. Later he traveled to McLean, Virginia, and applied for a job with the Central Intelligence Agency. He wrote a battery of tests, which he said were simple. They told him there was no place in the outfit for someone with less than a high-school education and who spoke only one language.

"You need people like me," Tait told the CIA.

"Not any more. We don't do that stuff. We'll get in touch with you if we need you."

* * *

In a town where men outnumber women seven to one and hookers fetch $300 a blowjob, everyone loves a female who gives it away free. Anchorage was such a town in the late 1970s and early 1980s. And bars like the Wild Cherry Saloon were places where gratuitous sex was likely to happen. Anthony Tait, bouncer and doorman at several downtown Anchorage bars, laughed at the women he called Quaalude Queens, though there was nothing regal about their behavior. They staggered around, flopped to the floor and had to be carried out.

Tait, five-foot-eleven and 180 pounds, looked like a young version of John Le Carré's George Smiley with his thick glasses. He watched one woman lose it 90 minutes after she downed quaaludes with her drink.

"I'm going to fuck every guy in this club," she announced to a wall of smiles. Nine or ten guys milled around a parked car in minus-20-degree weather for the rest of the evening and waited their turn to mount the woman who lay spread on the back seat.

The experience would forever shape Tait's perception and treatment of women. "I haven't got a whole lot of respect for some women," he said more than once.

Bikers occasionally came into one of the clubs where Tait worked and tried to impress him. They flashed rolls of money and snorted lines of cocaine off the bar.

"Listen," Tait would tell them, "if you want to do that, do it somewhere else or use my office, but don't do it here on the bar in front of me." He didn't want the club to lose its liquor license. Such incidents were uncommon, though, because bikers were not allowed to wear colors in discos where patrons were well dressed. But cleaner-cut members of the Brothers Motorcycle Club cruised the bars, slipped quaaludes to some babe and the next thing you know, half a dozen guys pumped her in the parking lot.

Tait didn't dislike bikers. He hadn't seen enough of them to develop a hatred. But he had a sharp eye and a

sharper memory. And the Brothers Motorcycle Club
brazenly paraded business in Anchorage.

Tait either liked or disliked people. There were few
in-betweens in his world. He didn't like pimps and he
didn't like black guys who worked white women. One
night, while he served drinks, a black pimp in a cream-
colored suit got on his nerves, banging the bar with a
jeweled hand as he demanded service. He asked repeatedly for an Alka-Seltzer in club soda. Tait told him he
didn't have any. The man demanded it. Tait mixed
the drink with Ajax. He stirred it well and passed it to
the customer. The man tensed within a minute and a
half. His stomach knotted and cramped. He sweated. He
clenched his butt, coolly slipped off the stool and pen-
guin-walked to the door. A huge, runny brown patch
stained the backside of his cream-colored pants. Tait had
several tricks to make troublemakers shit themselves. A
person with loaded drawers tends to fade into the night.

Tait first met the Brothers in 1976. For the two previous years he worked as a bull cook who washed floors
for a company on the North Slope region of Alaska with
Dan Wilcox, a Brothers associate. Tait's father had
helped him falsify the application for the North Slope
job. On it, Tait said he had graduated from high school
and had a year of college. (In fact, he completed grade
10.) He used an uncle as a reference. He said he spoke
Thai fluently. He lied about his military service, the type
of discharge he received and his court-martial.

One of Wilcox's two sisters lived with Anchorage
Brother Charlie Potter, and Wilcox and Tait went to visit.
Tait met Brothers Montgomery (Monty) Elliott and
Chester Williams. Elliott was not a mope like most
Brothers. He drove Corvettes and packed his cocaine in
salmon cans. The bikers talked to Tait about guns. Tait
watched Elliott handle his .380-caliber Mauser with leather
gloves to keep his fingerprints off the metal. Tait emptied
his pockets and showed them his Walther PPK and Colt
Cobra snub-nose .38. Elliott commented that Tait carried a
lot of artillery for someone on a visit to Anchorage.

"Doesn't everybody?" Tait replied with a laugh.

Tait returned to the North Slope, where he lost his job because he refused to shear his long mustache to conform to company health standards. In late 1976 he moved to Haines, Alaska, to live with his mother, then returned to Anchorage for a few weeks in 1977 in futile search of a job.

He moved to the East Coast, where he worked construction and security jobs in Baltimore until the spring of 1978. Then he sold cars, but didn't make much money. He returned to Anchorage in the fall of 1978 and told people he had seen action in Vietnam and was wounded. He showed them a 16-inch scar on his left leg he said was caused by a piece of shrapnel. He said a gunshot wound in his hand occurred when he grabbed a gun from someone who tried to rip him off in a hotel hallway. In fact, Tait had reached over to take a .45-caliber pistol from a friend as they sat around the house. He grabbed the gun by the muzzle, and his friend depressed the trigger as Tait pulled the gun. The bullet blew a hole the size of a 50-cent piece through his hand.

By spring, Tait had moved in with his younger sister and was on welfare.

Dan Wilcox decided around that time that Tait was the man his mother needed as bouncer at her 4th Avenue liquor store. Anchorage's 4th Avenue was a serious skid row, with four bars next to the liquor store where Tait worked. He was fit for the job: he pumped iron, practiced martial arts daily and ran five miles after work. Tait used the liquor store as a means to add to his gun collection. When someone pulled out their wallet late at night to buy a bottle and Tait noticed they had a gun, he scared them. "You'd better give me that gun right now. The police are looking for someone with a gun. Someone was just shot outside."

The customer would hand over the gun, and Tait would keep it.

Two Brothers walked into the store one day. They

brought in the sister of another Brother. She had gone to school with Tait and they chatted. The bikers, who ran a bar around the corner, were impressed that he knew the woman. Two days later, she returned to the liquor store.

"Hey, we're looking for a bouncer," she told Tait. "Do you want to bounce three nights a week?"

At the same time, the owner of Plaza Bingo offered Tait a maintenance and janitorial job—and 50 percent of all bad cheques Tait collected for him.

Tait quit his job at the liquor store and made good money at the bingo parlor and as a bouncer in the biker bar, which offered a special bonus—women. Strippers gave him a $20 tip at the end of the night and up to $100 if he subdued an overly aggressive customer. There were other gratuities to be had in strip joints, and he quickly picked up work at other clubs. When he left the bingo parlor after two years he had become a familiar face to the bikers.

Tait worked as doorman at several dance clubs. It was the end of the disco decade, and he described the clubs in two words: pussy galore. One club had fastened to the wall a log into which ringbolts were screwed. Groups of unruly patrons were handcuffed to the device so they didn't wreck the place before the police arrived. People were allowed to carry guns as long as they were not concealed. The loser of a fight usually ran out to his or her car and returned to shoot the winner. Tait confiscated many guns and built an impressive collection.

Tait's ability to beat people into the floor if he couldn't charm them with his diplomacy earned him a reputation in Anchorage.

His military background and his knowledge of bombs and guns made him an attractive prospect for the Brothers.

Two

Tait entered the world of outlaw motorcycle gangs in late February 1982.

A Brother talked to Tait inside a bar where he bounced. "Come on outside," the biker said.

He walked toward a pickup truck and pointed to a rigid-frame chopper strapped to the bed. "What do you think?"

"It's pretty nice. It's a Harley."

"If you want it, it's yours for $2,500."

"I don't have that kind of money now."

"That's all right. You can pay us when you get it. If you want to pay a buck a week or ten bucks a week. Just take the bike. There's a stipulation. You have to start hanging around."

Tait took the bike. He paid for it, changed the carburetor, fixed the bike up and painted it. The first few rides taught him that rigid-frame choppers were not comfortable machines. They jarred vertebrae. He exchanged his frame for one with a swingarm and souped up the engine with the help of his new biker friends. He had no idea what hanging around meant. He thought it meant hanging out with the guys in bars. It was really the first step of induction into the gang, a period when the bikers assess the raw material and decide whether he rated being promoted to the next level, a prospect, or prospective member.

Tait took his new Harley on the Brothers' first run of the year: the April 1 Frozen Few Run to Fairbanks, 360 miles north of Anchorage. Tait ran into an old friend, Robert Foley, to whom he had sold an AR-15 semi-automatic rifle in 1978. Foley was involved in a shooting incident and asked Tait to give a bill of sale and sworn statement to police as proof he did not steal it. Tait obliged his friend. When they met in Fairbanks, Tait boasted that he now hung around with the Brothers. Foley liked to ingratiate himself with the bikers, and told them Tait had once cooperated with police. Outlaw bikers are not supposed to help cops.

Coincidentally, a grand jury then handed down 40 sealed indictments against the Brothers, and Monty Elliott decided Tait was a rat and wanted to kill him. He convinced his fellow Brothers he was right.

"You're full of shit," Tait told the six-foot-four, 225-pound Elliott.

Tait and Elliott fought until both tired and stood and looked at each other.

"That's enough. Have you learned your lesson?" Elliott asked.

"No. Have you learned yours?"

Another Brother jumped Tait. He wasn't as good a fighter as Elliott. He telegraphed his punches and Tait beat him in half a minute.

"Listen," Tait said, "I don't give a shit what it takes and I don't know how I can prove myself to you guys, but I don't know what the fuck you're talking about with these indictments. I know Foley asked me to go to the police to tell them that I sold him the gun and if you don't believe me, bring him in here and I'll do it right now. And then I'll kick his ass, too."

That was the last time Tait was called a rat.

Elliott sold Tait a house trailer for $2,000, to be paid over time. The trailer was once valued at $24,000.

Tait met his first Hells Angels in April 1982, when seven California Angels showed up in Anchorage to celebrate the Brothers' fifteenth anniversary at the Indian

House restaurant and bar 30 miles outside Anchorage. The prospects waited hand and foot on the Brothers and Angels inside while Tait the hangaround provided security outside. A group of citizens showed up at their regular watering hole.

"Looks like he's going to need some help," an Angel told a Brother.

"Naw, just watch him."

Tait stood on the steps as the group approached.

"Good evening, ladies and gentlemen, did you all bring your invitations?"

"Huh?"

"Sorry, the bar's closed tonight. This is a private party and unless you have an invitation, the bar's closed to you."

They stood there for a couple of minutes.

"What are we going to do? We live here. This is our bar."

"Well, the bar's closed tonight. The bar's been leased to a certain group."

They drove away. San Francisco Hells Angel Carl James (J.R.) Serrano later approached Tait. "Hey, man. That was pretty fucking classy."

Serrano thought Tait was so cool he hung around with him for the following week in his trailer one block from the Dorbrandt Street clubhouse. Serrano's attention did the hangaround no harm with the Brothers.

The Brothers asked Tait to become a prospect during the Memorial Day Run in May. Protocol required Tait to stand before the bikers and make his intentions known. Tait could flatter the underwear off a nun. Or at least he wished he could. Among his goals in life were to create a better society where his idea of justice ruled, to ride the space shuttle—and to fuck a nun.

The Brothers were no match for his smooth tongue. Most prospective members mumbled crap about bikers being cool. Tait told them how much he admired the brotherhood and each member individually, how he never saw such a strong bond of unity among men except in special-forces groups, how being a member would fulfill his need for a home and lifestyle, and how the discipline reminded him of the military. The bikers ate it up, and Tait became a prospect in early June 1982, a position he had to hold for one year before being considered for membership. He was given the bottom rocker of the Brothers Motorcycle Club colors. It read "Alaska." The rest of the colors are given when a prospect becomes a full member and are worn on the back of a vest or jacket. They are the biker's most valuable possession.

"Here, you've got 15 minutes to get this thing sewed on."

Tait handed it to member Dan MacIntosh who sewed it on in his leather shop.

Thus began a happy period in Tait's life. He saw more of his father, who flew in from a remote job site to be with his son. And he immensely enjoyed intimidating people at the request of club members.

Several Brothers in a bar one night glared at a "nigger" who hustled white girls. They didn't like black guys who screwed white girls.

"Hey, prospect," a Brother told Tait. "Go get rid of his ass. Get him out of here and tell him not to come back."

Tait walked up to the man. "Get the fuck out of here and don't come back."

"Hey, fuck you."

"Who you talking to?" Tait slapped him in the face several times. "Typical nigger," he thought. Tait swept his arm across the bar and dumped several drinks on the man.

"Now get the fuck out of here. You're too chicken-shit to fight."

Tait turned to walk away. The man pulled a 9-mm pistol.

"He's got a gun," a woman screamed.

Tait turned. The man shot him twice in the chest. Tait never got the chance to touch the man—the crowd jumped the black man and thrashed him—but he did pick up the guy's gun. Tait, like most bikers, wore body armor.

Tait let the Brothers know right off he wouldn't be a regular gofer. One greasy, snaggletoothed '60s-type biker tried to pass his responsibilities on to prospect Tait. This biker was always broke and lived at the clubhouse, which he was supposed to clean. But every church night, which was Friday, the sink was stacked with dishes and the bathroom reeked. Tait was blamed at church for the mess.

"He lives here," Tait said. "He's supposed to clean the clubhouse."

"You're the prospect."

"That doesn't make any difference. He's got a job to do, he's got to fucking do it. I don't wash dishes. If you want the dishes washed, I'll go get some fucking broads and bring them over here and have them clean the goddamn clubhouse. But I don't clean up clubhouses. That's not part of my job. I'm a fucking prospect, not a maid."

Some Brothers thought the speech showed class. Others thought Tait overstepped his authority.

"We want the clubhouse cleaned up tonight."

Tait went to a strip joint and picked up three women. "We're having a little party over at the clubhouse a little later, but we need to get it organized and straightened out before we can have the party. If you girls want to come over to the party, you'll have to make sure it's all organized before you get in."

"Shit, yeah."

They couldn't get into Tait's car fast enough. They washed dishes, cleaned the bathroom and left the rest of the building spotless—all in 90 minutes. Then they had sex with all the bikers. Tait's status improved immediately among his brothers.

The greasy biker was eventually kicked out of the clubhouse and out of the club. Tait brought women over twice a week to keep it clean. No one complained about his attitude, but at weekly meetings several Brothers lodged sexual-deprivation complaints against Tait, who early on was nicknamed Tony Uno and Gentleman Tony because of his way with women. He got more than his brother bikers and they thought he infringed on their quota—after all, he was clean-cut and smooth-talking—and constant sex was supposed to be one of the perks of being a biker; boasting about it was another. One member of the now relocated Los Angeles County chapter claimed to have been the last man to screw Marilyn Monroe: he said he mounted her corpse on the morgue slab before the autopsy.

Hells Angel lore is rife with tales of sex and violence. Their idea of female emancipation is to take the handcuffs off a woman after they've had her. Sometimes they don't even do that, Tait learned as he spiraled deeper into the lifestyle of the abyss. And turnouts, as they're called, are passed around in group sessions.

The Hells Angels allowed the Brothers to become a prospect club for them in late June 1982. They had to give up their Brothers colors and wear only a bottom rocker that said "Alaska" and "MC" in red and white. Tait, as a prospect, had to remove his bottom rocker until the club was accepted as a Hells Angels chapter. The Hells Angels are monopolistic. They not only want to control every game in town, they want to own them. They don't like competition, especially from other bike gangs.

In 1982, there were 28 to 30 Brothers in Alaska, divided among the Fairbanks, Anchorage and Nomads chapters. The Nomads lived in Anchorage but couldn't tolerate the structure and discipline of the militaristic Anchorage chapter. They didn't have regular meetings and were often in trouble with the law. One member and a prospect were stupid enough to rob an after-hours club with their patches on. The Brothers had been around Alaska since the early 1960s. Like other bike gangs, they dealt and did drugs. By the early 1970s, many members were heroin addicts. Discipline faltered and the gang disbanded for a few months. They re-formed under strict Hells Angels rules. They had met the Hells Angels in the 1960s and sold their drugs in Alaska. A California Hells

Angel flew to Alaska regularly with a suitcase full of drugs. When the plane touched down in Anchorage, the California Angel gave his luggage claims check to a cab driver—usually a Brother—who picked up the suitcase. If stopped by police, he would claim he was asked to pick up the suitcase and deliver it to a hotel. That would break the trail.

The Hells Angels groomed the Brothers and taught them how to take care of business. The Brothers would have become Hells Angels in the 1970s if not for an unfortunate incident in 1976 in Healy, Alaska, when several Brothers gave statements to police who investigated a shootout between the bikers and a railway worker. The Hells Angels do not trust people who talk to cops.

In the mid-1970s, the Hells Angels urged the Brothers to make Alaska a one-patch state. The Brothers beat and shot members of more than a dozen rival gangs over the years. They stormed clubhouses and stripped them of their colors. By the early 1980s, the Panhandlers Motorcycle Club was the last gang the Brothers had to eliminate. They rode to Juneau, beat Panhandler members and wrecked their clubhouse. Several months later, the Brothers wanted to ensure the Panhandlers had not been revived. They sent prospect Tait to reconnoiter in 1982.

"We don't have the address. The only thing we can tell you is there's a bridge that looks like it's made with an Erector set."

Tait bought a map of Juneau and marked all roads that crossed rivers. He drove around until he found a steel-beam bridge. He hitchhiked along the road the clubhouse was on until he got a ride from former Panhandlers. He asked if he could use the phone in the former clubhouse. Nothing inside indicated the club was active. It was just a garage with a few bikes and posters. The Brothers asked Tait to hang around for a week to ensure they didn't have a church. They asked him to break in and snoop through the clubhouse. Tait couldn't be bothered. He lied and said he did.

*   *   *

While the Brothers vied to become Hells Angels in
Alaska, a rare occurrence opened the eyes of some law
enforcement officers to the extent that the Hells Angels
were entrenched in the drug business. Rats were few in
the biker underworld, where members were encouraged
to support each other for better or worse. Besides,
snitches had short lives.

But the brotherhood that bound outlaw bikers began
to unravel as the notion of equality fell by the wayside in
the late 1970s. Some Hells Angels made big money in the
drug business, and suddenly they had something to lose,
something to protect. Their bank accounts came first and
the brotherhood second. When a member threatened
their income, they beat or killed him. The Hells Angels
Motorcycle Club was no longer an organization that
sheltered social misfits. It became an enclave for some of
the underworld's most cunning drug manufacturers and
dealers. Typical 1960s bikers, content with a few bucks
in their pockets, threatened the modern bikers' illegal
enterprises because their outlandish behavior drew too
much police attention. The most aggressive Hells Angels
strived to clean up the club. They got rid of those who
didn't bring money into its coffers. They didn't want
riffraff. They wanted hustlers. Brotherhood lost out to
the buck. Love for a fellow outlaw turned to lust for
lucre.

The cleansing and mistreatment by fellow brothers
disillusioned some Hells Angels. They turned to another
brotherhood for help—law enforcement. They ratted on
former friends, mostly after they narrowly escaped being
killed by them. They explained the club's inner workings
to cops, who couldn't believe that a bunch of scumbags
were so criminally shrewd. Thus began the awakening of
law enforcement to the threat that outlaw motorcycle
gangs posed—a threat so large and complex that it still
would not be fully grasped decades later. But every
informer added more information to help convince

police that motorcycle clubs were no longer fringe opera-
tors in the underworld. They were major players who
cleverly shielded their operations behind the veil of
brotherhood they gradually eroded and replaced with
lawyers.

Oakland Hells Angel Sergey Clement (Sir Gay)
Walton was a powerhouse in the club when he became a
police informant in 1980 after 22 years as an Angel. He
cut a deal to shorten his drug sentence and lengthen his
life. He called his wife and asked her to join him in hiding. Linda Hill Walton, a Hells Angel associate, told him
to fuck off and reported the rat to the club. Sergey
Walton was debriefed for nearly two months at the end
of 1982, at the same time as the Anchorage Brothers
became full-fledged Hells Angels. The main debrief was
conducted by Special Agent James B. Flanigan of the
Bureau of Alcohol, Tobacco and Firearms in San
Francisco.

Walton told of the entrenched drug-manufacturing
business within the Hells Angels and offered fascinating
insights into all the workings and politics of the organization. His testimony revealed the day-to-day operations
of the Angels in California and inspired a few young
police officers to keep a closer watch on the bikers.

Walton said a drug war between the Northern
California Hells Angels and chapters in southern
California in 1965 and 1966 had changed the makeup of
the club as political power shifted north from the club's
first charter in the south. The Hells Angels Berdoo (San
Bernardino) chapter, founded on March 17, 1948,
started to sell drugs to other chapters in 1964. At that
time, there were only five Hells Angels chapters in the
world: Berdoo; Frisco (founded 1954); Oakland (1957);
Auckland, New Zealand (1961); and Richmond,
California (1962). A North Sacramento chapter had
folded in 1957 and was revived in 1973. By 1970, there
were 18 chapters, 45 by 1980, 70 by 1985 and 85 in
1995.

Since 1958, the most powerful chapter has been run

by the most influential Hells Angel—Sonny Barger. Barger is a self-proclaimed American legend. Sharon, his wife, sells T-shirts, sweatshirts and tank tops that read "Sonny Barger—An American Legend." She sells caps bearing his most famous quote: "I never thought freedom was cheap." (Sonny Barger believes the difference between a good member and an outstanding member is the guy's old lady. If she lets him have his way and disappear for weeks at a time and doesn't get on his case, the guy is more likely to participate in club activities.)

The media created Sonny Barger in the mid-1960s as they looked for rebels to worship, and he used the media when he found it convenient to do so. Barger spent 13 years behind bars and saw many of his fellow Hells Angels jailed for crimes that ranged from buggery to drug manufacturing to murder. Yet he always insisted that the Hells Angels Motorcycle Club was made up of a sorely misunderstood bunch of guys who happened to like motorcycling and whom the government continually framed. Sonny Barger—An American Sniveler.

Ralph Hubert Barger was born in Modesto, California, on October 8, 1938. His parents separated when he was six months old, and his father moved Barger and his sister to Oakland to be raised by their grandmother. Barger became fascinated with motorcycles when he watched an Oakland motorcycle cop park on the side street near his house and catch cars that ran a stop sign on the main street. He graduated from his bicycle to a motor scooter. He joined the army at 16 and got an honorable discharge after 13 months when they found out he was too young. He left the army with his first tattoo on his left arm: a snake coiled around a dagger—the symbol of the U.S. infantry, whose motto is Death Before Dishonor.

Barger bought his first motorcycle when he got out of the army: a temperamental 1934 45-cubic-inch Indian Scout that hardly ran during the two months he kept it. He replaced it with a 1941 61-cubic-inch Harley-Davidson when he turned 18. Barger and some friends who hung out at the same bar belonged to the Oakland Panthers, and they decided to form their own club. Don (Boots) Reeves had a Hells Angels patch. No one knew where he got it, but they thought it was cool. They had copies made and started the Oakland Hells Angels in 1957.

Barger and his friends didn't know about the Hells Angels chapter in San Francisco, nor about the original chapter in San Bernardino (formed from the Booze Fighters in 1948), the chapter in North Sacramento or the (now-defunct) So Cal chapter in Gardenia.

Reeves was the first Oakland chapter president. He left after a year to hit the road as a country singer, and Barger, five-foot-ten and 145 pounds of tense sinew and self-assured charisma, took over in 1958. The original seven Oakland Hells Angels eventually crossed paths with legitimate Hells Angels. Together, they made rules to decide who could become a member so another group like Barger's could not declare itself Hells Angels. Even as a teenage biker, Barger was a control freak.

It was under Barger's guidance that the Hells Angels incorporated and issued 500 shares in California in 1966 for the "promotion and advancement of motorcycle driving, motorcycle clubs, motorcycle highway safety and all phases of motorcycles and motorcycle driving." They had the Death's Head patented in 1972. And the Angels had the audacity in the 1980s to register their name as a trademark, even though they took it from the air force in the first place. The only change they made to the name when they registered it was to drop the apostrophe in *Hell's*. The club had used both styles over the years.

Sonny Barger is the man behind the attitude. His foresight, drive and cunning shaped the Hells Angels into a fearsome gang. Barger did for the Hells Angels what Lee Iacocca did for Chrysler—he converted a sloppy, rudderless organization into a lean, mean, no-bullshit company. He trimmed idiot cavemen from chapter rosters and embarked on an expansionist course that swelled the club from five chapters in 1965 to 85 in

1995. The assimilation of other motorcycle gangs in the 1970s and 1980s differed only in bloodshed from the corporate takeovers that shake Wall Street. Taking over a club is a business transaction. The target club buries its corporate colors and takes on those of the new parent company. It contributes to the head-office treasury and in return receives expert advice and support when needed. Takeovers get sloppy when the sought-after club allies with other gangs to fight off the suitor. But most gangs willingly join the world's most feared outlaw bikers.

Barger was the shrewdest of Hells Angels. He survived as leader of an organization known for killing its presidents. He learned systems and figured out how to get around them. He knew the intricacies of the legal system, which he easily stifled, fragmented and frustrated. Every time the Hells Angels went to court, Barger learned how to beat the system. Knowledge shaped his attitude. The Angels pushed the courts not necessarily to beat a charge but to find out about police sources, equipment and techniques to keep one step ahead of the law.

Barger retained his charisma, although he curbed his rough-and-tumble ways of the 1950s and '60s. He changed with the times and made the club adapt to allow it to grow and prosper.

The club was Barger's family. He once said he heard that his mother had died in 1982. He had an adult son he never talked about because the boy would have nothing to do with the Hells Angels.

Sonny Barger spent so much time behind bars that he didn't consummate his marriage to Sharon Marie Gruhlke for two and a half years, until New Year's Day 1976, in a trailer at Folsom Prison.

Walton detailed for police the inner workings of Barger's Oakland chapter. Walton said everyone who sold heroin used it. The northern California charters, led by Oakland, decided Hells Angels would not do heroin. North and

South fought and shot each other in guerrilla warfare. Berdoo lost its power and Sonny Barger's Oakland became the dominant Hells Angels chapter. Oakland claimed the right to grant charters and set out to expand the club with chapters in Los Angeles County and San Diego.

The Oakland chapter remained dominant because Barger encouraged the best, brightest, toughest and most enterprising officers from other chapters to transfer to the Bay Area. The members are older and more mature. They have been through battles with other clubs and understand it is better to make money, not war. The Oakland chapter believes it knows what is best for the club and forcefully imposes its will to achieve its goals.

Walton had been president of three Hells Angels chapters: the short-lived North Sac, the Nomads and Oakland. He said the club's "No narcotics burns" rule applied to all drug transactions, but it was adopted only after three Hells Angels from the East Coast—Bouncer, Spesh and Monkey—moved to California to become members of Walton's Nomads. They burned some hippies on a $3,000 dope deal and word got back to the club. San Francisco president Bob Roberts wanted to pull their patches, and a brawl broke out at the Carousel Ballroom. The "No narcotics burns" rule was subsequently adopted at an Officers' Meeting in Daly City. Walton said drugs, guns and violence were the Hells Angels' real interest, not motorcycles.

Walton said the Hells Angels stole many of their weapons from the military. Agents from the Bureau of Alcohol, Tobacco and Firearms found machine guns in houses where Walton said they were hidden, and Walton's own mother surrendered machine guns to the agents.

Walton said one Hells Angel had 50 percent of the club's guns, plastic explosives, grenades and LAWs rockets stored with friends in the Santa Cruz mountains. The Hells Angels kept another cache of weapons by Skaggs Island, near Vallejo.

Walton explained how the Hells Angels methamphetamine business skyrocketed after Angel Manuel Rubio met Kenneth Alison (The Old Man) Maxwell in 1974. Maxwell, a chemist with Shell Oil in Richmond, manufactured methamphetamine for the club and taught many Hells Angels to cook crank: Kenneth (Kenny) Owen—Oakland, Robert (Norton Bob) Thomas—Oakland, Charles (Chico) Manganiello—Oakland. Owen, in turn, taught Michael (Irish) O'Farrell—Oakland. By 1980, half the Oakland chapter could cook, Walton said.

When Rubio first had The Old Man teach Oakland members how to cook, they were obliged to do so for Rubio. Kenny Owen wouldn't stand for it and quit the Oakland chapter to move to Vallejo. The Hells Angels eventually expelled Rubio from the club for his heavy-handedness.

Walton's main drug associate in the Hells Angels was Kenny Owen. Owen moved into one of Rubio's former methamphetamine labs at 900 Deming Way in Vallejo and made it the Vallejo chapter clubhouse. Walton's drug business with Owen started at a New Year's party in 1977, after Walton got out of jail. Owen told Walton they were going to get lab equipment. They picked up Hells Angel associate Henry Crabtree, who said the night watchman at Stauffer Chemical Company in Richmond would allow them to steal glassware. They split the haul. Owen cooked his meth in the mountains near Tahoe.

Walton said it was his idea to set up the Freedom Defense Fund in 1979 after most of the Hells Angels Oakland chapter was busted on a Racketeer Influenced and Corrupt Organizations Act, or RICO, charge. The fund was established at a California Officers' Meeting at Walton's shop across the street from the Oakland clubhouse. The officers voted to assess each California member $500 for the fund to help cover bail and lawyers' fees. There were about 250 Hells Angels in California at the time.

Hells Angels Walton, Kenny Owen, Bobby England, Jim Brandes, Gary Popkin and Burt Stefanson started a bail-bond agency called Fast Tap in San Diego just before the RICO indictments. Each Angel contributed $25,000 except for Walton, whose investment was substantial. He sold out his share shortly after the RICO busts and made a profit of several hundred thousand dollars, which he contributed to the Freedom Defense Fund.

Every Hells Angel who could cook crank did so during the RICO trials from 1979 to 1981 to fill defense-fund coffers. Owen, who was a fugitive at the time, cooked 20 pounds, worth $250,000 to $400,000 wholesale, at a ranch near San Andreas before he turned himself in. During the trial, he ran five lab houses in the Santa Cruz mountains. One mountaintop house was rented from a bank by Jim Brandes, who used another Hells Angel's name. Kenny Owen's wife, Laufey, visited Walton in Lompoc prison later and told him Miller was so successful he built an underground lab in a mine shaft covered by a shed.

It was Kenny Owen who figured out how to make phenyl-2-propanone when it became scarce on the legal market. He cooked the prop in a secret room in the shop across the street from the Oakland clubhouse. Three chemicals were cooked under pressure at 250 degrees for 18 hours. Owen also thought to connect the meth cooking flask to a house's sewer line to prevent the escape of the meth's telltale odor. Hells Angels who were released from prison from 1979 to 1981 inherited meth labs and equipment from other Angels who had made their money. Ninety-nine percent of the Hells Angels' money came from crank, Walton said.

Walton said it is safer to do dope for two years and get out before the cops get wise to you. It is also safer to deal with Hells Angels only, because they won't rat you out. The Hells Angels are successful because they stand behind their product.

Most Hells Angels run their labs on their own. Walton said Bobby England's lab, busted in the mid-1970s, was the only one directly connected to the club. Walton got suspicious of a pickup truck with a camper on the back that had partly open curtains and warned England, but England said cars always parked in that spot.

After the RICO bust, many Hells Angels cooked on the road, some of them in recreational vehicles. Some of the phenyl-2-propanone came from Australia and was shipped as wine. Later it was sent in cans, four to a box.

The RICO trials cost the Hells Angels a lot of money. Walton paid his own lawyer $150,000. The club paid a private investigator $250,000 from the Freedom Defense Fund. Hells Angels lawyers each got $100,000. A dozen other lawyers were paid as much. One lawyer received $200,000.

Murder of members for breaches of Angel etiquette or failure to perform duties was standard practice: between 1965 and 1980, according to Walton, more than a dozen Angels were killed, sometimes by drug over-doses to make it look like suicide. Many were shot.

In spite of murdering and betraying each other, Angels do often observe niceties. An imprisoned Hells Angel can, for instance, request visitors from the club to stave off loneliness. A hat is passed around at a meeting before a member is released from prison, and everyone donates. Oakland Hells Angels get $25,000 and a car when released. Walton got $28,000 when he got out of Soledad. Sonny Barger got $100,000 when he got out of Folsom. Hells Angels with a drug business contributed $10,000 each. Walton gave Barger a Corvette. Barger's house went up for auction while he was in prison in the mid-1970s and the club bought it for him.

Walton also said that the Hells Angels have many sources of intelligence. One bail bondsman tipped them off whenever he heard something from his contacts in the Oakland Police Department. Various Hells Angels had relatives in law enforcement from whom they could have pried information.

But the Angels don't just have security connections, they use codes of their own. Walton explained the codes in their personal phone books, which use a fairly simple letter-number key. They choose 10-letter words in which no letter is repeated and assign a number to each letter. For example:

```
J  A  M  E  S     B  R  O  W  N
1  2  3  4  5     6  7  8  9  0
```

The number 974-9602 is encoded as WRE-WBNA. When this encoded number is dictated on the phone, the caller refers to "the nigger singer" when the code is JAMES BROWN. The Angels love playing at being secret agents. It was a side of the club that Brothers prospect Anthony Tait never dreamed existed.

Three

THE BROTHERS IN ALASKA officially became Hells Angels on December 18, 1982, after 18 months of scrutiny by the club. Tait became an Angels prospect and was given a red and white bottom rocker.

Three Alaska Brothers waited outside the Oakland clubhouse during the mandatory unanimous vote by West Coast Officers. They were given the Hells Angels colors to fly back to Alaska.

In late December, the Anchorage treasury bought 25 round-trip tickets for members to fly to California to celebrate at various Hells Angels New Year's Eve parties. Some went to parties in the Bay Area. Tait's group rented three limos and visited the San Fernando Valley chapter along with San Bernardino members. Anchorage chapter vice-president and sergeant-at-arms Edwin Floyd (Eddie) Hubert didn't go. Hubert had visited California as a Brother in the 1970s and decided to take back to Alaska a woman he met at a clubhouse. She didn't want to go. He said she had to. The Angels took him for a ride in the country, threatened to kill him and scared him so badly he never returned to the state. Hubert avoided contact with California Hells Angels. He was not a courageous man.

Chapter president Richard (Sleazy Ric) Rickleman and Tait drove to San Bernardino, where a Hells Angel sold Rickleman a $1,000 slot machine for $2,000. Several days later, they ended up in Monterey and bar-hopped with local Angels.

"There's one place left we probably ought not to go to because if we go, we'll end up getting into a fight," a Monterey Hells Angel warned.

So they went to the Brick House, a bar whose owner was connected with the EME—the Mexican mafia—and ran a gym. The room was packed with muscle-bound Mexicans in white tank tops. Tait picked up his glass and looked toward the door. A guy flew through the door backwards, hit the wall and slid to the floor. Tait ran over to see what was going on and someone cold-cocked him as he walked out the door. His head snapped back and his glasses flew off. Tait turned to see the bar owner look stunned because he did not drop. Tait tore into him with a gang associate.

A cop bore down on him with his stick. Tait blocked the stick with a sweep of his arm, swung his arm over and around the stick and trapped it under his arm. A group of cops rushed in. Tait pulled the cop against him and flattened himself against the wall.

"I ain't fighting. I ain't resisting. I'm not going to get beat by a bunch of cops with sticks."

The cops couldn't help striking their fellow officer as they tried to hit Tait.

"Okay. I got him. I got him," the human shield finally yelled.

Four cops grabbed Tait by the arms and legs and pinned him on the hood of a car while they searched him, then they took him to jail. He stayed in California until the end of January to appear in court, where he paid a $50 fine for fighting. The incident helped make Tait's reputation in California as word spread about his ability to disarm and fight off a group of cops.

Tait returned to Anchorage to find his personal life in disarray. His girlfriend, Tina Thrasher, drank and caused problems in his absence. She was an alcoholic, and Tait didn't think she was a good influence on his five-year-old nephew, Douglas, who lived with them.

Tait had been taking care of the child after his drug-addict sister Minto Kathleen disappeared.

"If you're going to be stupid, you can be stupid else-where," he told her. She packed her bags and left. In the heat of argument, Tait forgot she was pregnant by him. She moved into her sister's cabin 300 miles south of Anchorage.

The Brothers continued to test their prospect. Two Brothers started a fight with a table of loud soldiers at the Wild Cherry bar. Tait jumped in and broke one man's nose with a punch. Before he could throw another, seven GIs surrounded him and swung. Charlie Potter, who started the fight, watched the action from the bar as he drank. The Brothers slipped out a side door, and Tait realized he was on his own. He beat three soldiers. The other four ran out the door. Tait followed into the snow. He chased two GIs around a car until one man fled down the street. Tait was breathless. Another GI blindsided him and threw him to the ground. He lay on Tait and punched at his head. Another GI jumped on his leg.

"Break his fucking leg. Break his fucking leg," yelled a soldier who kept his distance.

Tait worked his arms under the man who pinned him and threw him off. The GI on his leg ran off. Tait grabbed his tackler by the hair and beat him fiercely. He wanted to end the fight because he knew from experi-ence the police would soon be there. Just then, Ed Hubert walked out of the bar and pressed a handful of snow to his face.

"What happened?" Tait asked.

"Some sonofabitch punched me."

"Who is it? I'll go get him."

"No, it's all right."

Two more Brothers walked out. They talked. The club's huge Samoan bouncer sauntered out, took a few steps past Hubert, turned around and drilled him in the side of the face. Hubert staggered. The Samoan took off down the street with Tait on his tail. Tait gave up the chase half a block later.

Tait made his reputation with the Brothers that night. Hubert, who took over the presidency from Richard Allen (Sleazy Ric) Rickleman, was a big man and a big fish in a small pond. He liked to have Tait's muscle around.

Now that Alaska was part of the Hells Angel family, it became another state to which Hells Angels could transfer. It was a particularly attractive area for one California Hells Angel who paved the way for it to be taken into the Angel fold. Arnold Paul (Animal) Hibbits left California and became a member of the Mat-Su, or Matanuska-Susitna, chapter. He settled in a cabin outside town where he could hunt, fish and hone his knife-throwing. He was an old-time Hells Angel with a reputation for viciousness. Hibbits was at Altamont in December 1969 when Meredith Hunter was stabbed to death by Hells Angels in front of the stage as the Rolling Stones played. He moved to Alaska not only for the lifestyle but to keep tabs on the new members to ensure they became proper Hells Angels. His antics added to Hells Angels lore in Alaska.

As a bouncer at the Arctic Fox, owned by Hells Angel Monty Elliott, Tait often had to "persuade" customers who'd angered Hibbits to disappear before things got rough—before Hibbits noticed.

Ever since his days working in the liquor store, Tait had had a knack for spotting guns. He stood in a Fairbanks bar one night and watched Oakland Hells Angel Quick Rick Bowles argue with a woman.

"Fuck you," Bowles said and walked away.

She approached him a couple of minutes later and sweet-talked. She commented on the spurs he wore in the middle of winter.

"Those are neat. Can I see them?"

Quick Rick lifted his leg. She yanked it and threw him over. He jumped up and grabbed her by the hair. She clutched his beard. He punched her in the head.

"I'm going to fuck you up," she threatened as she scrambled out.

She returned with a snub-nosed .38-caliber revolver. Tait saw it only because light glinted off the stainless steel. He grabbed the top of her hand, bent her wrist and pocketed the gun for his collection.

Not all prospect work involved muscle. Tait typed out a proposal the Alaska Angels wanted to present at the West Coast Officers' Meeting in California. Across the top he typed HELLS ANGLES. He printed 30 copies. The members confronted him.

"How do you spell Angels?"

"A-n-g-l-e-s."

"How do you spell Angels?"

"A-n-g-l-e-s."

The Angels stood silently, looked at Tait curiously, then laughed.

"What the fuck's so funny?"

"How do you spell Angels?"

"Oh, yeah. A-n-g-e-l-s."

"What does this say?" they asked as they showed him the proposal.

"This says Hells Angels."

Tait became a full-fledged Hells Angel on July 14, 1983. He was unceremoniously given a full patch to sew onto his jacket above the bottom rocker he wore as a prospect. The top rocker read "HELLS ANGLES." Everyone laughed. Tait was in no rush to get his obligatory Hells Angels tattoo.

Two weeks later, Tait and Dirty Dave Gonzales drove to Custer, South Dakota, in Tait's pickup truck for the Hells Angels annual U.S.A. Run, at which hundreds of members from around the world party hard for three or four days and nights. The two men were poles apart in class and style. Dirty Gonzales was the epitome of the scuzbag biker. Tait, because of the way he publicly treated women, was Gentleman Tony.

Once, Gonzales visited Hells Angel Tommy Clifton's home.

"Hey, Tommy, okay if I fuck your old lady?"

"If you think you can, go ahead."

Gonzales walked into the kitchen, where Molly cooked him some food. He punched her out and raped her on the floor. Clifton hadn't thought it would go that far. His relationship didn't last much longer.

Gonzales exposed more of his crudity to Tait during the long drive to South Dakota.

"Man, my herpes are killing me," he said.

"What are you talking about?"

"I got herpes bad. I got to get some sun on my dick."

"Really?"

Gonzales dropped his drawers around his knees, pulled out his dick and wiped rubbing alcohol on open sores. The alcohol burned terribly, and Gonzales twisted like a pretzel to get his mouth close enough to his dick to blow on the sores.

"What the hell's that going to do?"

"Well, the alcohol dries it out. But the sunlight helps dry them out too."

Gonzales cut a piece of tape and wrapped it around the foreskin to keep the tip of his penis exposed to air and sunlight. All of a sudden, a Customs station was up ahead. Gonzales scrambled to get his pants up before Tait stopped the truck.

After the run, Tait traveled to Yakima, Washington, to visit his mother. Then he drove his pickup, with his Harley in the back, to San Bernardino, California. The truck was stolen from outside his hotel by San Bernardino Hells Angels. The next day they bemoaned their brother's bad luck while he visited them. They sold him parts—wheels, tires, chains, headlights and a transmission—for a good price. Tait sued the insurance company for $15,000 because he wanted more than the $4,000 they offered for his stolen truck and motorcycle. The company settled out of court for $4,000. Tait took the parts he bought and built a new motorcycle in Anchorage. Registration papers showed the transmission on his rebuilt bike had the same serial number as that on his stolen one.

Tait's name showed up on other registration papers

at summer's end. Tina Thrasher gave birth to their
daughter, Crystal, on September 13, 1983. Tait would
see little of her.

The Hells Angels expanded rapidly in the 1980s. The
monopolistic club took over motorcycle gangs in countries all over the world and systematically set out to eliminate competitors through violence and intimidation.
They peacefully took over the Satan's Angels in British
Columbia in 1983 after a lengthy courtship during which
visiting Angels assessed the Canadian bikers' ability to
take care of business. The Satan's Angels proved this by
wiping out all other gangs in the province. The Hells
Angels' plan to control the West Coast from California to
Alaska was nearly accomplished. All that remained were
the states of Washington and Oregon.

Chapters were opening up all over the world as well-
established gangs selected by the Hells Angels made the
grade during their probationary period. From 1980 to
1983, the Hells Angels established chapters in Holland,
Australia (two), Denmark, California, France, West
Germany (two), Massachusetts, New York, Minnesota,
Alaska (three) and British Columbia (four). They had
truly become an international organization.

The Hells Angels suffered their first major blow as a
club in West Germany in 1983. The government finally
tired of the criminal activities of the Hamburg chapter's
members and their flagrant violation of stringent anti-
Nazi laws—the Hells Angels wore the swastikas that in
1969 Sonny Barger recommended members not wear to
improve the club's image. The Germans are sensitive to
organizations whose members commit crimes while
wearing uniforms, and their laws against such associa-
tions are strict. In October, the German minister of the
interior served notice on the Hells Angels that it was
banned.

The notice came two months after a raid by 500

heavily armed police on a Hamburg bar to arrest 24 Hells
Angels on charges of running a white-slavery ring. Police
also seized weapons, drugs and cash in 80 houses and
brothels. More than a hundred police in Zurich arrested
nine Angels the next week. The FBI arrested Andrea
Roman Brown, the 26-year-old president of the Hamburg
chapter, in New Hope, Minnesota, and charged him with
extortion and being a member of a criminal gang. The
Hells Angels were alleged to run a prostitution ring that
sold women to Switzerland, the Netherlands and Austria;
they kidnapped a prostitute and sold her for $5,500 to
work in Switzerland; they controlled 60 prostitutes in
Hamburg's red-light district.

In the written decision by German authorities there
appeared a description of the Hamburg chapter's organization and activities that might apply to any chapter any-
where.

I. The Hamburg Hells Angels Motor Club fulfills the
   conditions required for a prohibition pronounced by
   the Federal Minister of Interior . . .

   1. This association was entered into the Register of
      Associations in Hamburg on June 23, 1978. The
      members Hein (first president), Pietzschke (sec-
      ond president), Wunsch (first treasurer) and
      Nikolajczeyk (manager) are currently working
      in the formal executive committee. However,
      the association's formal executive committee
      does not correspond, as far as its members are
      concerned, to the actual leadership. In reality,
      the leaders in Hamburg are the members Grabe,
      Amtmann and Kopperschmidt.
         The registered association's organization and
      activities date back to the "Bloody Devils" in
      Hamburg in late 1971, to which some of the
      leading full members of the association
      belonged. After meeting with the Swiss Hells

Angels, that group set up internal rules that correspond to the association's present "laws."

2. The Hells Angels Motor Club has 15 members. Besides the 14 full members, there is one associate member participating in the registered association's activities. The association receives active support from at least another 17 persons. The association may have full members aged above 18 and honorary members. The decision on membership is made by the general meeting. By accepting membership, the member recognizes the association's charter . . . The formal charter does not sufficiently reflect the association's true principles and objectives. Besides the rights and duties described in the charter, there are—mostly unwritten—rules for members. The duties of members are based, inter alia, on the "Laws of the Hells Angels MC Germany," according to which members must subordinate themselves to the will of the community, obey a certain "code of honor," act as "outlaws," and therefore are obliged to violate existing laws. They further must not make any statement in criminal proceedings and regularly have to pay contributions. Where the member has violated certain rules, he must accept a fine. The so-called sergeant-at-arms sees to it that internal laws are obeyed and any punishment executed. Members must follow instructions from this person or other leading members without gainsay. Besides the coat of arms, the possession of a roadworthy motorcycle "above 500cc" is the external sign of membership.

Full members must attend weekly meetings at the "Angel-Place" in Hamburg . . . The "Angel-Place" was the association's club premises and its licenseholder the mother of one of the full members. In the club room attached to the premises, common goals, their promotion, organizational matters, etc., were discussed and coordinated.

3. The association's purpose as shown in the charter—motorcycle riding on a voluntary and solitary basis—is a pretext and does not correspond to actual facts. The association's members take a disapproving view of regular employment. As early as 1978, they therefore decided to commit punishable acts in order to obtain income. The association's purpose and activities are therefore linked to the commission of criminal offenses. The criminal objectives of the association are determined by its leading members.

a) Some members of the Hells Angels Motor Club are living on the earnings of various prostitutes. The procurers were supported by all other members in an effort to keep the women from leaving for fear of considerable reprisals; otherwise, the women had to pay a certain amount or were taken back to the procurers, for whom they were forced to continue working.

Members further promoted their goals by exerting pressure on new prostitutes to secure their work for a member and discussed possibilities for other members with a view to transferring certain prostitutes.

The Hells Angels Motor Club has described itself as the largest procurers' organization in St. Pauli, Hamburg.

b) Another source of income of the association and therefore a determining factor in its criminal goals was a protection racket practiced in bars near the Neuer Pferdemarkt in Hamburg. Several tenants of bars in the vicinity of the association's premises "Angel-Place" were forced through the massive and violent appearance of members in uniform clothing to cater for their

wishes free of charge and to pay "protection
fees" amounting to DM 1,500 and 2,500 a
month. In these encounters, some members
inflicted bodily injuries. On payment of the fee
they promised they would no longer appear in
those bars with more than two "uniformed"
members at a time. These agreements were
known to all members, who promoted the association's goals by either avoiding, or massively
visiting, the bars concerned.

c) A further goal of the members was to illegally
acquire, transfer and carry various firearms,
which in turn were used to promote the criminal objectives of the association, but also constituted a source of income through their sale.
Certain firearms were, according to a decision
taken by the general meeting, available to all
members.

4. The activities of the Hells Angels Motor Club
are cutting across the borders of a Federal State.

a) Apart from its appearances in Baden-
Wurtemberg and in neighboring countries, the
association regularly came to notice in Hamburg
and Schleswig-Holstein. On these occasions, the
association's members were identifiable by their
uniform clothing, the association's logo and coat
of arms, and their heavy motorcycles, mostly of
the Harley-Davidson make.

b) To further its procuring activity, the association
maintained contact with other groups and procurers' rings within, and without, its charter's
area of applicability. Members of a Frankfurt
group agreed to get new prostitutes from the
Frankfurt area. One or several members of the
group "Hot Wheels" agreed to help in the search
for one of the association's prostitutes who had
escaped. In return, the Frankfurt group was
assured of the support of all members of the

Hells Angels Motor Club. Another group in Hamburg, the "Steamers," assisted the association in the pursuit of its actual purpose.

The association considers itself a fully integrated part of a worldwide organization of the Hells Angels, which currently has 56 chapters, among them the Hamburg association and a group of the Stuttgart Hells Angels. Particular care is taken to maintain contact with the parent group, the Oakland chapter in the United States. The association was also in contact with other foreign Hells Angels, especially in U.S.A., Switzerland, France, England, Denmark, the Netherlands, Australia and Canada. International contact was maintained by means of regular mutual visits and assistance. Full member Otto, the association's "European Secretary," was its liaison member for foreign groups.

II. The purpose, and activities, of the Hells Angels Motor Club are in violation of the criminal laws.

1. Under the association's internal laws, members are obliged to attend the weekly meetings on Wednesdays, as a rule held at the "Angel-Place." The premises serve as a clearing house for all news and messages received for members. The activities agreed upon in the meetings are strictly executed. Decisions must be absolutely obeyed by the members. The purpose and objective of the association is the commission of offenses, which are prepared in the meetings. The club premises constitute the point of departure for the association's criminal activities.

In these premises, force was exerted upon women in order to make them prostitutes for the association's members. Also kept there were weapons. The protection racket also originated from there.

2. Leading full members of the association have committed numerous offenses for gain and in agreement with the association's purpose and objectives.

a) The leading full members of the association run several brothels in Hamburg and Zurich . . . The German prostitutes working in Zurich are controlled by Swiss Hells Angels on behalf of the association.

Other women were forced to be prostitutes for members of the association under threat of violence. On April 16, 1982, a prostitute was multiply mistreated in the association's premises and detained in order to force her to work for a full member.

b) In early 1982, several full members made violent appearances in Hamburg bars. The tenants were assaulted and patrons terrorized. Under the impression of these events, one tenant paid a "protection fee" of DM 2,500 a month to the association.

In a newly opened bar, leading members demanded a 10 percent share of the turnover. The tenant paid amounts of DM 1,500 on at least two occasions.

c) Since the association's creation, leading full members have illegally acquired firearms, put them at the disposal of other members or resold them to third parties.

• On September 21, 1982, two U.S.-made pump-action guns from Switzerland with the proper ammunition were found in the association's premises during a police search.

• On December 5, 1982, during the European meeting, two American pump-action guns, a double-action revolver and ammunition were found in the car of the Stuttgart group's president. These weapons had been obtained through a full member of the Swiss Hells Angels.

- Searches that were made of the club premises, a hide-out attached to it and the apartments of several members on August 10, 1983, produced numerous long guns as well as handguns.

3. The offenses committed are to be attributed to the Hells Angels Motor Club. They were committed with the knowledge, and approval, of the club's actual leaders. They are in an inherent relation to the goals of the association, and the latter's leading full members were involved in them.

    The offenses were planned during meetings in the club premises and then perpetrated accordingly by members. The mutual involvement of leading members in each other's offenses is based on their common membership. In connection with the protection racket and the arms violations, the association came forward as a whole or represented by part of its members. During the commission of offenses, and at other times in the public, members were wearing uniform clothing and were identifiable by the club logo and symbols. The motorcycles, the purchase of which was an obligation for members, were partly used in the commission of offenses . . .

    [The club's] activities are to be considered as organized crime and can only be stopped by prohibiting it.

    Lesser measures are not sufficient. An interdiction directed against the association's activity would not effectively put an end to its criminal goals and the activities arising therefrom. Since criminal offenses are the foremost source of income of the association and its members it is not to be expected that an interdiction of its activity would prevent its members from committing further offenses.

Experience shows that criminal convictions of members were not sufficient to stop the association's criminal activity. Also the expected conviction of members for membership in a criminal association and other offenses would not change this. In spite of the detention of some members it is to be feared that in view of the association's involvement with numerous other groups its unlawful activities will continue. Under internal laws, imprisoned members are supported by the association. This applies not only at the internal level but also in relation to other groups and the compulsory international solidarity of the Hells Angels. Any—primarily financial—support by members who are in freedom can only be based on criminal offenses as the essential source of income . . .

The immediate execution of the prohibition order and the dissolution of the Hells Angels Motor Club as well as the confiscation of its assets are in the public interest. It is to be expected that following the delivery of the prohibition order the association will make an increased effort through its unimprisoned members and outside contacts to seek income by illegal means. Effective measures against the association are therefore possible only if the order is executed at once. It cannot be excluded that assets and documents belonging to the association are removed for subsequent use in the continuation of its criminal activities.

Four

ANTHONY TAIT LIKED HIS WOMEN a little on the trashy side, and he had a passion for redheads. Brenda Lee Fowler was a stunning 20-year-old stripper and hooker whose driver's license address was "streets of Anchorage."

Brenda was born an army brat in Camp Lejeune, North Carolina, in 1962. She ran away from her Anchorage home at 13 and moved in with John Jones and his half-dozen children. Jones, then 71, was by all accounts the city's most accomplished pervert. He had sex with all but one of his daughters and buggered his son. He was a World War II veteran who plied hundreds of young girls with alcohol and painkillers intended to aid his injured back. Jones kept three or four cases of wine coolers in the house to loosen up girls who wouldn't fuck voluntarily.

Jones slipped a quaalude or Demerol to a girl after she quaffed two or three coolers. Next thing you know, he'd drop her panties and lick or fuck her. He took Polaroid pictures of naked girls who stretched open their vaginas. He had suitcases full of photographs: girls passed out, conscious, dildoes shoved into every opening. He had a varied collection of dildoes and butt plugs, vibrating, inflatable, strap-on, arm-sized.

Jones turned on a bedside tape recorder when he got

a girl into the sack and talked while he fucked her or she sucked him. "Oh, you like that. You like when I fuck you in the ass." Anchorage had fewer than a quarter of a million residents. Jones went through quite a few families' daughters.

Brenda Fowler was one of John Jones's playthings. It paid the rent. So the transition from giving it up freely to charging for it came easily.

Tait worked the door of the Arctic Fox in November 1983. The bar was owned by fellow Hells Angel Monty Elliott and Pat Hurn, sister of Angel Michael Hurn. He was not allowed to wear his colors on the job. It intimidated people who didn't need to be and invited jerks to start fights. Even members could not wear colors, T-shirts or Hells Angels belt buckles in the bar. However, the Hells Angels brought legal action against any bar that refused to let them wear club colors.

"Let's see your ID," he asked a good-looking redhead who walked in with her girlfriend.

"I don't have to show you my ID," she snapped. "I'm here to see Monty."

"That's all good and well," Tait said stonily, "but if you want to sit in the bar you got to have some ID."

"I'm here to see Monty. I don't need ID," she said, trying to pull rank on this dumbass bouncer it seemed the Angels hired to present a respectable front at the door. She had worked as a stripper for Monty Elliott in 1978 at a bar called the Strip.

"Look, don't give me a hard time," Tait said quietly.

Fowler gave him a hard time.

"Lookit, baby. You can do what you're told, show me the ID, or you can just get your fat little ass on out of here."

"I don't have a fat ass!"

"You either get out of here or I'll just throw you out the fucking door. I've done it before. It don't matter how pretty you are. I'll just throw your ass out into the street, into the snow and the slush."

She grabbed her coat and her friend and stormed

out.

Three days later, Tait chatted up a couple of whores over a drink at the Great Alaska Bush Company. He had his patch on. He scanned the tables and saw Brenda get friendly with a customer between dance sets. He smiled and tipped his drink to her. She gave him an evil glare and continued to hustle the customer.

Later, Brenda explained her run-in with the bouncer to the bartender at the Whale's Tail lounge in the Captain Cook Hotel. Tait walked in.

"That's the guy right there."

"There's the redheaded bitch herself right there," Tait said.

Four days after that, Tait took one of his many squeezes to his favorite bar, the Whale's Tail. She was also a dancer at the Bush Company. Brenda walked in with a guy and sat in a booth. Tait smiled at her. Her face tensed. Tait laughed.

Half an hour later, Tait got up to take a piss. He walked down a flight of stairs, and as he reached the landing, he heard a rapid click of high heels on the flagstones behind him.

"Excuse me, sir," Brenda sang. "May I have a word with you, please?"

"Yeah, sure. I'm just going downstairs."

"So am I."

"No, you're not. You're following me. You came down to talk to me for something, didn't you."

"Well, yes, I did."

"What's the story?"

"I really have to apologize to you and I'm really sorry about what happened." The rest of her words ran together and it sounded like gibberish to Tait. "I didn't know."

"That's all good and well," he said. "But you should just pay attention when people tell you to do something. You should do it and shut up."

"I just thought you were some guy giving me a hard time, trying to pick me up. That happens a lot."

"I can understand that. You're a beautiful girl. You're

real pretty."

"I've never met you before, have I?"

"No, of course not. I'm different. I'm not like the rest of the guys."

"That's what I noticed right off. I'm Brenda Fowler."

"I'm Anthony Tait. You can call me Tony if you like."

"I'd like to buy you a drink to make things up to you."

"That's fine," he said. "But what about your friend?"

"Oh, he won't mind. He's just a friend."

Brenda bought Tait and his squeeze, Carol, a drink. She walked over later and handed him her business card. "This is my home number. If you would, call me."

"All right."

Tait called Brenda a week later and left his home number on her answering machine. She called a week after that and asked him out to dinner. She was supposed to pick him up at 6:00. He called her house at 6:15 and left a message on the machine. "If you're standing me up, you're just shit out of luck. I'm not the type of person who deals with this thing."

Ten minutes later, a limousine pulled up in front of Tait's house. The driver got out and knocked on the door.

"Brenda sent this limo to pick you up to go to dinner. By the way, there's a present in the back for you."

There were two presents on the seat. Tait opened the big one first. It was an expensive shirt with matching tie. The second box contained a rock of cocaine as big as the first joint of his thumb.

"This isn't good at all," he thought. "I don't like this."

The driver dropped Tait off at a downtown restaurant.

"Are you standing by?"

"Yeah, for the whole evening."

"I'm going to leave this stuff in the back of the car."

He placed the parcels next to two bottles of champagne Brenda had bought.

Tait and Brenda had dinner, but she was jacked up on coke and she picked at her food. After dinner they hopped into the limo.

"We need to talk," Tait said.

"How do you like your shirt?"

"That's fine. The shirt and tie are real nice."

"How do you like your other present?"

"That's what I need to talk to you about. I don't do cocaine at all. I don't fuck with it, I don't use it, I won't put it on my dick for you to blow me. I don't do any of that shit."

"You don't?"

"That's right. I don't use drugs. If I do, I smoke some grass once in a while. It's all right here."

Brenda put the rock of cocaine in her handbag.

"By the way, I have to tell you. You spent a lot of money on this champagne. Let's try and take it back and exchange it for a couple of bottles of good wine."

"You don't drink champagne either?"

"No. It's garbage. It gives you a headache. It's ridiculously overpriced. We can take this stuff here and I know the liquor store you got this at and we can probably get a couple of really decent bottles of wine. Do you want to go over to your place or my place?"

"Oh, no. I got a room reserved for us at the Big Timber Motel. One with a hot tub and mirrors on the wall."

"Okay."

Tait didn't call Brenda for a week after spending a night during which, he says, he "fucked her into submission." She showed up on his doorstep one night jacked on cocaine and pissed right off.

"Hey, what's the story? You fuck me and that's it? I like you. I want to have a relationship."

"Well, you're here, aren't you?"

"What do you mean?"

"Well, you want to have a relationship. Why don't you start right now? I'd really like a blowjob."

Tait took Brenda into his arms and sat her on the

edge of his bed. She was so stunned by the request she couldn't act. He opened his bathrobe, took out his dick and stuck it in her mouth. "How do you like that?"

She slipped the penis out of her mouth, held it and looked up. "I really like you. I like men like you. You're powerful."

Brenda was a doper, stripper and hooker. It was all she knew, all she was trained for. She promised Tait she'd stop hooking. He had her wait tables and work in an electronics store. He kept close tabs on her when he was in town. He called her at odd hours to see if she was in. Of course, she did the same to him. But Tait was destined to be a traveling man. And that gave Brenda a lot of free time.

Brenda first showed her inclination to take care of business when she discovered one of Tait's other love interests. He met Vivian Burger, who danced under the name Danielle Marks at the Alaska Bush Company, in the hot-tub room of the Big Timber at a birthday party for Marks and another girl a week or so before he met Brenda Fowler. Marks got so drunk she missed a shift at the Bush Company and was fired. Marks told Tait she was arrested several times for prostitution in Los Angeles. Tait invited her to live with him in the duplex he shared with his father, who worked across the inlet and spent little time at home.

Marks spent three weeks in the duplex and three more weeks in Tait's new home before he kicked her out when she refused to work and bring home money to pay the rent. She moved in with an Anchorage cab driver and drug dealer. Tait was busy with Fowler and didn't see Marks until the spring of 1984, when he visited her in Humana Hospital, where she was being treated for a stomach infection. She asked Tait if she could rent his house trailer, and they made an arrangement. When Brenda found out about Marks, she visited the trailer with a girlfriend and pretended to deliver a pizza. They beat Marks viciously.

Tait had an eclectic taste in women and often philosophized that despite being involved in a relationship, "a man is like a dog. He's going to run around and sniff other fence posts." So it was with great satisfaction he learned that one of Brenda's friends was the stupendously endowed Cindy Pelligrini. He thought Cindy "had the nicest set of tits I've ever seen on a broad."

Cindy often visited Brenda and Tait at home. One night Tait suggested a threesome with the redheads. It was a practice Brenda would often encourage.

Five

FROM HIS EARLIEST DAYS in the Brothers, unbeknownst to them, Anthony Tait played both sides of the street. He rumbled with rounders, buddied with bikers and punched and intimidated his way through the underside of society. But he also harbored a long-seeded desire to legitimize his authoritarian dark side: he wanted to be a cop. He never pursued the career, he just liked the idea of being a cop. Tait had at times passed himself off as a cop. He thought, looked and acted like one. He hung out in cop bars when he wasn't in strip joints or biker bars. He gave the cops he met bits of hearsay he picked up from bartenders, hookers or his biker friends. The information interested the cops enough that they listened to him. He met them in more sedate watering holes such as the Whale's Tail Lounge in the Captain Cook Hotel and the Signature Room in the Hilton.

He befriended Larry Robinette, who worked vice for the Anchorage Police Department in 1982. Tait chose older men as friends. He learned from them and they treated him like a son. Tait and Robinette had dinner at each other's houses and met downtown for lunch. Tait fed Robinette trivial information on the Brothers and petty criminals. He was fortunate he was never seen talking to cops.

Alaska is a land of opportunity where few people

restrict themselves to one job. If there's a market for their talents, they fill it. Robinette was a jeweler. He made Tait an expensive gold nugget watch and two gold rings. He also sent some action Tait's way. Robinette rented a room in his house to a cocktail waitress from the Keyboard Lounge, the police bar in Anchorage. Brigitte was a French woman eager to get Tait in the sack. Robinette set them up in 1984.

"Brigitte wants you to come over to the house tonight."

"What for? It's her night off."

"I don't know, but I won't be home all night."

The light clicked on in Tait's brain. He visited Brigitte and decided, "She's a typical senseless female. She's driven all kinds of nails in the wall to hang belts on, hang clothes on." But the girl wanted to play a little slap and tickle, and Tait was not the type to forgo an opportunity to please a woman. He saw her only twice because he lived with Brenda at the time.

Another cop Tait befriended was Ron Becker, also with the Anchorage department. Dan Wilcox was robbed at home by a man dressed as a woman. Tait recognized the modus operandi and told Wilcox he knew the man. Wilcox asked him to tell the police and promised not to tell the Brothers that Tait talked to the cops.

Tait and Becker grew close after a long night of booze and violence that started at the Whale's Tail Lounge. They hopped from bar to bar until last call, and then Tait took Becker to an after-hours bar. There were only 10 people in the place. Two of them fought. Becker jumped up, told them he was a police officer and ordered them to stop. One man turned and knocked him silly with a punch to the head. Tait beat both men and hustled them out the door. He put an ice pack on Becker's head and they continued to drink until Becker passed out. Tait took him out to his pickup truck and sat him in the passenger seat in minus-20-degree weather.

Tait returned to the bar for two more drinks, then decided Becker shouldn't drive his police car. He took him to his place and stretched him out on the couch at 2:30 in the morning. Becker got up at 7:30 confused and embarrassed for being smacked by a drunk and saved by Tait. He didn't see Tait for two months, though Tait continued to eat at a restaurant Becker owned. Months later, Becker went off the deep end. His son, also a police officer, died in a car crash, and Becker began to drink heavily. He called Tait in the middle of the night and called him "son."

Tait was not a formal informant. He just told his police friends what he knew. Becker tried to follow up on some of the information. Robinette fed it to the FBI. Tait was impatient. He believed things should get done when he thought they should. One night in early 1982 he sat in a bar with Robinette, Becker and several others. They talked about the Brothers Motorcycle Club.

"Why in the hell don't you do something about these people?" Tait asked with his typical bravado and condescension. He had always believed cops could do in real life what they did on television. He also felt he could do anyone else's job better. He was adept at telling people how things should be done. "They run all over your town roughshod. They fuck everybody. They deal dope. They piss on cop cars."

Robinette explained that police infiltrators were identified by bikers within weeks.

Anchorage is a small city where faces quickly become familiar. The Anchorage Police Department had about 300 officers and the FBI had 22 special agents in town. The city cops didn't have money or manpower for long investigations into the criminal activities of the city's bikers.

"That's bullshit," Tait said. "I could do that on my own. I could get in there and find this stuff out, you know, before three weeks."

"You're full of shit," one man at the table said.

"You're out of your mind," Robinette said. "You don't know what you're talking about."

"You know what, I'll get in there, I'll find out what

the hell's going on and if I can't do it, the bet is a steak dinner and a bottle of whiskey—not Calvert's, either."

Tait was a shrewd gambler. The Brothers had already given him a Harley and asked him to hang around. Robinette did not know this that night. And Tait did not realize it would take a lot more than three weeks to gain access to useful information.

Tait met with Robinette once a week in a bar in 1982 to pass on what he learned. Tait and Robinette had no plan; Tait just told him what he saw. Tait had little to report during his prospect year, because prospects are not privy to club secrets. He got bored and fed up that the cops didn't act on his tips. But the information he gave them didn't merit action because it was gossip, outdated or could not be substantiated. Tait told Robinette he wanted to quit. Just when he was ready to pull the plug, he got his patch, and the criminal side of the gang opened up to him. This second wind kept him going until the spring of 1984. Tait didn't see much of Robinette in 1983 as he got more deeply involved in club activities.

Robinette was friends with Gordon Tait. The three of them sat down one night in the fall of 1983 and Robinette explained their attempt to penetrate the Hells Angels.

"We're going to try and pump these assholes."

Tait's father offered support. Tait used him as a sounding board and someone to bitch at when he needed an ear. Gordon Tait earned $70,000 to $80,000 a year working as a cook for Chugach Electric, and for the past couple of years had given his son up to $1,000 a month in pocket money. Father and son also had a joint bank account from which Tait could withdraw. The father spent $300 to $400 on dinners with his son that included 25-year-old scotches at $17 a pop. Gordon Tait didn't have much to spend his money on. He didn't drive. He enjoyed life's pleasures. He would call Tait from the fly-in camp he worked in 50 miles away.

"Hey, get four cases of Budweiser and two bottles of

R&R and a bottle of E&J brandy over here as fast as you can."

Tait packed the bottles as soon as the liquor store opened and paid $20 to have the booze flown to his father.

Tait and his brother Andrew suggested to Gordon he save money for his old age.

"I'm not going to have an old age. And you two shits are going to put me in a cardboard box and dump me on the side of the street somewhere."

After Gordon Tait listened to Robinette tell of his plans to infiltrate the Hells Angels, he told his son he needed some props. He rented a huge house in December 1983 for $1,200 a month. It had two and a half living rooms, a large kitchen, an eight-seater hot tub in a cedar room in the basement, a pool table and a wet bar. Gordon Tait was home four days every two weeks. Tait had women over so often his father commented that the house had "hot and cold running cunt. If I had what you have as a young man, I probably wouldn't have gotten married."

Tait felt his father now tried to make up for time they had not shared after his parents split up. Tait learned from his expanding circle of woman friends that his father was quite a lady's man. If the elder Tait had a failing, it was that he never took time to understand and appreciate scotch. In fact, he hated it.

In March 1984, Tait once again wanted to pack it in and go play cops and robbers elsewhere. "I'm sick of this, Robbie. I'm out of here. I'm going to pull the pin, leave town and try and get a job as a cop down south."

"Let's just try and see if we can get somebody interested in this," Robinette said. "I'll talk to a few people." He convinced Tait it was not worth busting a few Hells Angels on the meager information he had so far provided. Robinette saw Tait's potential as an informant inside the world's most notorious outlaw motorcycle gang. He knew the FBI was the only law enforcement agency in Alaska with the money to pay, and the interest to develop, such an informant.

Tait continued to press. "What are we going to do? I'm sick of this. Let's do something. Let's get on with it. I'm just wasting my life if we're not going to do anything."

Tait took Brenda to the Hells Angels U.S.A. Run at Lake of the Ozarks in Perry, Missouri, that June. Hells Angel Edward (Deacon) Proudfoot, a mail-order minister with the mail-order Church of the Angels, married them officially on June 14. New York City president Sandy Alexander and another Hells Angel wrote the wedding vows.

By July 1984, Tait had been a member of the Hells Angels for one year. He decided he had all the information he would ever get. He planned to copy the gang's entire security file from three briefcases in Ed Hubert's attic, hand it over to the police and go south to become a cop. Robinette persuaded him to hang tough. He hung out with the gang, went on runs and pounded nails on a construction job all summer. Most Alaska Hells Angels were not as well off as their southern brethren and worked to make ends meet. Toward the end of August, Tait had enough money saved up to fly himself and his tools to Maryland, where he planned to get a good construction job with a friend.

"Look, I've got somebody who's kind of interested in this," Robinette told him. "Let's hold up."

Tait spent most of September hunting and returned refreshed to Anchorage in October. He decided to sell his car and motorcycle by January and leave Alaska while it was in the deepest grips of winter. "Look, this is bullshit," he told Robinette. "I want to cut the strings and get the hell out of here."

"I've talked to somebody and the FBI wants to meet you," Robinette replied. Once again, he was a step ahead of Tait and kept him interested.

Although he had been a full-fledged Hells Angel for more than a year, Tait had yet to get his club tattoo.

Monty Elliott paid more than $500 in 1984 for Tait to get it while on the road. The Death's Head and the words "Hells Angels" along with "Alaska," were inked on his right deltoid.

In November 1984, Tait submitted titles to his house trailer and motorcycle as $26,000 in surety for a bail bond. The Hells Angels in Alaska had an arrangement with Fred's Bail Bonding whereby members posted a surety and whenever they were arrested anywhere in the United States, they just showed their tattoo to get bail.

He applied for an American certificate of citizenship the following month so he could get a passport, which his chapter suggested he get to fly to Japan to assess a local club. Tait's lack of a criminal record and clean-cut looks made him their best candidate for international trips.

FBI Special Agent Kenneth Marischen was well known on the Anchorage social scene. The six-foot-seven former semi-pro basketball player stood out in a crowd. He was gregarious, had an appraising eye for women and was a good drinking companion. And he was part of a federal/state/local task force that tracked Hells Angels. Late Friday or Saturday nights he included the Keyboard Lounge on his tour of bars because owner Jimmy Seward treated cops well.

Marischen often sat at the back of the lounge with Larry Robinette. In early December 1984, Robinette pulled Marischen aside.

"Would you be interested in taking information from a person who is in the Hells Angels?"

Marischen wondered why Robinette didn't handle the source himself. Was he trying to foist a problem source on the bureau? Robinette assured him he thought only the bureau had the resources to do anything worthwhile with the source. Local agencies could afford only a one-time bust. He suggested the source be used in a nationwide investigation of the Hells Angels.

Marischen had been in Alaska since October 1982.

He was a bureau agent 17 years before being transferred to Anchorage at his request. The posting was much sought after by hunters, fishermen and outdoorsmen, and Marischen liked to stalk game. He said he'd meet the source after Christmas.

Marischen orally briefed his superior, Anchorage Special Agent in Charge Larry Nelson, about his plans to debrief Tait. The FBI was near the end of Operation Roughrider, its first major investigation of the Hells Angels, and bureau offices across the country were kept abreast of goings-on within the club. Cops throughout the States requested information from the FBI in Anchorage about the movements and drug dealings of Alaskan Hells Angels, whose phone numbers appeared on phone toll records of members in other states. The FBI needed more information on the club.

Unbeknownst to Robinette, Ron Becker also tried to set Tait up with the FBI. He arranged a meeting with FBI Special Agents Billy Andrews and Bruce Talbert in mid-December. Andrews ignored security precautions and asked Tait to come to the downtown federal building for the encounter. The agents interviewed Tait, although they knew little about the Hells Angels, and filed a report. Tait told them he had been sergeant-at-arms for the Anchorage chapter and state security officer since the summer. He proved himself worthy of those jobs as a prospect. All he wanted to do was hand over the club's security files and tell the FBI all he knew about the Hells Angels. He gave them a rundown of the club's current membership and hierarchy in the Anchorage, Fairbanks and Mat-Su chapters. Andrews, in his report, noted inaccurately about Tait: "He is very familiar with weapons and received his training from the military while serving in Vietnam."

Marischen returned from holidays in early January 1985 and met with Tait right away.

Tait was blunt. "This is all I've got and I'm ready to pack it in. I'm ready to quit because I want to leave. I want to get a job. I want to get on with my life."

That didn't sound like much of a plan to Marischen. An experienced agent, he probed Tait until he found the right buttons to push to get him to work for the FBI as an informant. Those two buttons were money and ego. Tait complained about the money he blew while he got information from the Hells Angels. Now he wanted money for his efforts. It would become the focal point in his conversations and dealings with the FBI. Tait also needed to be stroked. He needed to know he was doing a good job. No one could stroke an informant better than Marischen. He was given sensitive jobs during his first year in Anchorage, one of which was media-relations officer.

Marischen convinced Tait he would like to shut down the Hells Angels in Alaska with his cooperation. But given Tait's desire to pack up and leave, Marischen picked his brain quickly to get what he could. He compiled a list of questions he wanted answered. Some of them were basic: How many Hells Angels are there in Alaska? Who are they? They met over several days and talked for hours. Tait knew much about Alaska operations but little about the Hells Angels nationwide, since he had not traveled much within the club. Marischen went through the background checks and debriefs needed to open Tait up as an informant.

He dragged out the debriefing sessions while he discussed Tait's potential as an informant with FBI supervisors, including the two agents in Washington who overlooked Operation Roughrider. They pointed out that once Roughrider went overt, or public, Tait could tell the FBI of threats against the Roughrider source and FBI agents. They were enthusiastic about the opportunity, finally, to control a source active inside the Hells Angels who did not have a criminal record. Past sources had all been on the outside, or members who quit or bargained information for lighter sentences. No one had ever given them current intelligence.

Tait and Marischen hit it off well from the start. Both were rough-and-tumble guys who eschewed suits and ties for plaid shirts and cowboy boots. It was one of the few times in his career Marischen developed an instant rapport with an informant. It would help them in hard times, especially if Tait caught on to his control's tricks and manipulations.

Marischen had passed the Missouri bar exams before he joined the FBI's St. Louis office in 1966. He worked fugitive cases and kidnapping and extortion cases for 11 years at the Los Angeles Division. Sometimes he was at the center of historic events.

Marischen stopped at a bar on the way home after work to see a female informant on Wednesday, June 5, 1968.

"I just heard that Bobby Kennedy got killed," she told him as he walked in. "Is it true?"

"Naw, I would know. I just came from the office."

At that time, FBI agents couldn't take radio-equipped bureau cars home, and since pagers had yet to be invented, they were out of touch with the office. Marischen found a pay phone and called work.

"Get your butt back over here. All hell's breaking loose."

Marischen was one of the two agents at the hospital where Kennedy was taken after Jordanian fanatic Sirhan Sirhan shot him twice in the head with a .22-caliber pistol in the kitchen of the Ambassador Hotel. Marischen was put on the phone with FBI Director J. Edgar Hoover, which was unnerving for a young agent. When Hoover was told Kennedy might die, he ordered Marischen and the other agent to stand by Kennedy's side and report on his condition regularly. Marischen spent the night with Pierre Salinger, Kennedy's press secretary; Pat Lawford (Kennedy); and Ethel Kennedy and other family members.

Marischen was put in charge of a four-man apprehension crew when 19-year-old Patty Hearst was kidnapped by the Symbionese Liberation Army in 1974. They acted on tips and raided buildings where Hearst was thought to be held captive.

In the late 1970s, Marischen worked a year and a

half on an undercover surveillance team that never went near the office. The agents went straight home after they followed their Soviet spies for the day. If he had learned the need for security and how to keep a low profile by that stage in his career, the assignment sharpened his wits.

Marischen was then assigned to track terrorists and uncovered a five-man terrorist team as the war between Armenians and Turks heated up in North America. In 1980, a terrorist with the Justice Commando of Armenian Genocide walked in front of the Turkish consul general's car when it stopped at a red light and shot him through the windshield with a .45-caliber pistol. Marischen's team solved the killing and several bombings, which led to the first U.S. prosecution of a terrorist gang. The other terrorist group that kept Marischen busy was the Armenian Secret Army for the Liberation of Armenia.

Marischen, an avid hunter and outdoorsman in search of a slower-paced life, requested a transfer to Alaska and was sent to Anchorage in October 1982, two months before the Brothers Motorcycle Club became Hells Angels. The Anchorage office is a seniority position because it is treated as a foreign bureau. It's a high-expense office where the FBI doesn't send junior agents, and turnover is low. Marischen wore many hats in the small office. He was informant coordinator, in charge of administering the informant program, spokesman and media coordinator, and SWAT coordinator.

Tait was adamant he be paid for his information. He lost his construction job in January 1985 after the owner, a Hells Angel associate, lost a contract and the entire crew was fired. Tait told Marischen he got fired because he took too much time off to talk to the FBI under the pretext of going to the doctor or the dentist, and he demanded to be reimbursed for money he had spent. Tait had the misguided notion that the FBI was able to mount complex and expensive operations on the spur of the moment. He finally said he needed money to fix his motorcycle immediately. Marischen didn't know that the Alaska Hells Angels had a down time from November 15 to March 15, so Tait didn't need the bike for another two months. Marischen gave him an envelope that contained $500. Tait considered it an insult.

"Listen, I've spent all of this money of my own. Here's umpteen thousand dollars' worth of receipts to show you where the money went. It's all spent on this. What about it?" Tait wanted all his expenses, from rent, telephone bills and travel costs to motorcycle and entertainment costs, paid by the government. Tait intensified the pressure. He told Marischen he couldn't continue without money. He said he pawned his belongings for cash.

The pattern for their interactions was set. Marischen began to formulate a plan to control his informant and to make Tait perceive his FBI handler as a friend and sympathetic ear inside a large but stingy bureaucracy.

In mid-January, Gordon Tait suffered a stroke. He died one week later. The scene at the funeral home reflected Tait's divided loyalties: police officers on one side of the room, Hells Angels on the other. The cops were friends of Gordon's. The Hells Angels offered their support to Tait, although one Hells Angel was an accomplished chef and had traded recipes with Gordon, who had cooked for up to 100 people at a time on work sites. Tait's mother and sisters were not pleased his friends showed up. The Angels questioned Tait about the cops.

"Everybody here has their own parents and their own family and your parent's friends don't have to be your friends."

Tait's pager beeped several times an hour. Marischen wanted to know what was happening at the funeral home. Tait, as always, was ready for violence. He carried a Beretta 92 9-mm pistol and six 20-round magazines and a Browning Hi-Power 9-mm pistol with four magazines. "Any shit starts, I'm going to riddle every fucking asshole here," he thought. "That's going to be the end of it." Tait always talked about ending things.

In February, the FBI gave Tait a polygraph test to ensure he wasn't a double agent. FBI Special Agent Peter J. Flanagan from the Chicago Division administered the test in an Anchorage motel. He then interviewed Tait for his report.

Examinee, who is currently in a position to furnish information regarding the activities of the Anchorage Chapter of the Hells Angels Motorcycle Gang, has offered his assistance to the FBI and has to date provided a large quantity of information regarding Hells Angels members and activities.

The purpose of the polygraph examination is to determine the truthfulness of examinee's statements that he has not offered his assistance to the FBI at the direction of the Hells Angels, that he has not told any of the Hells Angels members of his contact with the FBI, that he is not now involved in any serious criminal activity nor is he involved in any scheme to deliberately mislead the FBI.

It is the opinion of the examiner that examinee's recorded responses to question A and B are indicative of being deceptive. It is further the opinion of the examiner that examinee's recorded responses to relevant questions C and D are not indicative of being deceptive.

The relevant questions asked are as follows:

A. Were you instructed to contact the FBI by anyone you haven't told me about? No.

B. Were you instructed by any club member to contact the FBI? No.

C. Have you told anyone about your contact with the FBI you've withheld from me? No.

D. Have you told any club members about your contact with the FBI? No.

During the post-test phase of the examination, the examinee stated, in regards to his being instructed to contact the FBI, intelligence-gathering and source development were routinely discussed at the Hells Angels weekly meetings. Examinee stated even though associating with any law enforcement officers was frowned upon, members were encouraged to develop sources of information regarding the Hells Angels within the various law enforcement agencies. Tait maintained that he had been truthful to those relevant questions asked, regarding his being specifically directed to infiltrate the FBI by the Hells Angels.

Flanagan included a separate report for Tait's file:

During the pre-test phase of the polygraph examination, Tait advised that although his current narcotic use is limited to marijuana, one joint of which he had the previous evening and a second joint approximately 9:00 this morning, he did previously have a problem with cocaine use up until 1980. (It made him sick). He stated through his own work, he was able to completely kick the cocaine habit. Tait added that although he described his present health as good, despite feeling weak and tired, he has been under tremendous strain as a result of his recent decision to assist the FBI along with his father's recent death. He advised that although he is not currently under a doctor's care, due to all of this recent pressure, he has considered seeing a psychiatrist.

Following the polygraph examination, Tait advised that although he has only been in contact with the FBI for a short while, his decision to assist law enforcement was made many years ago when he sought membership in a motorcycle club known as the Brothers. He advised that his plan then was to work undercover by gaining the confidence of the other members so as to provide intelligence information to any law enforcement agency which could require his assistance. Tait advised that it was his recently deceased father, who was a British sub-

ject and worked for the Palestine Security Forces,
who counseled him on intelligence-gathering.

Tait advised he has previously assisted the
Maryland State Troopers with two drug buys back
in 1970, and has more recently assisted the
Anchorage Police Department on occasions. In
discussing his associates, Tait advised that the
only person he trusts 100 percent is President
Ronald Reagan, and stated, "If it doesn't work out
he will probably have to try to contact President
Reagan," due to the "magnitude" of the information he possesses.

Regarding any attempt by Tait to infiltrate the
FBI on behalf of the Hells Angels, he denied having
been specifically instructed by the Hells Angels or
anyone else to do so. Tait advised that at the club's
weekly meetings, intelligence gathering is discussed and members, although not encouraged to
associate with any law enforcement officers, are
encouraged to try to develop and cultivate sources
within any law enforcement agency who might be
working against the Hells Angels. Tait advised that
in the spring of 1983, he attended a "Radiological
Monitoring Course," sponsored by a local agency,
which consisted of officers from various law
enforcement agencies and included the state police.
Tait advised that during the course, he became
friendly with the state police officers, leading them
on to believe that he was a police officer, and continued to meet with these officers on a weekly basis
after the completion of the course until the group
slowly faded away and interest stopped. Tait
advised that he told the Hells Angels members
about this "infiltration." However, he never actually gained any intelligence information from it.
Tait advised that as far as any "sources" he has cul-
tivated, they primarily consist of bartenders, prostitutes and some army personnel from some of the
local military bases.

While the FBI tried to ensure that Tait was not a double agent, the club's long-established intelligence network within law enforcement served to protect its multi-million-dollar methamphetamine-production business thousands of miles to the south. Law enforcement knew since the late 1960s that Oakland Hells Angel Kenneth Jay (K.O. or Kenny) Owen was the club's premier methamphetamine manufacturer. He always eluded them, although they picked up traces of his trail and busted him on many lesser infractions. Drug Enforcement Administration Special Agent Laura Hayes decided in 1984 to attack Owen's drug business from a different angle. She traced the origins of precursor chemicals he used to make meth and followed the shipments to his doorstep.

There are three ways to synthesize methamphetamine. The fish-bowl synthesis, where methylamine and phenyl-2-propanone are mixed with other chemicals; the hydrogenation synthesis, where ephedrine is reacted with hydrogen under pressure; and the red phosphorus synthesis, where red phosphorus and ephedrine are reacted in the presence of a form of hydrogen iodide.

Methylamine and phenyl-2-propanone are controlled substances in California. The clandestine chemist can synthesize these compounds, which are more difficult to make than methamphetamine, or can take the calculated risk of stealing them or buying them under false pretense from chemical-supply houses. Phenyl-2-propanone is legally used in photo processing and has a distinctive long-lasting odor. Its smell, or rather that of its precursor—phenylacetic acid, used as an odor-retaining base in some perfumes—has led many a police officer to a clandestine lab.

The hydrogenation synthesis requires specialized knowledge and expensive equipment to inject explosive hydrogen under pressure into a pressurized vessel, where it interacts with ephedrine to form methamphetamine. The process produces highly explosive ether or acetone. The red phosphorus synthesis produces toxic fumes if the chemicals are mixed too long or heated too high.

The history of clandestine labs and the manufacture of methamphetamine in California can be traced through successive legislative attempts to curb the problem. The common way to synthesize methamphetamine until the 1980s was the fish-bowl method, and the California Department of Justice and the DEA tried to curb the exponential growth of clandestine labs from the 1960s to the 1980s with laws that controlled the sale and purchase of, among other chemicals, methylamine and phenyl-2-propanone. The laws drastically, though briefly, reduced methamphetamine production. Clandestine chemists learned they could synthesize phenyl-2-propanone with phenylacetic acid, which suddenly became a much sought-after chemical. Clandestine labs were back in business.

In 1983, California passed a law to restrict the sale of phenylacetic acid. This caused underground chemists to import methylamine and phenylacetic acid from states where the chemicals were not controlled. Methylamine is legally used in pesticides and dyes. Phenylacetic acid is used primarily to make penicillin. Its second most common use is the manufacture of methamphetamine.

Laura Hayes's case against Kenny Owen started in October 1984, when undercover DEA Special Agent Michael Duda learned that a chemical company owner planned to send someone to Fort Lauderdale to pick up seven cylinders of pressurized monomethylamine. A woman picked up the cylinders, which were five feet high, 12 inches in diameter and weighed 125 pounds each.

The chemical company was well known to the DEA as a documented source of chemicals, glassware and equipment used to manufacture methamphetamine. It had been named in 14 DEA investigations since it was formed in 1980. The company appeared legitimate, but business records seized under a federal warrant in 1982 showed 75 percent of its business was in precursor chemicals. Seized receipts showed frequent cash sales of ephedrine, methylamine, ether and phenylacetic acid in amounts of $10,000 or more. The receipts did not identify the purchaser or reveal the amount of chemical sold. Much of the company's business was done elsewhere than at its store. Large shipments were placed in ministorage units rented by the buyers.

The federal search warrant led to the co-owner being arrested for violating state reporting requirements on sales of methylamine. The DEA cited his extensive criminal background: he was mentioned in 31 DEA investigations. Since 1973, he was linked to the importation and manufacture of cocaine, marijuana and methamphetamine. He allegedly set up a meth lab in San Francisco in 1975. The same year, he was linked to an organization that flew marijuana and cocaine into the United States in private planes. He was said to be behind the laboratory that processed the cocaine hydrochloride. Todd Loomis was arrested in 1977 after he delivered 14 pounds of cocaine to an undercover DEA agent in Florida.

The DEA's investigation of the chemical company owner in 1984 showed he was as active as ever. DEA agent Michael Duda learned that in December the owner would again send someone to Fort Lauderdale to pick up another eight cylinders of monomethylamine, to be delivered to the same customers in the Bay Area who received the seven cylinders in October.

DEA agents in Fort Lauderdale installed a radio transponder in the cap of a cylinder and placed a tracking device on the yellow 1972 Ford Custom Wagon used to pick up the gas. DEA agents then followed the converted bus across the country. The driver met with two men at a hotel in Stateline, California. The two men followed the driver into San Francisco in a green van. Several vehicle swaps were made before one man drove the Custom Wagon to the Bay Area Rapid Transit station in Richmond, where he parked and used a phone. A blue Cadillac with two men showed up. They talked briefly.

The driver of the Cadillac, who bought large quantities of precursor chemicals for methamphetamine from the chemical company, was a chemist who manufactured methamphetamine for the Hells Angels. The DEA had known of Hill's connection to the Hells Angels since 1979.

The passenger in the Cadillac, Hells Angel Kenny Owen, got into the Custom Wagon and drove it to the Woodshop, his warehouse-workshop across from the Hells Angels' Oakland clubhouse. The blue Cadillac followed and parked next to the building.

The building at 4010 Foothill Boulevard was in the name of Linda Walton, wife of Hells Angel Sergey Walton, who had become a police informant in 1980. Several Hells Angels had run businesses out of the building.

A few days later, the Custom Wagon was driven to the Hells Angels compound of five houses on dead-end Mark and Stella streets in Oakland. The five houses were surrounded by a high redwood fence. The Hells Angels had owned the houses for 10 years and the property was in the name of Linda Walton. The Custom Wagon was parked near a house Kenny Owen had recently moved out of.

While the DEA watched the shipment of monomethylamine gas, DEA Special Agent Donald Wood learned that the chemical company owner had ordered 2,200 pounds of phenylacetic acid for the same customer. Wood arranged for the acid to be in Phoenix, Arizona, and placed a tracking device in one of the barrels. DEA Special Agent Charles Henderson took delivery of the acid and placed it in a mini-warehouse storage unit.

DEA Special Agent David Schickendanz then called a prearranged number. Two men showed up in the yellow Custom Wagon and said they would drive the phenylacetic acid to California that day. They asked Schickendanz if he had checked the barrels for beepers. He said he had not and took the keys to the Custom Wagon, which he drove to the storage unit, where the barrels were loaded into it. Schickendanz returned the keys to one man and said he checked for beepers.

That man drove to Stateline, California, where he

booked into a motel. The two men, who chauffeured the monomethylamine, arrived in a white Mercedes. They drove the Custom Wagon to the Woodshop.

Laura Hayes drafted her search warrant affidavit. Surveillance of the transponder emissions showed the chemicals were still in the compound and the Woodshop. It would be difficult for the DEA to make a case against Kenny Owen if the chemicals were not seized in the same building. Loomis paid $43,000 for the chemicals, which had a street value of $237,000.

The Hells Angels had enough precursors to produce more than 1,000 pounds of methamphetamine. The DEA learned that Todd Loomis ordered another 6,600 pounds of phenylacetic acid, enough to produce 3,300 pounds of drug. Some of the chemicals went to Everett Hill, whose criminal record for controlled substances stretched back to 1949.

Federal search warrants were executed at Owen's Woodshop and his former house in the compound. FBI Special Agent Jay E. Colvin and ATF Special Agent Theodore Baltas were part of the raid team. They found empty cylinders that had contained the monomethylamine gas in a common garage at the compound. The cap with the transponder was found on a nearby workbench. Recipes and formulas for methamphetamine synthesis were found in the attic of Owen's former house. But the gas itself was nowhere to be found. The raid on the Woodshop produced half the metric ton of phenylacetic acid and the container in which the transponder had been secreted. But the other chemicals that would have given rise to manufacturing charges if found stored with the phenylacetic acid had vanished. Somehow, the cops had been duped. Owen's craftiness had fouled their investigation, and the Hells Angels' premier crankcooker slipped through their fingers.

Tait packed his father's ashes in three liquor bottles. He filled a half-gallon R&R jug, a Johnnie Walker swing

bottle and half a bottle of Dimple Scotch. He left two on
the mantel at home where he would habitually talk to
them. He took the Dimple Scotch bottle to Scotland a
couple of days after the cremation, he cut a piece of turf
out of a family grave that contained four bodies—one
was a turn-of-the-century police sergeant—and dumped
the ashes into the soil.

Tait stayed in Europe six weeks and scrupulously
kept receipts so the FBI would reimburse his expenses,
although U.S. law prohibited him from working for the
agency outside the country. His first stop was the London
home of Guy (Tricky Tramp) Lawrence, the Sonny Barger
of Europe. Hanging out with Europe's most powerful
Hells Angel opened doors for Tait. But the door to Tricky
Tramp's house was opened to him because the English
Hells Angels mistakenly thought Tait was sent over by
West Coast Officers to investigate a rift between the
Amsterdam and Rio de Janeiro chapters that gave rise to a
motion at the Hells Angels Euro Meeting to strip Rio of
its charter. Tait picked up grumblings about the Rio
chapter as he visited various English chapters, but it
would be a week before he learned the details. In the
meantime, the Windsor chapter lent him a prospect's bike
to get around.

English Hells Angels who saw Tait with Tricky
Tramp talked openly in his presence about their criminal
activities, which were mainly burglaries, car thefts and
minor dope deals.

The Euro Meeting in Southampton in February 1985
was a typical Hells Angel blowout, with blowjobs for all.
The English Angels produced a turnout called Delicious
Dee, "a skanky bitch with razor scars across both wrists
who'd been rode hard and put away wet," according to
Tait. She satisfied all 50 guys at the party at least once
and most twice. For once, Tait kept his hormones in
check. He figured she must have crabs or the clap.
Despite his celibacy on this night, he would find on his
return home that he had picked up some carnal crus-
taceans after all.

The problem between the Amsterdam and Rio de Janeiro chapters had begun when the European Angels tried to score cocaine in Brazil. They couldn't find any and asked their Rio brothers to buy some for them. The Rio Angels spent the money but didn't buy coke. They said they wanted to wait to get a better exchange rate. Despite claims to the contrary, Hells Angels around the world fuck each other over regularly. The Rio Angels didn't even ride mandatory Harleys, but chose stripped-down Japanese bikes they called Demon Machines.

The Amsterdam Angels couldn't understand why their Rio brothers wouldn't sell them coke. They finally scored some from a Rio Angel's girlfriend. That pissed off the Rio Angels, who abandoned the Amsterdam Angels in an isolated house in the countryside. The Dutch Angels walked back to civilization and the Rio Angels put them up in an apartment that had rope cots instead of beds. The Dutch Angels brought the matter up at the Euro Meeting. Brothers shouldn't treat brothers like that, they said. They wanted to pull the Rio charter.

The European Angels asked Tait, "Why don't you find out what's going on and take it back to the OM in Oakland and talk to Oakland about it?"

Tait flew to Amsterdam and got their side of the story.

Several European chapter presidents tried to contact Tait in Alaska while he was on his way back from Europe. They left messages with Anchorage vice-president Ed Hubert. Hubert had sponsored Tait into the club and was proud as hell his protégé rose so quickly in prestige and respect within the gang that international presidents called him. Hubert didn't hesitate to throw his weight behind a winner, especially if that winner was his sergeant-at-arms and bodyguard.

Early in April, the FBI obtained from the Department of Justice authorization for criminal authority for Tait. He could now commit crimes as part of the investigation into the Hells Angels. He was also authorized, at Marischen's request, to carry a concealed weapon because of the dangerous nature of his task. This circumvented the need to get a weapons permit, which is issued by local police forces only. That would have created a paper trail and security risk. Marischen and his superiors decided early not to involve other agencies in the investigation. Even agents who worked with Marischen had no idea what he was up to.

A few days later, Tait flew to California to attend his first West Coast Officers' Meeting in the Oakland clubhouse, at the request of the European Hells Angels. The clubhouse was a former dance studio with hardwood floors that Sonny Barger often boasted about. Tait told the officers what he learned at the Euro Meeting, and after the WesCOM, the president of the Rio de Janeiro chapter was ordered to fly to Amsterdam to settle the matter.

Although Tait attended his first OM under the pretext that he needed to plead Amsterdam's case, he relied on the stingy resources of the Anchorage chapter to get him to Oakland. Gerald Michael (Pee Wee) Protzman and another Angel alternated as elected representatives of the Alaska Hells Angels at the West Coast Officers' Meetings. Their airfares and expenses were paid out of the club treasury. Alaska Angels were among the poorest in the club.

Marischen recognized Tait's potential and the opportunities for him to make a heavy dent in the Hells Angels organization if he could only get out of Alaska, but he never thought his informant would get out of state. Alaska Angels were a ratty, rag-tag bunch of bikers who lacked the sophistication of their California brothers. Tait seemed stuck in no-man's-land. Marischen and Tait devised a plan that would allow him to attend all WesCOMs and meet the more criminally active Hells Angels. Tait approached Ed Hubert with the idea.

"Hey, I can fly for nothing. Why don't I take over the responsibilities of attending the WesCOMs? I can get free tickets, but only for myself and in my own name, because my sister works for the airlines."

The offer took the financial onus off the Alaska chapters, though it created jealousies among Hells Angels who were elected to attend WesCOMs but couldn't afford to attend the meetings out of their own pockets. It was a crafty move with one flaw. Tait did have a sister who worked for an airline in Alaska. This gave credibility to his story, since some of the bikers knew of her. But it is never wise to involve one's family in an operation, especially when they don't know about it. Tait was later elected the official Alaska representative to the WesCOMs. Marischen hoped his charisma, his ability to bullshit, his coming from far-away, mystical Alaska, his access to easy money, his military expertise with explosives and weapons and his supposed combat experience in Vietnam—stories he made up to impress people over the years—would open doors for him in California.

The Hells Angels had another issue to settle: whether to grant a charter to a Japanese bike gang. Two Japanese bikers wore bogus Hells Angels colors to California in 1983. They were stripped of the patches and sent to Anchorage to be looked over by the newest Hells Angels chapter. Tait, who was a prospect at that time, had to house and entertain them because he spoke pidgin Japanese. Tait talked to two Oakland members about the Japanese bikers in April 1985. The club decided Tait should be part of the contingent of Hells Angels to fly to Tokyo to assess the wannabe bikers because he spoke the language and knew some of the Japanese gangsters. All of a sudden, Anthony Tait was a major player in the Hells Angels Motorcycle Club.

Six

Tait arrived in Tokyo in April 1985 for a three-week stay. Several days later, the Alaska Hells Angels sent Tom (T.J.) Joiner as an extra vote. The club paid their airfare only; Tait and Joiner were expected to cover their expenses in a city with an exorbitant cost of living. Tait wired Anchorage for money and received $1,000, which he and Joiner stretched for a couple of days.

The Hells Angels don't grant new charters readily. They sent 21 American and English Hells Angels to Japan.

The Japanese bikers decided to become Hells Angels after two San Francisco Angels started to supply them with methamphetamine. The Frisco Angels spread their wings into the international market and had reasons other than brotherhood to press for a charter for the Japanese bikers, who were to be called the Tokyo Nomads. Tait finally got the Frisco Angels to admit in front of the rest of the group that they wanted a foreign market for their drugs. He also turned the Japanese bikers against each other. He prompted one of them to beat up first the club vice-president, then the president. That whittled down the number of Japanese bikers who wanted to become Hells Angels. They did not know that violence was part of the lifestyle.

The Club secretary and another member then bad-mouthed the member who beat the vice-president. They wanted him out of the gang because he wanted to tell the Hells Angels that the secretary worked on an automated fingerprint identification system developed by NEC Electronics. Only five computers in the world were equipped with the system. They were in Washington, D.C., Australia, Portugal and Anchorage. The secretary didn't want the Hells Angels to know that he had lived in Anchorage for six months with the Alaska State Troopers while he worked in a senior position on the project and did not contact the Hells Angels. The secretary kicked the potential informant out before he could rat on him.

"I'd call bullshit on him," Tait told him. "I'd go kick his ass."

"Oh, is that what you do?"

The incident gave Tait enough ammunition to convince his fellow Hells Angels that the Tokyo bikers were not worthy of being granted a charter.

Tait also found out during his stay in Japan that not all Hells Angels are as tough as they pretend to be, especially the English Angels. Fester from the South Coast charter got carried away as he played pinball in the Hard Rock Café, and slammed the machine around. Charming Chuck Zito, a martial-arts expert, told him to chill out. (Zito had been a bodyguard for Liza Minnelli and taught Sylvester Stallone how to box. In return, Stallone gave him a gold boxing-glove pendant.) Fester told Zito to shove it. Zito, as Fester remembered through an alcoholic haze, coolly threatened to severely beat him.

"I'm not going to fuck you up now. I'm going to fuck you up tomorrow when you're sober so you can remember it better."

A panic-stricken Fester woke Tait and cried out his story. He begged Tait to ask Zito not to beat him. Fester returned home unscathed.

Operation Roughrider went overt—public—on May 2, 1985, while Tait was in Tokyo. More than a hundred Hells Angels and associates were arrested across the

United States on drug charges in the most damaging investigation to that date of the club's involvement in the drug trade. An informant who befriended several Hells Angels had traveled from chapter to chapter with an undercover FBI agent introduced as his partner and bought drugs from the bikers for several years. Tait had provided Marischen with the itineraries of Hells Angels for whom they had arrest warrants; he had merely asked his colleagues what their travel plans were. Charming Chuck Zito and One-Eyed Bert Kittel surrendered at the U.S. embassy in Tokyo. They were jailed, then deported to the States and arrested as they stepped off the plane.

While Tait jetted around the world on Hells Angels business, Marischen continued the tedious and laborious process of ascertaining Tait was legit and proving it to the bureaucracy.

Tait was opened up as an informant on January 23, 1985. He had to undergo a "suitability and pertinence inquiry" before he could be made an organized-crime informant. Marischen had to convince himself and the bureau that Tait could and would give the FBI information about crimes over which the bureau had jurisdiction: drugs, explosives and conspiracy to commit murder. The process was slow because Tait was shut down as an informant while out of the country, although that did not prevent him from communicating with Marischen from abroad. Tait was converted to a fully operational source in late March.

Tait pestered Marischen about money when he returned from Tokyo in May. He wanted to be reimbursed for his expenses promptly. Marischen couldn't afford to defend the bureau while he tried to win Tait over. He pretended to side with Tait and bitched against the FBI bureaucracy. In Tait's eyes, they were both the victims of a system needlessly weighed down with paper-shufflers. To pull off this scam effectively, Marischen needed someone to whom he could pass the buck. At the same time, he wanted to flatter Tait with a show that high-ranking FBI officials were interested in him. He turned to Larry Nelson, the special agent in charge of the Anchorage Division.

Nelson had to assess the potential of using Tait as an informant against the Hells Angels. He had to ensure all options were covered. Marischen would use Nelson to flatter Tait and redirect his antagonism. A control must have little friction with an informant. Nelson would know he was being used, but in a division as small as Anchorage, field agents and supervisory staff developed close relationships and knew when to help each other.

Tait's rants against the FBI's reluctance to pay him quickly reached one of many melting points in May. Marischen could side with him only so much as he bitched about his money problems, reinvented the system in a way he thought it should operate and claimed he should get all the money he wanted immediately so he could spring into action and do all the great things he knew he could do. He thought the FBI could make one phone call and get him a false identity.

At the same time as he was trying to placate Tait, Marischen tried to answer questions in his own mind. "Is he shucking and jiving us? Is he trying to get information from us by the questions that we ask?"

Running an informant was a double-edged sword. If Tait was a double agent, the FBI could look bad and end up giving the Hells Angels a good idea of what they did and didn't know. But Marischen also had to take advantage of Tait while he had him. He filled the blanks in the bureau files. He updated dossiers on all Alaska Hells Angels. He answered questions for the Anchorage multi-agency task force—FBI, state and local police—he worked with. He found out as best he could where the Hells Angels got their drugs and who they associated with. Marischen pressed to get all he could in case Tait pulled the plug. When it seemed he had persuaded Tait to stay on, he flattered his ego some more. "I will get the head of the FBI in Alaska here," Marischen finally said.

They met in an apartment the FBI had used as a dead drop for a pornography investigation. (A real address arouses less suspicion than a post office box.) Tait took immediately to Nelson's authority. When Marischen built his rapport with Tait by bad-mouthing the system in echo with Tait's concerns, Nelson took the heat. When Marischen jumped into Tait's shorts and expressed the same exasperations, Nelson looked him straight in the eye and said: "That's the way the system works." Tait could accept that, for the moment, from the head of the FBI in Alaska.

The Anchorage Division of the FBI had a yearly budget of $4,800 to pay informants when Tait walked into their office in December 1984. By April, the bureau paid Tait $4,000 a month in cash they got from Washington. The FBI paid his living expenses, telephone bills, airfare, anything Tait could attribute to the case. But money was still an issue, because the FBI never paid on time.

Marischen also had to contend with Tait's continuous need for an ego fix. That Tait was the first law enforcement source inside the Hells Angels greatly boosted his ego. Because past informants talked after they left the gang, mostly to plea-bargain for reduced jail sentences, they offered dated information.

Marischen didn't want to do drug buys in Alaska because that meant Tait would have to be seen in bars and on the street selling drugs. Anchorage was too small a town to pull that type of scam.

Once, Tait took Brenda to California for a week. They returned to Anchorage and stood in the baggage-claim area when a well-proportioned blonde bounced up to Tait.

"Hi, Tony. How you doing? Long time, no see."

Tait stalled. He knew he'd remember this babe's name. How could he forget?

"Oh, sure, you remember me."

Brenda stormed out. She couldn't stand old flames.

The woman pulled out her identification: Alaska State Trooper, Narcotics Division. She said she had a dog outside to sniff his luggage. She was bubbly and happy and Tait told her to go ahead. Then her male partner showed up. Tait didn't like him. He ran his dog back and forth over Tait's bag.

"If you don't get your dog off my bag, I'm going to boot him right in his ass."

The trooper got testy. Tait got testy.

"You found any dope?"

"No."

"Then get the fuck out of here. You've had three runs on the bag. That's all you're entitled to take. Get the fuck out of here."

Tait called Marischen and asked how the troopers knew which flight he was on. Marischen said he called them, warned that a biker scumbag was on the plane and asked if they could check out his bags. Marischen wanted Tait clean and wanted Tait to know it.

A former Outlaw from Kentucky wandered into Anchorage in the spring of 1985. John Cleave (John Chrome or J.C.) Webb fled after a run-in with another biker over a stolen motorcycle. He traveled up the west coast of the States until he could go no farther unless he did so by plane. Webb found the Hells Angels and told them he wanted to become a member. There were rumors, typical in the paranoid criminal underworld, that Webb was a snitch in the San Bernardino area before he headed north. The Hells Angels interviewed Webb and monitored his responses on a voice-stress analyzer to determine whether he lied. Another Kentucky would-be biker, Mark (Meatloaf) Loving, showed up around the same time and asked to hang around. The Angels were ready to kill Webb and Loving when the analyzer indicated stress under questioning. Tait pointed out they had not calibrated the machine and that the loud and violent questioning would stress out anyone.

Ed Hubert asked Tait, as Hells Angels security officer for Alaska, to fly to Kentucky to do a background check on Webb, who paid for the trip. The Anchorage chapter paid part of his living expenses in Kentucky, the FBI paid the rest. Marischen took advantage of Tait's official trip to broaden the investigation.

Marischen wanted to capitalize on Tait's quick rise within Hells Angels ranks. He would now attend West Coast Officers' Meetings regularly in California and moved in the gang's international circles. It wouldn't be long before he gained access to the Hells Angels' criminal cliques. Marischen informed FBI headquarters in Washington when his operation expanded into California. He wanted FBI agents in the Bay Area to meet Tait and figure out ways to use him. They set up a meeting at a Las Vegas hotel during a stopover on Tait's trip to Kentucky.

FBI Special Agents Timothy McKinley and Jay Colvin from the Bay Area and Tom Gates from Los Angeles met Marischen and Tait, who flew in to Las Vegas on separate planes to prevent a chance sighting of Tait with any agent. Marischen was well known because he appeared in newspaper articles as FBI spokesman in Alaska; the Hells Angels hated McKinley for his persistent investigations of their criminal activities in Oakland and San Francisco.

Marischen thought Tait's ego would be stroked by this meeting with agents from other jurisdictions. It showed Tait he was no longer a local Hells Angel hick in Anchorage but a mover and shaker who commanded attention in the heartland of the Hells Angels. Marischen was brief with the agents. "Here's our access, here's our availability. I'll make him available to anything you have going. You tell me, I'll bring him down and set him up to see what your needs might be. Give me some input what you think he can do for you in your territory."

McKinley had instructions to interview and evaluate Tait, then craft an investigation to exploit the unique opportunity to run an informant inside the Hells Angels. He was impressed with what he saw. Tait did not have the downsides typical of organized-crime informants. He was not a drug user, he didn't seem to need to work off a beef against anyone in the gang, he was never the subject of a law enforcement investigation, he was sane and seemed reliable.

On the other hand, McKinley was uncomfortable with Tait's naive impression that the government could act immediately on his suggestions. If he informed that a particular telephone was used for criminal conversations, Tait expected the phone to be tapped within hours, even illegally. McKinley thought Tait was too good to be true—the best double agent he ever met—and he wasn't going to be fooled by a biker spy. McKinley had seen Tait before he ever spoke to the FBI. That was when he investigated Hells Angel Robert Andrew (Beautiful Bob) Vickery, whom Tait stayed with during a visit to California.

McKinley decided early that should Tait prove legitimate, the bureau would use him as a walking recording platform. The Hells Angels hired expensive lawyers and were unrestrained by truth in court. Their private investigators dug up dirt and fabricated innuendo to discredit witnesses against the club. But they could not fight against their own words. If Tait had access to club meetings and high-ranking members, McKinley didn't want to rely on verbal reports. He wanted conversations taped so they could never be denied. He also wanted to safeguard the investigation in case Tait screwed up, did something stupid or refused to testify. Cases could still be built on the tape recordings. But many technical bugs had to be worked out and the groundwork laid before an operation could begin.

McKinley was no novice biker-investigator. He nearly single-handedly enhanced the FBI's reputation through aggressive pursuit of outlaw bikers, which the bureau refused to recognize as a criminal threat to society until the mid-1980s. The FBI was rightfully mocked by seasoned biker-investigators for its suit-and-tie approach to organized crime. The bureau had a reputation for being decades behind other law enforcement organizations when it came to investigating organized crime. It was only in the 1960s, when Attorney General Robert Kennedy slapped some sense into bureau director J. Edgar Hoover, that the FBI recognized traditional organized crime—the

Italian mob—as worthy of investigation. Before then, Hoover would not allow his agents to pursue the mob.

McKinley started to look at bikers in 1979 after Hells Angels allegedly threatened a federal judge. The Angels had threatened people for years, but it took a supposed threat on a judge to get the FBI interested. FBI investigators realized they didn't even know the names of Hells Angels members, let alone where they were. The only information the bureau had was outdated and inaccurate.

McKinley was sent to San Diego in 1981 to sit in on a wiretap of Hells Angels involved in an extortion. He returned to Oakland with some ideas on how to investigate the club. The FBI called several agents to Washington to discuss ways to investigate the big four outlaw motorcycle gangs: the Hells Angels, the Outlaws, the Bandidos and the Pagans. Within a decade, they would add the Sons of Silence and the Dirty Dozen to their list as bikers grew wealthy with drug money and sophisticated through legal advice.

Baltimore FBI agent Kevin Bonner contacted McKinley in 1982. Bonner was the undercover agent in Operation Roughrider, which investigated the drug dealings of East Coast Hells Angels. He ran an informant called Vernon Hartung, who befriended Hells Angels and introduced Bonner as a yuppie drug dealer. Hartung knew Frisco Gary Kautzman, then president of the Hells Angels San Francisco chapter, and they visited Kautzman in California to get his blessing to start a chapter in Baltimore. Hartung said he needed money and agreed to sell Kautzman's methamphetamine in Baltimore. Kautzman shipped it to him via UPS.

Toward the end of Roughrider, McKinley put in a bid to get Hartung and Bonner back in Oakland to buy drugs from Howie Weisbrod, a former New York City Hells Angel. That got him legal authority to plant a bug in Hells Angel Big Al Perryman's house. FBI agents broke into the house and hid the bug behind a heavy cabinet. King the Wonderdog, a 260-pound English mastiff who played with a 90-pound stone cannonball, was the agents' only fear. McKinley had a silencer-equipped pistol to kill the dog if need be.

As McKinley talked to Tait in Las Vegas a month after Operation Roughrider went overt, he used knowledge from that case to plot an investigation that would get much closer to the heart of the Hells Angels. Hartung, as a drug customer, was not positioned to provide quality information about the inner workings of the club. As he pondered the possibilities, McKinley realized that if it weren't for the experience gained from Operation Roughrider, he could have endangered Tait. Roughrider gave him a healthier respect for the difficulties of investigating the Hells Angels. They were not the dumbass bikers many law enforcement people believed. They employed sounder tradecraft than did the police who tracked them, were more disciplined about what they said on the phone and actively gathered law enforcement intelligence. Roughrider made the FBI appreciate how sophisticated the Hells Angels were.

Roughrider, like all cases against the Hells Angels, also toughened the gang. They became more sophisticated businessmen. They were wary of who they dealt with and got expensive legal advice on how to avoid prosecution. One Hells Angel printed across sheets of paper that contained a formula to manufacture methamphetamine: "RICO DEFENSE MATERIAL."

Hells Angels in San Francisco and Oakland had an awesome ability to detect tapped phones. Ten consecutive taps by McKinley and other bureau agents were discovered on the twelfth and thirteenth days of operation. On those days, the caliber of conversation went to hell. Calls dropped from 150 a day to two. Suspects used pay phones and warned callers: "Be careful what you say, there's termites on the line." Others screamed into the phone: "Motherfucking feds. You FBI slime pigs. Eat shit and die."

McKinley suspected someone in the Pacific Bell legal department tipped off the Hells Angels—someone over whose desk the paperwork crossed 12 to 13 days after it was filed. The FBI found that pen registers on phones of suspected criminals showed calls made into private phone company numbers where employees had computers with access to wiretap records. Phone company officials swore to investigators that wiretap information was super-secret. Investigators found it wasn't a case of who in the phone company knew about the wiretaps, it was a question of who did not know.

The FBI wasn't so blameless itself. When the bureau rented a line for a fictitious business from which to listen to wiretaps, it was booked through the government sales office. Anyone who scanned the computer would question why Acme Dry Cleaning's phone bill was paid by the government.

Tait arrived in Louisville, Kentucky, on June 1 to check into J.C. Webb's background. He ventured little outside his Best Western hotel room and the pool room. He didn't want to run into Outlaws. He took a taxi to the clubhouse the gang had vacated a year earlier and photographed it. He drove by houses where Outlaws had lived and places they hung out. He photographed a downtown bank with "Louisville" on its sign to prove he was there.

The FBI did the legwork. Bureau agents pulled Webb's security file and provided Tait with information to feed his chapter. Tait could tell them where Webb lived, who he hung out with and other information that greatly enhanced his credibility as a security officer in the eyes of his fellow Angels. Neither the FBI nor Tait had to knock on doors and arouse suspicion. All the legwork was done on computer.

Webb, five-foot-eleven and 200 pounds, had a criminal record that dated back to 1971, when he was charged with violating narcotics control laws and possession of hashish. He had charges for receiving stolen property, possession of narcotics, forgery, trafficking in a controlled substance, trafficking in marijuana for own use, possession of marijuana, possession of dangerous drugs for own use and assault.

Marischen recognized that he couldn't operate Tait solely as an informant forever. He needed to develop an operational plan, but knew little of the Hells Angels operations outside Alaska. He was secretive by nature and didn't like to let people in on Tait's secret, but he had little choice. He must plan an operation flexible enough to broaden in scope as Tait's power and influence in the Hells Angels grew.

Marischen made sure from the start that Tait's name didn't appear on FBI documents. He code-named his informant Hammer.

Marischen laundered information he sent to FBI headquarters for dissemination around the country so Tait could not be identified. Sometimes he described the source as "she." Sometimes it was non-gender. When Tait started to provide information on Officers' Meetings in California, Marischen couldn't afford to put an Anchorage tag on the reports. He arranged with the FBI's San Francisco office in 1985 to open a security file for a source in that city to launder Tait's information. That would throw suspicion off Tait should the Hells Angels get their hands on the information.

Marischen also paid Tait in cash to prevent paper trails that private investigators in the employ of the Hells Angels could follow. Ed Hubert's wife worked for an Anchorage bank and might stumble across a government cheque in Tait's name. The more information put on paper, the greater the chances an unauthorized person would discover Tait's identity.

Marischen decided to equip Tait with a transmitter to broadcast to a nearby receiver all conversations within earshot. Such a transmitter would give law enforcement its first-ever chance to listen to and record Hells Angels churches and discussions Tait had with members. To date, cops relied on word-of-mouth reports or waited for the opportunity to seize and copy meeting minutes during raids.

Marischen and Tait discussed many ways to conceal a transmitter. They wanted to hide it in the handle of a knife and run the wire antenna around the belt. The bureau refused because a knife is a weapon that could be used to hurt someone and generate lawsuits. Instead, they wanted to hide the transmitter in Tait's Hells Angels colors and run the antenna around the jacket lining. But Tait pointed out that Hells Angels don't wear colors when they commit crimes. They don't wear them much outside club functions to keep a low profile.

The FBI technical section in Quantico, Virginia, sent Marischen a photograph of a large, thick belt buckle with a switch on the edge. It looked like something Maxwell Smart would wear. They also sent a transmitter taped to the inside of a baseball cap with a battery pack. The hat would have knocked out a dog if dropped.

Marischen decided the most practical way to hide a secret transmitter was out in the open. He had it installed in the shell of a pager. The on/off switch on the pager would allow Tait to turn the transmitter off whenever he suspected the place he entered was equipped with radio scanners that could detect his equipment. Even then, it was highly unlikely the Hells Angels programmed their scanners to the frequency of the crystal that Quantico technicians installed in Tait's transmitter: they picked the frequency of a New Jersey garbage pickup unit.

It took Marischen a while to find enough proper equipment to make usable recordings. His first receiver was a hand-held monitor plugged into a cassette recorder. The prevalence of groundwater in Alaska limited the transmitter's distance, and its signal was easily blocked by walls and bodies. The front wall of the Anchorage club-house was covered with 5/8-inch steel plate. Marischen sometimes could not hear anything at a safe distance from the clubhouse. He had to park his car 20 yards from the Hells Angels compound, plug the receiver and tape recorder into the cigarette lighter to keep the battery going in minus-30-degree weather, and abandon the car.

Marischen found out McKinley had a briefcase

equipped with a receiver, a recorder, an antenna and batteries. The mini reel-to-reel recorder sported enough tape to record for three and a half hours. Marischen asked his technical agent to send for one. He received an old unit and wondered if someone had tried to foist something on him.

Law enforcement knew little about outlaw motorcycle gangs in the mid-1980s. Cops clung to and perpetuated myths that should have long been dispelled. Fewer than a dozen police officers across the U.S. knew what the gangs were about. They even hounded the scum on their own time. They had a wealth of information between their ears and shared it with anyone who asked. Their greatest frustration was trying to convince their superiors that bikers were worth investigating. They watched with amusement, curiosity and then disdain as so-called experts with little investigative experience showed up at conferences with the whole biker scenario figured out and charted. The "experts" tried to offend and shock audiences with sordid tales of biker sex and violence. They rarely checked their facts and repeated myths, lies and misconceptions. While sophisticated bikers like the Hells Angels evolved and ran downright slick drug operations, these experts talked of a long-gone past.

A U.S. Marshal arrived in Anchorage from San Diego in the spring of 1985 at the request of the Anchorage Police Department to give his dog-and-pony show on outlaw bikers. He liked to talk to Hells Angels and had a particular member in mind when he flew to Alaska. An Angel called Tony Tait had given him a hard time at a run in Custer, South Dakota, two years earlier. He wanted to know more about this clean-cut hardass.

Ken Marischen got a call from a highly placed Anchorage police officer who knew the FBI was working with Tait. "You gotta know that a U.S. Marshal is snooping around. He's been asking about Tony, Tony's background and his position with the Angels. Where he's getting his money and his travels and his drug dealings. We didn't say a thing. We said, 'Go see Ken.' "

"Go see Ken" should have tipped off the U.S.

Marshal. It meant back off because the FBI is either working a case on Tait in which the Marshals Service has no jurisdiction, or Tait worked for the FBI. The U.S. Marshal never contacted Marischen. He tried to find out where Tait lived so he could visit him. He asked local police officers to drive him to Tait's house. Marischen played it cool and the U.S. Marshal finally left town.

Hells Angels don't often ride their motorcycles any more. When they do, it's for scheduled runs or funerals. There's nothing like the death of a prominent, respected and influential Hells Angel to show the locals what the expression "rolling thunder" really means. James E. (Fu) Griffin Sr., a longtime member of the Oakland chapter, died accidentally in Fresno, California, on July 5, when he drove his new Firebird into oncoming traffic while handing methamphetamine to his 15-year-old passenger.

Intelligence officers from all levels attend biker funerals to update photographs and watch who associates with whom. Funerals allow them to get closer to bikers than they ordinarily do.

FBI Special Agent Tim McKinley stood in a school across from the funeral home and watched a Hells Angel in a white cap make his way along the sidewalk like a politician. He stopped and greeted everyone he knew and some he didn't. His patch said he was from Alaska. It was Anthony Tait, whom he met six weeks earlier in Las Vegas. McKinley talked to Karen Sanderson, an intelligence analyst for the Western States Information Network. She noticed the Hells Angel with the white cap because he was too clean-cut to be an outlaw biker.

"Who is this guy and why is he a Hells Angel?" she thought.

Sanderson voiced her opinion to McKinley. He grunted and didn't pursue the conversation. Sanderson then recognized that the Angel was Anthony Tait. She had seen his photograph in her files. She focused on him and picked out all the details she could at the burial. He wore a patch on his colors that said "Frozen Few." She wondered what it meant.

Tait photographed Sonny Barger and other prominent Hells Angels who tossed dirt onto the casket as it was lowered into the ground.

In July, Tait, weak with pleurisy, and Brenda had a vicious argument about nothing in particular that ended when he slapped her across the face.

"You no-good motherfucker! I'll get you for this!" Brenda ran out of the house they had recently moved into and down the street screaming.

Tait ambled to the front door and sat on the steps to warm his body in the sun. A police car pulled up. Then another. Then another. The first Anchorage officer to walk into the yard was Tait's friend Dick Coffey.

"Hey, man," Tait said, "what's happening? What the hell are you doing here? You're not supposed to be here."

"I got a call here for some domestic violence."

"Domestic violence? I'm sitting here dying. I can't even get up." Tait noticed Brenda cowering behind a police officer. "What the fuck's going on?" he asked.

"We got a 911 call that there's a fight here and someone's been hurt," Coffey said.

"Ain't no one hurt," said Tait.

"Ya motherfucker!" Brenda screamed. "You hit me!"

"Is that what this is about?" asked Tait.

"Yeah," said Coffey.

"Yeah, I slapped her after she threatened me. She followed me from room to room. I'm on narcotics for my lung. I can't breathe. I can't walk. I can't do anything. She's just on me and I can't take it any more."

"What do you want me to do?" Coffey asked.

"Why don't you take her and her shit and get her the fuck out of my life."

"What does he want you to do?" Brenda screamed. "What do you mean? You own him too? You own that cop too? Motherfucker!"

"Hey, Dick. There's a bag of trashbags under the sink. Pack all of her shit in it and have her go with it."

"Okay."

"I'm coming in. I'm laying down on the couch. I can't do any of this."

Coffey helped Tait get up and into the house.

"By the way, make sure she doesn't take any of the firearms in the bedroom or in my office."

"All right."

The cops hauled out six garbage bags of Brenda's stuff. Coffey walked back into the house and looked down at Tait on the couch.

"Got everything. By the way, that's a nice bearskin. Where did you get it?"

"I shot it."

"You shot it? Well, she's got it. It's gone."

As Coffey talked to Tait, Brenda told officer John Reed, "Man, he's a hit man for the Hells Angels. He's a killer. You see all the shit he's got?" She pointed out the weights, striking boards, light and heavy bags and speed-bag in the back yard. "He's always out there punching and kicking those bags, lifting weights, and he's always going to the range and shooting. He's a trained killer. He teaches karate." Tait had taught karate off and on since his days on the North Slope in the mid-1970s.

Reed acted quickly. When a Hells Angel's old lady starts to rat on her old man, you get as much out of her as quickly as possible before fear sets in and she clams up. He called the one person he knew who was equipped to handle Hells Angels intelligence. Someone to whom he regularly passed on street information. "I have a deal for you," he said over the phone. "I've got Brenda Fowler in my patrol car and she wants to roll on Anthony Tait, her boyfriend."

Kenneth Marischen almost fell off his chair.

"Are you interested?" Reed asked.

"You bet. Where can we meet?"

Marischen pulled his car up to Reed's on a street corner. He tried to stay cool and non-specific. "I'd sure like to talk to you."

He sensed that Brenda's animosity toward Tait had

started to wear off. He feared if he didn't connect with her now, she would blow up some other time and become a real security risk for the case. He called Larry Nelson and said he needed a place to talk to an informer immediately. Nelson dated a woman who had access to empty houses. He told Marischen where to pick up a key. Reed drove Brenda to the house while Marischen raced to get the key.

"Do you want me to stick around?" Reed asked.

Marischen was afraid Brenda's information would be too specific. "John, if you don't mind, I'd just like to talk to her alone."

"You got her." Like a true professional, he never questioned Marischen about the incident. He knew he would be informed of anything he needed to know.

Marischen ushered Brenda into the house. She told him things she never told Tait. She worked as a prostitute for an escort service called A Taste of Honey, owned by Anchorage madam and massage-parlor owner Bambi Cracker. Cracker paid for the phone number listed in the Yellow Pages that rang at Brenda's apartment, where she lived when the relationship with Tait soured, which it often did. Brenda's stage name was Honie when she danced at strip joints like the Great Alaska Bush Company and the Kit Kat Club. She described herself as a performer and had a range of exotic costumes she peeled off to excite and arouse men. Her dancing brought her business. Guys flew her to the North Slope to turn tricks at Prudhoe Bay in Deadhorse. She talked about drug dealers on the North Slope and claimed she saw $13-million in cocaine.

Brenda talked about Tait. She showed Marischen color Polaroid photographs of bruises on her face and body caused by his fists. She claimed he broke her nose. Marischen thought the photographs looked dated. Although she was pissed off at Tait, she said he didn't do drugs or sell them. She told Marischen that other Hells Angels, such as Ed Hubert and Sleazy Ric Rickleman, sold drugs.

Tait had a passport, traveled a lot, was gone three weeks every month, kept $3,000 to $5,000 in a drawer, received phone calls in the middle of the night and went out of town shortly after he received mysterious phone calls. She said Tait claimed to be a Hells Angels hit man who killed people in California. She also said Tait had automatic weapons and grenades. Tait told her he served in Vietnam as an Airborne Ranger who went on search-and-destroy missions. He said he received a Purple Heart for a hand wound. Brenda said Tait couldn't tell the truth because he didn't know the difference.

Brenda told Marischen that Tait sold quaaludes in 1984 but stopped when he didn't have enough money to buy more to sell. He always carried a gun, which he tucked into the back of his pants when it wasn't under the seat of his truck when he drove.

Every morning when Tait got up he had a cup of tea and watched the adventure movie *The Final Option* on video. He rewound the tape to watch exciting parts over and over. Then he went to his room to disassemble, clean and reassemble his guns.

Tait took away Brenda's high heels and dresses and made her wear jeans and camouflage clothing. He taught her how to use guns and knives. She even held his watch for him on club runs when he wasn't fit for guard duty.

"If things don't go his way," she said, "he makes them go his way forcefully. He is very violent."

Marischen had no choice but to open Brenda up as an FBI source. He didn't like going behind Tait's back, but here was a tremendous opportunity to corroborate what Tait told him. It also gave him leverage to sell Tait to FBI headquarters at the beginning of the case, seven months after Tait first sat down with Marischen.

"I've got his girlfriend. Unbeknownst to him, I've got the Hells Angel's girlfriend and I've got the Hells Angel. Now, you tell me a better way."

The bureaucrats were sold.

Marischen officially opened Brenda's source file on July 26. He found out she used many aliases: Diana

Simpson, Brenda Shumacher, Rochelle Jones. She wanted her file opened under the codename Honie. Besides her personal track record, Brenda had a criminal record that included driving under the influence of drugs and impersonation of a police officer.

Marischen wanted to keep Tait and Brenda together. They had a history of breaking up, but always got back together. It was safer for Tait and the case if Marischen could use them to keep tabs on each other. Manipulation is a skill greatly aided by luck and hormones.

Tait found a note tacked to his front door one month later. It read: "We need to talk. We'll do lunch. We'll do it in a neutral ground."

Brenda opted to buy her way into his life the way men bought their way into her pants. She gave Tait two gold chains of her own that she'd had cleaned and freshly boxed.

"So what's the story?" Tait asked.

"I just want to know if we can start seeing each other again. You don't have to let me live with you. You don't have to . . ."

Brenda was back in Tait's life.

The Hells Angels U.S.A. Run was held for the second consecutive year at Lake of the Ozarks in Perry, Missouri, in July and August 1985. Marischen's budget didn't allow him to travel with his informant, but he wanted Tait to have an FBI contact in the area in case he needed help or a major crime was being committed. Marischen called the senior resident agent in Springfield, Missouri, who was the brother of a friend. "Here's what's happening. If a guy called Hammer calls you and needs some help or needs to furnish information, or whatever he needs, help him."

The agent agreed without asking questions. He called Marischen two days later.

"Any problems?" Marischen asked.

"You know a guy by the name of Tait?"

Marischen shivered. "Why do you ask?"

Apparently a group of intelligence and security people

had been standing around keeping an eye on the bikers
when an officer of the U.S. Marshals Service showed up
and told them they didn't have to hang around.

"He came up and said, 'You guys can all go home.
You don't have to be here. We've got this thing covered.
We got a guy inside by the name of Tait that's working
for us.' "

"Holy shit."

Marischen knew some dumbass wannabes in his
time, but he was going to turn this one into a has-been.
The U.S. Marshal had figured out from his talks with
Anchorage police officers that Tait was an FBI informant
and now he pretended he was in on the action.

Marischen told Larry Nelson. Nelson blew up and
both men got on the phone to FBI headquarters in
Washington. They couldn't believe a U.S. Marshal would
roll on a source knowing he was a source. And even if
Tait wasn't a source, the U.S. Marshal set him up to die.
An FBI supervisor called the U.S. Department of Justice,
which is responsible for the Marshals Service, and lodged
a complaint.

While Marischen continued to lay the groundwork
for an investigation, Tait fed him information, some
banal, some interesting. When Tommy Clifton left the
Fairbanks chapter, he kept his new motorcycle and
"donated" his old one to the club—an Angels tradition.
Tait also reported that the Fairbanks chapter bought a
quarter to half a pound of cocaine to sell to build up its
treasury. And Anchorage Hells Angel Dan McIntosh had
as a friend an Anchorage police officer called Biff.

The West Coast Officers sent Tait to the Hells
Angels World Meeting during the World Run in England
in August 1985. They now saw him as a world traveler
and reasonable diplomat who cared about club issues.
Elliot (Cisco) Valderrama represented the Oakland chapter, and Angels from Frisco and San Bernardino also
attended. The main issue on the agenda was a complaint
by English Hells Angels that they could not communicate with their brothers in France, who had breached a

promise to learn English, the club's language of business, within two years.

After a heated discussion, it was Tait who came up with a solution: the French must learn to speak English by the time of the next U.S.A. Run, or they were out.

Tait thought the other topics and rules discussed were pathetic. A member can't wear a Hells Angels belt buckle unless he has been in the club 10 years. A member cannot be expelled unless present at the meeting where the vote is taken. The member can be forced to attend, even if he has to be kidnapped. Only known informants or police officers were exempted from the rule.

Rule 28 in England: "No cops, no niggers, no snitches."

Hells Angel Bilbo from the Wessex chapter got into a bar fight and removed his colors. He fled when police arrived and forgot them. London Hells Angel Goat ran from a fight in Paris. Kent Hells Angel Herman showed a letter obtained from a woman in Interpol sent to intelligence agencies around the world asking for names of Hells Angels who would attend the U.S.A. Run.

The president of an English chapter smuggled crank from France in his motorcycle tire. He walked the bike, with a flat tire, off the ferry through Customs. He gave members advice about the drug at the next club meeting. "Any of your customers who buy this to shoot up, you'd better tell them not to because it's got some bits of rubber in it. They'd have to strain it first."

Back in Alaska, Tait took care of routine club business—retrieved patches from lapsed members (once by threatening to kill the man), found out what drug deals and other activities members were up to—and reported back to Marischen.

In September, Marischen informed Tait that he must agree to periodic unannounced urinalysis tests to prove he didn't use drugs. Tait agreed. Marischen's operational plan was beginning to take shape and it included controlled drug buys from Hells Angels. Experience taught him trials would be easier if he proved his witness did not use drugs while he worked as an informant.

Tait was at the West Coast Officers' Meeting held at the San Francisco chapter clubhouse in mid-September 1985. It was reported that Oakland Hells Angel Irish O'Farrell was involved in negotiations to get royalty money from a drag bike toy to be marketed by Revell. The toy was a Hells Angel bike authorized by Cleveland Hells Angel Kevin Cleary. Royalties would be paid directly to the Hells Angels Motorcycle Club to be redistributed. Part of the money would go to Kevin to pay for his racing. The rest would go to the club and the Hells Angels Defense Fund.

The officers discussed whether to end the ongoing war with the Outlaws Motorcycle Club. Canadian and San Francisco Hells Angels ran off a group of Outlaws at the Sturgis Run in South Dakota in August, although the municipally staged event is open to all bikers. The Hells Angel clubhouse in Charlotte, North Carolina, was blown up the next day. Cleveland Hells Angel Donald (Donnie) Mahovlic said his club got along well with the Outlaws and West Coast Angels were messing that up. He said that Kevin raced motorcycles through the south and had good relations with the Outlaws.

Three pages of FBI radio frequencies were handed out for distribution to members. Some of the frequencies bore the notations Blue, Gold, San Francisco, E. Bay, Room Bug, Federal Room Bug.

Events that center around sex are Hells Angels institutions. The annual Whorehouse Run was a must for bikers who like to end a day's ride with a night of riding. Although the run is held by two California chapters, all Hells Angels are welcome to join in three days of fun. Tait rented a Camaro to follow the pack. He attended many motorcycle functions in rented cars. He hooked up with the San Fernando Valley Hells Angels at their clubhouse in Chattsworth, where the run began. They met the San Bernardino chapter at the Cocky Bull on

Highway 18 in the high desert. From there they rode through the backside of Death Valley where they stopped at landmarks such as Furnace Creek and Dante's View. They rode at night to stay cool. Tait leaped his Camaro off a side road near Furnace Creek and did some four-wheeling to impress the boys. They ended up in Beatty, Nevada.

Beatty has a strip of low-rent whorehouses, such as Fran's Star Ranch, the Stage Coach and the Exchange, where you can gamble, eat, drink and get laid for $15. The whores set egg timers outside the door: fifteen minutes for $15. One Hells Angel roamed up and down the hallway and turned the timers back while his brothers enjoyed lengthy 15 minutes. The timer bells never rang while the Hells Angels were in the saddle.

Tait learned while in southern California that the Brothers Speed and the Outsiders, two small clubs with chapters in Washington and Oregon, might become Hells Angels. Washington and Oregon were two places where the Hells Angels were determined to keep out the rival Outlaws Motorcycle Club.

Also while in California, Tait visited San Francisco Hells Angel Carl James (J.R.) Serrano at his apartment in Daly City. Tait saw two blocks—one-inch thick, eight-inches long and three-inches wide—of what Serrano called "black Lebanese hashish" on the kitchen table. They were wrapped in white muslin embossed with a skull and crossbones. Serrano told Tait he sold hash by the kilogram.

Marischen attended the annual meeting of the International Outlaw Motorcycle Gang Investigators Conference in Toronto in late September. He met with Tim McKinley from Oakland and Tom Owens from FBI headquarters to discuss the direction of the case.

Marischen also confronted the U.S Marshal, whom he believed jeopardized the case and Tait's life. Marischen wanted to stomp him. He walked into a wash-room to cool off before he confronted him in a hospitality suite.

"You fucking asshole. I ought to punch your god-damn lights out."

The U.S. Marshal replied that he couldn't believe a law enforcement officer would complain to another officer's agency.

"You need to get yourself fired on that sonofabitch. You just stay out of it. I'm not telling you anything. You just stay out of my way and stay away from this particular case."

Members of his organization also confronted him.

The next West Coast Officers' Meeting was held in San Jose, California, in October. It was a routine account of club business. Chapters reported in order of how long they had held their charter. San Bernardino, or Berdoo, always reported first, as it was the original chapter, followed by San Francisco and Oakland. Oakland reported it had two clearing accounts at banks for the Hells Angels Legal Fund (HALF). The chapter asked for travelers cheques rather than cash. They gave as much cash as they could to an attorney who represented Hells Angels charged in Operation Roughrider, to "wash" it through his sources. The chapter donated a computer to him for his professional services.

The Richmond, California, chapter recommended guidelines for the admission of new chapters:

1. All potential new chapters must have a five-year history as a club and still have 50 percent of the original charter members.
2. Clubs that prospect for Hells Angel membership must have members only, no hangarounds or prospects.
3. All members must speak English.
4. Clubs must have at least six members.
5. Clubs must submit a personal criminal and political history of each member.

The San Jose chapter recommended that California runs be restricted to members, prospects and hangarounds.

Guests would not be allowed unless escorted, to deter rats such as FBI informant Vernon Hartung in Operation Roughrider. The chapter also feared law enforcement would have legitimate grounds to prosecute them if their new chapter in Ireland was infiltrated by terrorists. They recommended more thorough background checks overseas.

The Ventura chapter reported that Rocky was out in bad standing and anyone who caught him should beat him. (Most Hells Angels don't know other members' full names for security reasons.)

Vancouver Hells Angel Richard (Rick) Ciarniello reported police had 27 warrants to serve on Hells Angels from the Sherbrooke and Montreal chapters for the killing of North chapter members. The warrants included five counts of murder. He said the cops had a singing Angel—an informant. He handed out a list of steps U.S. Angels with criminal records must take to enter Canada. (It was typed on Vancouver Hells Angels letterhead. Each chapter has custom-designed letterhead and other business paraphernalia that feature the club name and the Death's Head. Members have rubber stamps of the Death's Head over the name they use to sign letters and Christmas cards.)

It was reported that the next East Coast Officers' Meeting would be in New York City on November 11. Attendees would be shuttled from the clubhouse to a secret location because the feds had access to the clubhouse, which was seized during Operation Roughrider. The East Coast Hells Angels planned a fund-raising benefit at the Limelight disco in New York to raise money for legal fees incurred by the Roughrider busts. Tait worked as doorman that night and refused entry to Joan Jett, whom he did not recognize.

The Cleveland chapter reported on members' jail sentences so other members would know where they were. Frank, who was charged with murder, got two years for a guilty plea on a reduced charge. Harry faced five to 25 years for aggravated robbery. A murder charge was dropped.

The Salem, Massachusetts, chapter reported that a judge seemed to help the Hells Angels by making things easy.

The New York City chapter reported that Hells Angel William Joseph (Wild Bill) Medeiros was arrested, and the word was he rolled.

The Rochester chapter reported that James Henry (Mitch) McAuley, an organizer of the Limelight benefit, was charged with 28 counts of forgery with Hells Angel Michael J. (Mike) Quale. Their bail was set at $30,000.

The Binghamton, New York, chapter reported that Hells Angel Bear flipped out and was in the "nut house" classified as a manic depressive. He was given a six-month medical leave from the club. He thought the club was coming to kill him.

Phillip Scott (Phil) Utley pleaded guilty on a Roughrider charge and was sentenced to five years. James (Oats) Oldfield also pleaded guilty and was sentenced to three years.

Tait talked to several Hells Angels after the meeting. Many were upset that New York City president Sandy Alexander screwed the club badly on the Hells Angel movie *Angels Forever, Forever Angels*, on which the club spent millions of dollars, and made more money than he reported. San Bernardino president Jeffrey (Jeff) Cagle was stunned at how many longtime Hells Angels became police informants as a result of Operation Roughrider. "It's blowing my mind. All my heroes are up there singing."

San Francisco Angel Steve told Tait the crank market was flooded in the Bay Area and no one could figure out where it came from. He added that a police source warned him a directive was issued to stop all Hells Angels and their affiliate gangs for field interrogations.

Tait also learned that a former Anchorage police officer employed by the U.S. Postal Service in Anchorage warned Larry Allen, a local tattoo artist and drug dealer, when drug-sniffing dogs were in the post office and advised him when not to ship drugs.

Hells Angels officers in Alaska met in mid-October in the Anchorage clubhouse. As usual, the business discussed, apart from criminal activities and convictions, didn't interest Tait. It was reported that Carol Spearman, wife of Hells Angel William (Gypsy) Spearman, was arrested on a drug charge. Spearman bailed her out with money borrowed from the Anchorage chapter treasury. A friend of Carol's on the State Grand Jury was sympathetic to the Hells Angels and fed her information on local cases, including her own. They discussed whether Spearman would sing. "If there's any question, let's do her," Sleazy Ric Rickleman said.

It was reported that Anchorage prospect J.C. Webb received his patch and was a full member. The officers discussed pulling Monty Elliott's patch because he was a problem. He didn't hang around with club members, and even citizens complained about his coke habit. Elliott broke up with Karin Purcell, whose girlfriend, an Anchorage police officer, wanted to bed him.

Ed Hubert said he nominated Tait to become state sergeant-at-arms. Tait held that post in the chapter.

The Anchorage chapter introduced a new rule: no more alcohol or drugs one hour before or during church.

An Anchorage lawyer who handled most of the sticky stuff for the Hells Angels exacted a fee of a few hundred dollars and a prostitute. Club members considered him sexually perverted because of his antics with the hookers.

The Anchorage Hells Angels held their annual fundraiser at the National Guard Armory every fall. That year, Tait wore a tuxedo shirt and bowtie to serve drinks. Brenda Fowler wore a rented maid's uniform that Tait liked.

On October 23, Tim McKinley filed his opening memo on the proposed case against the Hells Angels with Tait as informant. (Marischen would work Tait as an informant until a proper case could be crafted.) McKinley identified 10 Hells Angels as subjects of investigation, including Oakland chapter members Kenny

(K.O.) Owen, Gary Popkin and Werner (Krusi) Sohm. A week later, FBI headquarters rescinded the authorization for Tait to carry a gun. Bureaucrats feared he might kill someone and the bureau would be held legally responsible. Tait continued to carry a concealed handgun for his own safety.

Tait's status was changed from organized-crime informant to top-echelon informant in November because his attendance at WesCOMs gave him access to the highest levels within the Hells Angels.

Tait flew to New York City on Saturday, November 9, but he was floored by the flu and missed the East Coast Officers' Meeting. He visited the New York City clubhouse briefly on Sunday and spent Monday in bed. Tait met with Barger, Richmond Hells Angel Richard Leonard (Indian) Miguel and Oakland Hells Angel Cisco Valderrama in the clubhouse on Tuesday. They discussed the Halifax chapter, whose members were continually arrested and re-arrested on release. British Columbia chapters sent members to bolster membership and morale in Halifax.

They talked about the problem with the Windsor, England, and Zurich chapters, which allowed members to wear Hells Angels belt buckles that other chapters restricted to 10-year members. The Richmond chapter sent an intimidating later to the English chapter and threatened to beat any English Hells Angel who wore the buckle in their territory.

Tait noticed that select Hells Angels wore tattoos believed to indicate they had killed someone. The tattoos appeared to have replaced the traditional Filthy Few tattoo, which had a lightning bolt to signal an Angel has killed. East Coast Hells Angels had an "AAA" tattoo for "Alexander's Avenging Angels." West Coast Hells Angels had a "BBB" tattoo for "Barger's Brutal Bastards."

About the same time, Marischen met in Oakland with McKinley, his supervisor Tom Lusby, Byron Sage from Washington, Bob Braver, the case agent on Roughrider out of Baltimore, and Kevin Bonner, the FBI undercover agent who handled informant Vernon Hartung in Roughrider. They plotted how to best use Tait nationally and worldwide. They also figured out ways to avoid problems they'd encountered in Roughrider. Marischen planned to meet Braver and Bonner along with Vernon Hartung in Austin, Texas, to pick his brain under the pretext that he planned a case against the Bandidos in San Antonio.

Back in San Francisco, Tait ordered two leather vests at $200 apiece from the Leather Odyssey in San Leandro. He drove to South City in San Francisco to meet with San Francisco vice-president John Makoto (Fuki) Fukushima, the gizmo-wiz who took the Hells Angels into the computer age. He pulled out his security file and gave Tait, for the Alaska security file, a report on the Big Four outlaw motorcycle gangs prepared by the Organized Crime Section, Criminal Investigative Division of the FBI, dated June 1985. He also told Tait that Oakland Hells Angel Big Al Perryman found a bug in his house.

Oakland Hells Angel Krusi Sohm lent Tait his girlfriend's bike to ride to Spatt's restaurant in Berkeley for Sohm's 10-year anniversary party. Tait also met longtime Oakland member Mike Lessard, who had just been released from prison to a halfway house.

At the restaurant, Tait sat between Kenny Owen and Gary Popkin, two Oakland Hells Angels. He went through a scenario created by his handlers to give the impression he made a lot of money. He ordered several entrees and ate a little from each while he offered them to his fellow diners. Owen was impressed by the gesture. Popkin couldn't care less; he let few people get close to him.

The WesCOM was held in the San Francisco clubhouse the day after Sohm's party. Fuki passed out copies of the FBI report on motorcycle gangs. It was announced that the Sherbrooke, Quebec, chapter's anniversary was December 5, and 17 of their 26 members were in jail. Sonny Barger's testimony before the New York Grand Jury was read.

After routine announcements from West Coast chapters, the minutes of the East Coast Officers' Meeting were read. The coasts kept in touch regularly: the East Coast Angels called the West Coast Angels every Wednesday night to brief them on what happened in the club. Minnesota Angel Patrick Joseph (Pat) Matter coordinated the list of who on the West Coast was to receive phone calls.

Tait went to the house of Gary (Frisco Gary) Kautzman in Vallejo after the meeting. He smoked a couple of joints of bad marijuana with Kautzman and listened to conversations picked up on bugs planted in his coffee pot and motorcycle shop office. Kautzman eavesdropped on his colleagues and listened for anyone breaking into the shop to plant bugs or steal.

Tait visited Big Al Perryman at home the next morning. Perryman told him his wife, Vickie, had noticed two small wires that protruded from a power cord while she moved furniture as she cleaned. She checked and found a bug. He did not want to keep it in the house, so he photographed it and gave the bug to Kenny Owen, who built a bug detector from a microwave radar detector that emitted a buzz when brought near a listening device.

Tait noticed a quarter pound of premium-quality "Humboldt County Heroin" marijuana. Perryman offered him some and they smoked. Tait later turned down an offered snort of crank. Perryman told Tait he lost his personal stash of crank when he left a quarter ounce in a New York cab.

"How did you take it with you?"

"I always carry it in my drawers."

Perryman was a happy-go-lucky, 375-pound behemoth so fat he often fell off his motorcycle. The Hells Angels discussed placing him at the back of the pack on runs after he once fell off and took down a bunch of Angels. Nothing embarrasses a Hells Angel more than a fall off a motorcycle.

Fat Albert, the Fat Man or Big Al had a mean streak

and was quick to stomp people and take care of business. When he wasn't mean, he was the club comedian and fashion plate. Perryman loved jewelry. He rented a limousine on a visit to New York and drove from boutique to boutique to buy $20,000 in gold jewelry and trinkets to give to the guys with him.

He also liked to roam at night. He ate well and a lot. He hired a catering company to bring him food at a run because he didn't want to ride all the way to town. Like most other Oakland Hells Angels, he was a longtime member astride the mid-century mark.

Tait received an airmail letter from London's Guy (Tricky Tramp) Lawrence in late November. It contained an updated jail list for English members and addresses where they received mail. Tait also learned that one of two trailers occupied by Dan McIntosh behind the Anchorage clubhouse was hooked up by intercom to the house of Mat-Su Hells Angel Michael Hurn. In early December, Tait found out that Hells Angels in Fairbanks were aware that a female Alaska state trooper worked undercover as a cocktail waitress in the Lonely Lady bar. Marischen warned the troopers and she was pulled out.

Fairbanks Angels ran into a former Dago chapter member called Funny Sunny Selig, who had falsely told the press in Seattle that he was Hells Angel leader in the state. They out-dated his tattoo. The Death's Head tattoo has an in-date to indicate when a member joined. The out-date indicates when he left.

McKinley sent a memo to FBI headquarters in which he cited "lack of DEA interest" in the case against the Hells Angels.

The next West Coast Officers' Meeting, at the San Bernardino clubhouse in December, turned into an intelligence session as officers watched a home movie of a 1982 Fourth of July party at the New York City clubhouse. The film was shown so everyone could have a look at Vernon Hartung. A gray-bearded, taller and heavier man than Hartung was identified as FBI undercover agent Kevin Bonner. The Hells Angels said both men should be killed. Oakland Hells Angel Charles (Chico) Manganiello said he saw Hartung and Bonner when they were in the Bay Area in April. He said Bonner had altered his appearance substantially since the film—he had lost more than 50 pounds and dyed the gray out of his hair. He was much younger than he appeared in the film.

Manganiello was observant. The Hells Angels misidentified the man with Hartung. He was another FBI undercover agent—Special Agent Butch Hogeson of the Baltimore Division.

Chico Manganiello was a longtime Hells Angel whose ego needed young girls and whose body required crank to keep going. If Santa Claus were a crankster, he'd be Chico Manganiello. Tait and Manganiello shared the drive from San Bernardino to Oakland after the meeting. Talk turned to drugs. Tait said a small group of one-per-centers—bikers who consider themselves outlaws—started to distribute ephedrine as speed in Anchorage. The Hells Angels would lose control of the area if they didn't start to manufacture and distribute crank. Manganiello described himself as a good crank cook and offered to teach Tait everything he knew about clandestine labs. He complained that most Oakland Hells Angels who cooked acted like mad chemists and just threw chemicals in.

Manganiello invited Tait to his large laboratory on a property he owned in northeast California. He said his vacuum extractor was so big it had to be moved with a forklift. He used a generator to produce electricity so the feds couldn't track his electricity bill. He offered to sell Tait monomethylamine gas for $1,000 a pound and phenyl-2-propanone for $5,000 a gallon.

Marischen and Tait were at a loss to find a safe place to meet by late 1985. Tait would be hard-pressed to explain being seen in the federal building that housed the FBI office. They parked side by side in the lot of a bowling alley just outside town or at the far end of the airport near the water. Security police caught them twice. Each time, Marischen hustled out of the car and badged the officer before he saw Tait. Faces get familiar quickly in a small town. Sometimes Tait parked his truck and hopped into Marischen's car as he drove by. But the Anchorage Division of the FBI had no undercover cars, and Marischen's vehicle was obviously a cop car—a Caprice with blackwall tires. Marischen even got the first pager in his division so Tait could contact him without leaving a number with a secretary or switchboard.

Early in 1985, Tait met Marischen and Larry Nelson in a second-floor apartment the bureau had rented in Marischen's undercover name. The furnished apartment allowed Marischen and Tait to meet safely and leave messages for each other, and Tait could drop off tapes there for Marischen. It gave both men a place to crash when they got tired. For Tait it was also a haven from Brenda when they'd been fighting.

Tait continued to press Marischen for money in December 1985. He wrote this note on Marriott Hotel stationery.

I don't think that seven months will be long enough, and I feel that you people don't trust me and that I am being used without much of a return for past services.

I would like to straighten out this cash thing. Some cash should be placed in the First Interstate account, $1,000 or so, not to be used unless I have to.

If I do have to go I want to stop in San Antoine and meet Bonner and discuss my future. I would like to get this on paper.

Why am I not invited to the White House Christmas party?

Seven

IN EARLY JANUARY 1986, Tait once again wanted to bail out. He wasn't convinced it was worth his while to hang in. He and Marischen talked back and forth. Marischen couldn't figure out how to stroke his informant's ego any more. If egos had hair, Tait's would be bald from all Marischen's attention.

Then one morning Tait brought Marischen the horoscope from that day's *Anchorage Times*. Tait is a Gemini. He read: "Avoid premature starts. You can afford to play the waiting game. Law is on your side. You have been carrying an unfair burden. It will be removed. You'll reach a wider audience, could receive public acclaim."

"That's good," Marischen said enthusiastically.

"I'm in," said Tait. "I'm in for the long run."

Marischen showed the horoscope to Tony Hodge, the assistant special agent in charge, with whom he often discussed the trials and tribulations of handling Tait. They laughed. "I couldn't have written this any better," Marischen said.

In town a week later for another WesCOM, Tait visited Kenny Owen's Woodshop in Oakland and noticed the odor of fresh methamphetamine in the second office toward the back of the building. Owen told him about the secret room behind the wall in the office. Owen kept the front door locked that evening.

Tait visited Big Al Perryman at home on Sunday.

Perryman said he had visited Sacramento "on club business" and pulled a Hells Angel patch worn by a citizen called Kevin Bretts. He took the man's valuables and told him to "get out of Dodge" within 24 hours. Perryman also said he and Sacramento Hells Angel John Robert (Frisco John) Stevens beat someone else in Sacramento with baseball bats. Frisco John was arrested and Perryman said he spent little time at home to make it difficult for police to arrest him. In that incident, Steven Cooper was beaten but ran out of the house before the two Hells Angels could kill him. He identified Frisco John, but could not identify his second attacker, who wore a red T-shirt with "Hells Angels" across the front. The FBI did not arrest Perryman so as not to compromise Tait, who had tipped them off.

Tait attended Oakland church that evening. Sandy Alexander was the hot topic. He had called Michael Charles (Sweet Mike) Carothers of the San Fernando Valley chapter and Ventura president George (Gus) Christie to say he was angry at the club because few Hells Angels spoke to him and they treated his wife, Collette, poorly. A New York City Hells Angel had beaten her. Carothers and Christie reported to Oakland that Alexander told them he would try to withdraw his guilty plea on federal racketeering charges in New York. Alexander had sold drugs to Vernon Hartung and Kevin Bonner. The Hells Angels learned from the affidavit of FBI Special Agent Mark Young that Alexander made tens of thousands of dollars selling drugs to Bonner yet he didn't report or share the profits with the club as required by the chapter. The Hells Angels also learned that Alexander registered the New York City clubhouse, a seven-storey tenement, in his name and his wife's rather than in the club's name.

Sonny Barger warned that the FBI was putting a "national RICO" together in San Francisco and cautioned members to clean up. He complained that child-molestation charges were pending against former Oakland member Winston McConney. Barger was upset because he was the second child molester in the Oakland chapter. Members voted to do nothing about McConney.

Members were told that Oakland had obtained from Sacramento sources a prosecutor's brief on outlaw motorcycle gangs prepared by the California State Department of Justice.

Tait struck up a conversation with Chico Manganiello, who told him he just returned from Portola where he had "been cooking since Christmas." He said he would return Tuesday to cook some more. He invited Tait to visit him at home the next day.

Tait dropped by Manganiello's house in Oakland on Monday. Manganiello offered Tait coffee, which he accepted, and crank, which he refused. Manganiello went into the kitchen and returned with a small clear plastic bag full of crank. He spooned the powder into his coffee. Tait pulled out a U.S. atlas and had Manganiello show him where Portola was in northeast California. Manganiello advised Tait to buy property in the area, as had Oakland Hells Angel Gary Popkin, and offered to give him a tour of the area. Manganiello said Kenny Owen, Bobby (Dirt) England and Richard (Spiderman) Grootendorst were good cookers.

McKinley started the rough draft of a contract between the FBI and Tait on Tuesday, January 14. The FBI's proposed case against the Hells Angels was approved during a conference with the Presidential Organized Crime Drug Enforcement Task Force the following morning.

Tait was about to enter the Oakland chapter clubhouse to visit Irish O'Farrell that night when two police cars boxed in a car that screeched to a stop outside Kenny Owen's Woodshop across the street. Two drunk men jumped out of the car. Tait crossed the street, banged on the door and told Owen about the men in the car. Owen said he knew them.

The driver, Blair Guthrie, a Hells Angel associate, yelled out, "Hey, Kenny! Hey, Kenny!"

He walked toward the Woodshop as the police

talked to him, ripped off his black leather vest as he got to the door and threw it in. He pulled the door shut, locked it and snapped the key in the lock.

The cops immediately took Guthrie and his partner down and made them lie on the road in the rain. Tait and Owen entered the Woodshop through a side door. Owen quickly checked the vest pockets and pulled out two small plastic bags that contained a crystal powder. He hid the bags, and then they walked to the front of the building to watch Guthrie and the cops. Owen explained to Tait that Guthrie carried two types of crank: dote and antidote. Dote was high-grade. Antidote was low-grade.

Owen wore a shirt that said "Hells Angels" across the front. Tait had his colors on. Suddenly the front door crashed open and six Oakland police officers stormed in. They had popped the lock with a screwdriver. Tait asked if they had a key to the place.

"Yeah, something like that."

Another pointed to Owen. "That's the one who took the vest."

"Then you're under arrest," said an oversized cop who grabbed Owen by the shirt and ripped his pocket.

"You can't do that," Tait said as he reached toward the cop. Another cop punched Tait in the throat and in the head. They shoved him backwards and held him down on a woodworking bench. They took Tait and Owen out of the building and sat them in a patrol car. Tait could hardly stand. They asked why he had $1,400 in his pockets.

"Listen, I'm from Alaska and up there that's lunch money."

The cops let everyone go after a sergeant showed up and realized the force could be sued for illegal entry and assault and battery. The Hells Angels were notorious for suing. The cops embellished their reports to save their asses. They claimed they saw AR-15s on the wall of the Woodshop. But Kenny Owen never kept guns there. The beating left Tait with a chronically injured back.

Tait had had no choice but to step in and help

Owen—he was a sergeant-at-arms. The gesture paid off.
Owen was immeasurably grateful, and he told Tait he
admired his loyalty to the club. Oakland Hells Angel
Michael Malve congratulated Tait for standing up to the
cops and gave him a key to the Oakland clubhouse. Tait
gave it to the FBI to copy, then returned it a couple of
days later when he left town. It was a small gesture of
honor among thieves: Tait wouldn't need the key while
he was out of town.

The next day Tait met with Fuki Fukushima at his
house. They discussed security files and the counter-
intelligence operations of the San Francisco chapter.
Fukushima worked at a Ford dealership and was suspected of taking police reports from the trunks of cars
that the Oakland Police Department brought in for
service.

He showed Tait a telephone roster with the names
and home phone numbers of DEA agents. Fukushima
said the roster was taken from the purse of DEA agent
Laura Hayes—who directed a case against the Hells
Angels—while she sat in a restaurant. The purse also
contained her credentials, badge and Smith and Wesson
Model 13 .357 Magnum service revolver.

The Angels monitored Hayes and another female
DEA agent on a radio scanner as they planned on a DEA
radio frequency to meet for drinks. They sent someone
to the restaurant to photograph the agents with a camera
fitted with a telephoto lens. Fukushima showed Tait the
photograph. He said there were too many cops for the
Hells Angels to watch them all.

Later that afternoon, Tait drove to the Frisco
Choppers store in San Francisco to talk to Vallejo vice-
president Gary Kautzman. Kautzman played several
radios simultaneously in the shop. He had learned while
he defended himself against drug charges laid in
Operation Roughrider that this hindered federal agents
who monitored conversations in the shop.

When Tait attended the West Coast Officers'
Meeting at the San Francisco clubhouse that night, four

Hells Angels equipped with two-way radios guarded the outside of the building.

Among the items discussed that night were some charity PR efforts. Fukushima reported that the annual San Francisco Toy Run was set for December 20. The toy run is a publicity ploy designed to portray Hells Angels as benevolent, though hardcore, bikers. They ensure they are photographed with teddy bears and other stuffed animals on their motorcycles.

The Daly City chapter said it would sponsor an exhibition about the Vietnam Memorial.

Among the administrative items was the announcement that Gordon Gary (Flash) Grow transferred from San Francisco to Oakland to become the new trademark secretary. Grow was picked by club officers because of his loyalty and devotion to the Hells Angels.

McKinley filed a memo with headquarters in Washington on Friday, January 31, in which he officially code-named the case against the Hells Angels CHARON, after the mythical boatman who ferried souls across the river Styx into hell. He added Chico Manganiello as a subject of the investigation.

McKinley received a call in early February from a man who said Kenny Owen bought equipment at an auction that could be used in a large-scale methamphetamine laboratory. The informant once owned the equipment: a 50-gallon Pfaudler glass-lined pressure-reactor vessel to make methamphetamine, a large vacuum chamber to dry the drug and a large steam generator to develop pressure to operate the pressure vessel. The informant said the Pfaudler pressure-reactor vessel needed two seals and a valve before it could be used. The Pfaudler distributor in Davis, California, was the only supplier of the parts.

Tait attended the tenth-anniversary party of the Hells Angels Charleston, South Carolina, chapter on February 7. Raids and arrests were the main topic of conversation. The Angels passed around photographs of James (Gorilla) Harwood, who testified against the club after his arrest in

Operation Roughrider. Lawrence J. (Butch) Garcia of New York City said his chapter wouldn't let former president Sandy Alexander live once he got out of jail because he "jacked them around" too much.

Ronald (Big Cheese) Cheeseman of the Mid-State, New York, chapter also made the Hells Angels hit list that night. Someone announced the gang planned to "do him" when he got out of jail. They couldn't pull his patch while he was in jail, but no longer considered him a member. Roughrider investigators found videotapes in Cheeseman's house of him having sex with a seven-year-old boy and an 11-year-old girl.

A Charleston Hells Angel told Tait that information out of Virginia showed the feds had an inside source in the Hells Angels.

A British Columbia Hells Angel reported that an FBI agent worked with the Royal Canadian Mounted Police section that investigates bikers in that province. The Hells Angels would send a photograph of the agent to other chapters.

British Columbia Angels complained that Montreal Hells Angels were a bunch of "gangsters" who had leased a fleet of cars and transported drugs behind the car's name plate and front dash and in the air-conditioning ducts. Robin from the Nanaimo chapter and Guy from the Vancouver chapter discussed the killing of the North chapter in Quebec in 1985. They said that a Hells Angel called Apache was the main hitter for the Quebec Hells Angels.

Quebec Hells Angels decided in March 1985 to kill most members of their North Chapter in Laval. All but two members were hitmen and these Angels regularly stole drug profits from the club. Five North Chapter Hells Angels were shot at a party at the Sherbrooke clubhouse, wrapped in sleeping bags and dumped in the St. Lawrence Seaway. A sixth member was killed a week later. Ironically, the chapter's most vicious member—Apache Trudeau—who had killed at least 43 people, escaped to testify against the club.

Before he left Charleston, Tait found out that Marischen had solved several problems they faced. Tait had trouble renting cars because he had no credit card. He needed a job to get one and since the FBI paid his salary, he didn't have a job he could substantiate. He needed support from an employer to get pre-authorization to rent cars. Once he knew what area he planned to visit, he could call the rental agency and give them a number they could call to check his employment.

Marischen called on a local businessman and friend to back Tait's job record. He was promised the favor would not be abused and asked no questions. Elmer Eller owned Alaska Art Tile, a retail tile distributor in Anchorage. The company had a wholesale branch called Alaska Pioneer Tile. Eller signed Tait up as an employee and allowed Tait to print up business cards that identified him as a wholesale salesman and buyer for Pioneer Tile. Tait could now explain his frequent trips as expeditions to buy tiles or to attend conferences. Eller even volunteered, should the need arise, to give Tait the regular employee discount if Hells Angels decided to buy tiles through him.

On his way back from Charleston, Tait attended a tile seminar on the *Queen Mary* in Long Beach, California. He learned about tiles, the jargon, what to say and do as a tile buyer and salesman, and picked up props to set around his apartment. Tait now had a solid cover.

Marischen crafted an additional way to explain Tait's FBI income. He could not say he worked full time because the Hells Angels knew he didn't. He floated the story that his father had left an estate that paid him a monthly stipend. People who knew Gordon Tait knew he didn't have that kind of money, and a decent investigation would show the story to be false. So Marischen approached fellow FBI agent Roger Lee, who had many Anchorage contacts. Lee suggested he speak to local attorney Wevley Shea, a friend who could be trusted. Marischen explained the situation to Shea with little detail. Shea was a professional. He didn't ask. He knew what Marischen wanted. He inserted Gordon Tait's name in his card file so anyone who asked would see that Tait was Shea's client. And if anyone asked, he would confirm he handled Tait's inheritance.

In the meantime, a man who identified himself as Mr. Maxwell visited the offices of west coast Pfaudler Company distributor Henry Sugar and ordered two seals and a valve for a Pfaudler reactor. The parts were shipped to the address given by Mr. Maxwell: Unlimited Welding, 4010 Foothill Boulevard in Oakland—the business name of Kenny Owen's Woodshop. Mr. Maxwell was Kenneth Alison Maxwell, known as The Old Man, who was on probation on a federal conviction for manufacturing methamphetamine.

One night in mid-February, Tait, wearing his colors, walked into the Crazy Horse Saloon and ordered a beer. The bar had a policy not to serve Hells Angels in colors because they caused fights and scared away business. The doorman spotted Tait's colors and told him he could stay as long as he removed his jacket.

"No, thanks."

Tait left without paying the tab, and the Anchorage Hells Angels launched a discrimination suit.

The clubhouse and bars were the hub of the Hells Angels social life during the cold winter months. J.C. Webb, Ed Hubert and Mark Greer had a high-school girl in the hot tub. Webb tried to talk her into having sex with all of them. She wouldn't. After half an hour, she got up. Greer sat on the edge of the tub. Webb grabbed his stun gun, sneaked up behind her and zapped her rear end as she started to get out. She turned, looked at the stun gun and grabbed Greer's cock.

"Well, who's first?"

The hot tub was often the focal point for social soirées at the clubhouse and members hung their swim trunks on pegs. One time, Tait found a large bloodstain in his trunks. He brought the matter up at church a few days later. "Listen, I want to know whoever brought their nasty fucking girlfriend over here on the rag and had her wear my swim trunks." He pulled the trunks inside out and showed the bloodstain. "Whoever fucking did this, this is terrible. You can take these and give them back to your girlfriend. I want you to know if there had been sharks in that fucking hot tub, there would have been blood everywhere."

Everyone laughed.

Tait liked to put people down. He used church as a venue to make disparaging remarks couched in humor. Dirty Dave Gonzales acted like an asshole one night. Tait looked at him. "Dirt, how would you like to be cryologically suspended for the next 250 years?"

"What does that mean?"

Everyone laughed. Russ Hagel said, "I don't know what that means, but it sure sounds pretty good. What is it?"

"Be frozen and be placed in suspended animation for the next 250 years."

Everyone laughed again.

By February 1986, Tait was so busy he had little time to meet his friend, 42-year-old cop Larry Robinette, twice a week for lunch. Robinette had made good on his bet many times over and had bought Tait six or seven steak dinners since he became a Hells Angel. They talked on the phone the third week of February and Robinette suggested they meet for lunch on Wednesday. Robinette got up around 8 o'clock that morning. He put on a pot of coffee, swept the snow off his car and picked the newspaper off the porch. He lay down on the couch to read the paper while the coffee perked.

Tait didn't worry when Robinette failed to show for lunch. It had happened before when duty called. He phoned his house that night but got no answer. He was too busy to call Thursday. He tried six or seven times Friday. He went to the Whale's Tail Lounge that night.

"I've got bad news," said the barman. "Robbie died. He's been lying in his house for three days."

McKinley found out that month that the codename CHARON was used in a counter-intelligence case, so he changed the codename of his proposed investigation to

CERBERUS, the mythological three-headed dog that guarded the entrance to hell.

Meanwhile, Brenda Fowler continued to supply Marischen with information on Tait. They had split up several times and she left town to work as a prostitute, but they always got back together. Marischen never ended her as a source because she was one bridge he could not afford to burn. Tait immeasurably increased the value of that bridge in March. Brenda called Marischen and tried to con him by claiming Tait had told her his secret.

"Kenny, are you meeting with Tony?"

Marischen panicked. "No, Brenda."

"Well, Tony says he's working for Kenny in the FBI and he's tall."

"I'm the only Ken with the FBI. He's full of shit. I don't know. Maybe it's somebody else."

When Marischen's heartbeat returned to normal, he walked into Special Agent in Charge Tony Hodge's office and shut the door. The case had become extremely sensitive when both Tait and Brenda signed on as informants. Only Hodge and Larry Nelson knew the situation. Marischen explained Brenda's call and they laughed.

"I'm the only Ken with the FBI."

They roared.

"She bought that? Goddamn."

They laughed some more.

Brenda later claimed she found out on her own that Tait worked for Marischen. She said she followed Tait once and saw him hop into Marischen's truck. She snooped through Tait's belongings and used his tape recorder to record his telephone calls. The tension between Tait and Brenda and Brenda and Marischen grew. Something was bound to happen.

It dawned on Tait a few weeks later that Brenda must be an informant for Marischen. He confronted his control in the undercover apartment with fists clenched and ready to pummel. He bitched against the bureau. He said Marischen didn't trust him. He accused him of going behind his back. Marischen let him vent his anger. Then he took the only route that could save the case. He offered Tait as little information as possible about his agent/informant relationship with Brenda. He never told Tait that Brenda went to the police. This woman surely would always be in his life for better or worse. Marischen needed Brenda to spy on Tait and he didn't want Tait to suspect her. He also didn't want Tait to beat Brenda for ratting on him. Marischen told Tait that Brenda only gave him information on a drug dealer on the Slope. That partly appeased Tait. The tension remained strong between the men for three days, then dissipated. Marischen felt like a matchmaker for a relationship made in hell.

McKinley found out in March that CERBERUS was also used in a counter-intelligence case. He changed the name to CACUS, a half-man, half-beast, armed with a long lance, who bedeviled the lost souls of thieves in the eighth ring of hell.

When Tait next visited Big Al Perryman's house, Bobby England and Chico Manganiello were there along with a woman. Perryman set a 10-inch round slab of polished rock in front of him and measured out a line of crank for everyone in the room. He passed the rock around. Tait felt he had to snort his line. It would be too obvious if he didn't and he felt uncomfortable doing his song and dance about having quit drugs for a medical problem. He inhaled the crank and left Perryman's house confused.

Tim McKinley was used to Tait's late-night phone calls. When his pager went off that night, he thought, "Another one of the midnight calls of Paul Revere."

Then the pager went off several more times. That was unusual. McKinley looked at the display on his pager. The number was garbled. He figured Tait was under a lot of stress to incorrectly punch in a phone number and his code.

McKinley put on his slippers and called Tait from a pay phone. Tait was upset and talked rapidly like a crankster or a 14-year-old kid on his first trip. He was rattled. He felt he fucked up. He had to do it. He felt terrible. He didn't feel good physically. His skin crawled. McKinley told him to stay in his room and he'd drop by in the morning. Tait was still stoned when McKinley walked into the hotel room at 11:00.

On April 1, Tait took part in an annual ritual for the Alaska chapters. The Frozen Few Run is one of the club's most demanding and demented events. It starts in 30-degree temperature in Anchorage and ends in freezing air 360 miles north in Fairbanks. Bones and muscles stiffen quickly at 60 miles an hour in April. The bikers continue to Chena Hot Springs resort, where they party for a weekend. The 1986 run was more exciting than most.

The Hells Angels pulled into the resort after dark and had dinner. Tait, as security officer, did an inventory of vehicles in the parking lot and noticed a dirtbag, which is what he called any unkempt person he disliked, and his girlfriend. He figured they'd leave when they found out who the new guests were, but the dirtbag knew some Angels and they talked into the evening. Tait went to his cabin at 1:00.

Until that weekend, the only incident of note during the Frozen Few run happened in a shower when Monty Elliott asked someone to pass him a bar of soap while he washed. Sleazy Ric Rickleman reached over and shoved the soap up the crack of Elliott's ass. Elliott waited until Rickleman was about to wash his long greasy hair and pissed in his shampoo bottle. Rickleman washed his hair with it and got pissed off when everyone laughed.

Tait got up at 7:30 the next morning and put on his longjohns, blue jeans, snakeskin wool socks, cowboy boots, a heavy shirt and official green Forest Service parka. As he hurried down the trail he noticed four people 50 yards ahead. He recognized a Hells Angel, a prospect, an associate and the dirtbag. The prospect suddenly jumped back. Tait approached from the side. At 25 yards, he saw the dirtbag had something in his hand.

"Hey!"

The dirtbag turned to look at Tait. The associate tried to shove him and the dirtbag swished his hand at his face. Tait stepped closer and saw the knife in the dirtbag's hand. He approached Tait, who backhanded the knife hand away with his heavy leather gloves and hooked the dirtbag in the jaw. He pried the knife out of the hand and flipped it into the snow. The dirtbag attacked. Tait kicked him to the ground and kicked him in the stomach several times for good measure. Something fell out of the dirtbag's waistband. Tait grabbed him by the hair and smashed his nose. Blood splattered the snow.

"Leave him alone." The dirtbag's girlfriend came around a cabin with an M1A .308-caliber assault rifle. Tait had a five-shot snub-nose .38-caliber belly gun in his pocket. He could put all five rounds in her chest and head before she could react. He decided to talk. Then she pulled back the action and chambered a round in her rifle.

"Get away from him. Get away from him!"

"Hey, lady. I work for the Forest Service. I work here at the lodge. I'm just trying to break this up." He got within 10 feet of her. A little closer and he'd grab the gun and beat her bitch ass.

"Don't let him get close. He knows karate." The dirtbag had regained consciousness.

She leveled the gun at Tait's chest.

He stepped back toward two cords of wood and a 55-gallon trash drum. "Hey, let's take it easy. All you need to do is get out of here."

"I want my fucking gun back!" the dirtbag yelled. "You guys got my gun."

Tait kept moving back.

"Watch out!" the dirtbag yelled to his girlfriend.

An Angel associate rested his gun on a sign and aimed at her. Angels came out of the woods with guns.

Tait got behind the woodpile. She crouched behind the
steel drum. She wore tennis shoes, jeans and a sweat-
shirt. It was minus 20 degrees. She waved the gun back
and forth. Seven or eight Hells Angels aimed AR-15
assault rifles, shotguns and pistols at her. They were
going to kill.

"Don't shoot! I'll handle it," Tait yelled. "Listen,
you'll never get out of here alive. You got no cover there.
They'll kill you and that'll be it." Tait was between the
Angels and the woman. "Let's talk about this."

Russ Hagel knew the woman from school. "We
won't kill you," he said. "You just got to go. Listen to
him."

"Look," said Tait, "we're freezing out here. Let's go
inside and sit in the back of the lodge and talk this over
and have a cup of coffee and you can go. Everything will
be done."

"Okay."

"Let's just walk in there."

Tait slipped off his glove and held his gun in his
pocket, ready to blast her. He walked into the lodge, past
the owner. "I need some backup. Call the police."

"Huh?"

"Call the police."

"Okay."

The owner used a radio telephone to contact the
nearest house with a telephone and they called the
police. Tait and the couple sat at the back of the lodge.

The dirtbag said, "Listen, I just want my gun and
we'll go." It was a Colt .45.

"I'll see what I can do. I can't guarantee. It might be
lost in the snow."

"No. That guy picked it up." He pointed to Charlie
Potter, who stood outside and looked in the window.

"I don't know if he did or not," Tait said.

"I saw him pick it up."

"I'll see what I can do. For safety's sake, you're going
to have to leave the lodge."

"Okay, we'll go."

Tait got them organized and walked them out to the pickup truck. The woman kept the rifle pointed at him. The Angels were going ballistic.

"They're going to leave," Tait told them. "There's no problem. Let's not have any trouble. Let them go and everything will be jake."

The couple got into the truck—and it wouldn't start. Tait told two prospects to get a couple of kerosene heaters.

"You stay in the fucking truck. I'll have them take care of it."

They put one heater on the radiator and one on the block. The motor started in 15 minutes. The couple drove off.

"All right," Tait said. "You know what's going to happen now. The police are probably on the way. This guy's probably called them. We're going to have to do what we can. They're probably going to send a SWAT team. We'll be fucked if they get here and we got all these guns. I want everybody to give me their guns, throw them in the trunk of my car, lock all this shit up and we'll all get naked and get in the hot tubs."

As sergeant-at-arms, Tait had the authority to confiscate the guns. The cops arrived and stormed the hot-tub room. Tait was the only Angel not in the water. A state trooper leveled his gun at him.

"Hold it right there."

"Hey, man. Can't you see I'm unarmed? I don't have any weapons on me except the one in my drawers. Do you want to see it?" He started to pull down his bathing suit.

"No, I don't want to see that. Everybody just stay in the pools."

The cops took the Angels and associates out one at a time and searched them and their belongings before they let them go. They seized a few knives. A Fairbanks prospect had stolen moccasins and embroidered mittens from a display case in the lodge, but no one would identify him when police found the items in his cabin. The Angels had to leave the lodge.

In early April, McKinley arranged for former
Oakland Hells Angel Sergey Walton to get a pass out of
jail to visit his mother. The next day, McKinley and ATF
Special Agent Ted Baltas debriefed Walton about Hells
Angels drug activities before he became a police informant in 1980. Three other people—an FBI agent, a
police detective and a lawyer—participated in the session, which was explained to Walton as an interview to
precede his grand jury testimony.

On April 17, eighteen months after Tait walked into
the FBI office in Anchorage, the bureau committed itself
to the investigation of the Hells Angels as a major case.
Tait was now an FBI contract informant. He would have
become one sooner if FBI headquarters in Washington
hadn't quibbled with the wording of the contract
McKinley drafted. He finally drafted two versions, which
Tait signed, and shipped them to Washington with a
note that read, "Have your pick." McKinley had never
heard of an informant being given a contract, but the FBI
wanted to ensure control over Tait, and bureaucrats covered their asses should the case sour.

The major-case status gave the operation more
money, but it also meant that McKinley, as case administrator, now had to prepare monthly expense vouchers for
headquarters. The civil service is often a tougher oppo-
nent than organized crime.

Tait's contract, signed by him, McKinley and Jay
Colvin, read:

Whereas the Federal Bureau of Investigation, here-
inafter referred to as F.B.I., is conducting a lawfull
[sic] investigation concerning allegations of criminal activities on the part of certain individuals who
are members of, or associates with the Hells Angels
Motorcycle Club in and around the western United
States and Alaska. But the ultimate purpose of said
investigation being prosecution of individuals
engaged in violation of federal and state law.
And whereas Anthony Tait is in the position to

and is willing to furnish assistance to the F.B.I. in this regard.

And whereas the parties hereto desire to record the respective interests, rights and obligations.

Now therefore the parties here agree as follows:

1. Terms and conditions. In furtherance of the goals and of the aforesaid investigation Anthony Tait agrees to fully cooperate with the FBI and shall truthfully and completely and accurately disclose to the FBI any and all information which he now possesses or may later possess concerning all aspects of this investigation and shall do so in a prompt and timely manner.

2. Anthony Tait agrees at the direction of the FBI and under the supervision of the FBI to meet with designated individuals and agrees to make or to have made by the FBI consensual visual, oral and wire recordings of such meetings and related telephone calls.

   Further, Anthony Tait will provide written authorization to the FBI to monitor and record such meetings and/or conversations prior to such monitoring/recordings.

3. Anthony Tait agrees and understands that Anthony Tait is not an employee, partner or member of a joint venture and not an associate or agent of the FBI. Nor will he identify himself or hold himself out to be such.

4. Anthony Tait shall have no authority, actual or implied, to obligate and/or bind the FBI to any contractual duty and/or obligation and any obligations so made are the sole obligation of Anthony Tait and not the F.B.I.

5. It is understood that the FBI at its sole discretion will control all investigative activities including any decision to terminate this investigation.

6. Anthony Tait hereby acknowledges that he has been advised to attempt to avoid any conversations

or communications with individuals under indictment which conversations deal with the legal defenses contemplated by his fellow conversants, save where those conversations are in and of themselves criminal in nature and such conversations regarding plans to murder witnesses.

7. Anthony Tait agrees he will at the direction of the FBI make himself available for periodic polygraph examination and will upon periodic request by the FBI provide an appropriate sample for urinalysis. It is recognized by both parties that it is the purpose of this clause to protect the interest of both parties in insuring the integrity of this investigation as well as the integrity and reputation of all individuals involved with the matter or matters under investigation.

8. Anthony Tait agrees to purchase at the direction of, and under the supervision of the FBI a new or late model Harley-Davidson motorcycle in good, safe mechanical condition. This vehicle is purchased as a reasonable and necessary business expense by Anthony Tait with monies paid him in connection with services discussed in this contract.

9. Anthony Tait shall obtain collision, comprehensive and liability insurance for said vehicle to be purchased with funds provided him by the FBI with specific coverages to be determined by the FBI.

10. Anthony Tait agrees not to operate said vehicle while under the influence of alcohol or controlled substances and to maintain the vehicle in good working order and in safe condition. Tait further agrees to at all times operate and maintain said vehicle as would a reasonable man under the same or similar circumstance and in compliance with applicable state and/or federal law.

11. Anthony Tait understands that a specific rela-

tionship between Anthony Tait and the owner/proprietor of a certain ceramic tile company located in the Anchorage area of the state of Alaska has been established in order to create an image of Anthony Tait being employed by said ceramic tile company. This image of an employment situation was and is intended solely to further the interest and goals of this investigation by establishing the false facade that Anthony Tait is a buyer for the tile company, thus in part explaining Anthony Tait's extensive travel that will be necessary to support his cooperation in this investigation. This relationship is not intended to benefit Anthony Tait either directly or indirectly.

12. Understanding the reason for this relationship as set out in the above paragraph, Anthony Tait specifically further understands that his position in this relationship is limited to holding himself out to the general public to be a sales representative of the tile company and use of appropriate business cards. Anthony Tait specifically understands that he is not in fact an employee, agent, nor representative of said tile company and hence has no authority expressed or implied to bind said company to any contractual or liability producing situation.

13. The parties to this agreement recognize that a situation may occur that in order to preserve the above described employment image as well as Anthony Tait's credibility as the subject of this investigation it may become necessary to obtain tile and/or related materials for a subject. In such a situation Anthony Tait shall first contact the FBI's designated representative and the owner/proprietor or said tile company prior to making any commitments in order to ascertain if and under what conditions the tile and/or related materials may be available.

14. Anthony Tait agrees when directed by the FBI to testify and furnish all information in his possession, custody or control which he has received during the course of or related to this investigation.

15. Anthony Tait shall not participate in any unlawful activities except insofar as the FBI determines that such participation is necessary to this investigation and the FBI expressly authorizes such acts. It is understood that any such violation of law not expressly authorized by the FBI may result in the prosecution of Anthony Tait.

16. Anthony Tait will not initiate any plans to commit criminal acts nor will he participate in any acts of violence. Anthony Tait agrees that he will do all that is humanly possible to dissuade subjects from violence and failing that will upon learning of plans either involving violence or potentially involving violence promptly notify the FBI.

17. Anthony Tait shall in no way either during the term of this agreement or thereafter reveal the confidential and sensitive nature of this investigation, nor identify any undercover agent to any unauthorized person or persons and further will not undertake any publication or dissemination of any information or material that results from this investigation without the prior expressed written authorization of the FBI.

18. In consideration of Anthony Tait's performance as set out herein the FBI agrees to:

A. Reimburse Anthony Tait for expenses incurred by him which expenses are deemed by the FBI to be reasonable and in furtherance of this investigation. Anthony Tait agrees that insofar as practicable he will prior to incurring such expenses consult with the designated representative or representatives of the FBI as to the nature and justification for incurring such expense. The FBI retains the right to direct Anthony Tait not to incur such expenses which it deems not to be in furtherance of its investigative goals.

B. The FBI, cognizant of the fact that but for providing assistance to the FBI in regard to this investigation Anthony Tait would be employed in a wage earning capacity, agrees to compensate Anthony Tait in that amount of $4,000 per month for the duration of this agreement. This money shall be dispensed by the FBI on a monthly basis at the first of the month following the specific month for which the money was earned. The money shall be dispensed as follows:

1. $1,500 per month directly to Anthony Tait.

2. $2,500 per month in additional funds shall be earned by Anthony Tait each month to be paid by the FBI on or about the date the indictment from the investigation becomes public.

C. Anthony Tait will additionally be paid $8,000 forthwith to facilitate his purchase of the Harley-Davidson motorcycle for use while in |the continental United States in connection with the indicated investigation as discussed above. It is understood between the parties that the $8,000 is for information previously furnished by Anthony Tait and for suggestions that he has made in the indicated investigation.

19. Parties hereto agree that liability for any negligent or internal act of any FBI employee shall be borne by the FBI. Liability for any negligent or intentional act or acts of Anthony Tait which acts were taken without prior expressed approval of the FBI are the sole responsibility of Anthony Tait. However, Anthony Tait does not waive any rights or claims to which he is or may be entitled to under the federal Tort Claims Act.

20. This agreement shall commence on the date of

the acceptance by Anthony Tait as signified by his signature to this document, and shall continue for a period of 24 months thereafter. This agreement may be terminated upon notice to Anthony Tait by the FBI.

21. And the last provision. This document constitutes the full and complete agreement between Anthony Tait and the FBI. Modifications to this agreement will have no force or effect unless or until such modification is reduced to writing and signed by the parties thereto.

By subscription of their signatures below, the parties herewith acknowledge they have read, do understand and will abide by the above statements. This contract signed by Anthony Tait and dated 4-17-86 as witnessed on the 17th day of April, 1986 by Timothy McKinley and Jay Colvin for the Federal Bureau of Investigation, Special Agents out of San Francisco, California, and for a party, for the Federal Bureau of Investigation in Washington, D.C.

The $2,500 per month to be put aside was for Tait's relocation when the case ended. The FBI had budget problems at the time and McKinley worried that if he didn't establish a relocation fund, there might not be money to do so when Tait had to be moved.

McKinley and Tait went out to dinner after he signed the contract. An anger seethed inside Tait. He stared at McKinley and decided to test him.

"Brenda's an informant, huh?"

In fact, though Tait didn't yet know it, Brenda had just left him and gone to Colorado. She stole $300 from his pocket and pawned his crossbow, binoculars, a cedar loon and a viola to pay for the airline ticket.

McKinley's first reaction as an FBI agent, for whom the confidentiality of an informant is the first commandment, was to lie. But McKinley had a sneaking hunch he had better not lie. "Yeah."

It was a lucky call. Tait had already learned from
Marischen a week earlier that Brenda was an informant.
Although he bullshitted and lied to people, Tait could
not stand being lied to. Tait then ranted against
Marischen. They talked most of the night about
Marischen's use of Brenda as an informant. FBI agent Jay
Colvin defended Marischen's actions. Tait eventually
adopted the attitude that he didn't like it but he'd live
with it.

McKinley decided to include an agent from the
Bureau of Alcohol, Tobacco and Firearms in the investigation to handle weapons and explosives violations. Ted
Baltas had investigated Hells Angels for the ATF since
1978 in the New England area. It was only natural that
he continue his inquiries when he moved to San
Francisco in 1983, where he met McKinley while they
worked Operation Roughrider. McKinley told Baltas the
FBI had another source in the Hells Angels and asked if
he'd like to participate in an investigation that could be
better than Roughrider. He didn't have to ask twice.
They had known each other for two years and respected
each other's work. They were both tied up in Roughrider
litigation until early 1986. By then, Ken Marischen had
worked Tait in Alaska for more than a year to see if he
was for real. The FBI couldn't be too careful. The Hells
Angels believed the government had RICO charges lying
around against the gang and periodically rounded up the
bikers. They were on a constant lookout for government
agents and paid highly for inside information.

McKinley and Baltas wanted to bring Tait into the
Bay Area because Sonny Barger and the Oakland chapter
were the heart of the Hells Angels and there are seven
Hells Angels chapters within a 50-mile radius of San
Francisco—the biggest concentration of Angels in the
world. If anything criminal was going to happen, it
would be in California. The investigation as originally
proposed focused on the Angels' involvement in the
smuggling of cocaine, the manufacture and distribution
of methamphetamine and moneylaundering. It explored

their dealings in unlawful weapons and bombs.
McKinley and Baltas knew from experience, informants
and previous cases that the Hells Angels manufactured
and sold drugs in the Bay Area. But they could not make
major cases against them. Many Angels had weapons and
explosives convictions. They tasked Tait with a general
intelligence-gathering mission.

"Get out there. See how you're received, see what's
going on, then we'll sit back and review what we've got
and see what particular direction we want to go in."

They were concerned Tait might not be accepted in
California. He was a relatively new member, he was
young and he wasn't physically overbearing—you
couldn't pick him out in a crowd. McKinley and Baltas
hashed it out. They had a good thing here, but how far
could they take it? They decided to take it slow and feel
their way through.

They started with the premise that the investigation
could not go on forever. They didn't want it to stagnate
while Tait got stifled at a lower level, so they created an
image and aura for Tait that would give him access to the
club's highest levels.

The Hells Angels are severely structured. The Alaska
members were looked upon as ass-dragging yahoos. The
agents wanted Tait to be seen as a wealthy world traveler
who appeared to get his money from dealing drugs. That
would appeal to Angel drug manufacturers and dealers.
His position as sergeant-at-arms for the Anchorage chapter and Alaska would bring him in contact with guns and
explosives. They set out to imbue Tait with a certain
amount of class.

They also agreed that nothing was to be done unless
it was talked about beforehand. The agents didn't want
to blow opportunities through improper planning. Tait
was warned not to act on his own. He was an agent of
the government, not a government agent. He didn't have
a badge or a gun. He wasn't a cop, but a source. He was
the eyes and ears of his handlers. They told him what to
do and when. On the other hand, Tait was the man in

the field. He knew what would work and what wouldn't. They consulted him and he could veto their decisions. Unlike most operations that involve an informant, a rapport formed between handlers and informant. The operation would become a team effort. The handlers watched Tait's back.

"You're not out there being a hero or winning medals," Baltas said. "None of us are. Your safety comes first. If something happens and this investigation gets compromised, your safety comes up, it all stops. Doors get kicked in, we come down, we get you out, it's over, forget it."

Tait knew they could never get in fast enough to save him.

Tait was given ground rules, one of which was "Don't bullshit us, we won't bullshit you. If you don't know, you don't know. If you can't do it, don't push. We won't push. Let's just take our time." He was warned not to discuss the investigation with anyone.

The Hells Angels' wariness, combined with their active intelligence gathering, prompted Operation CACUS to be security-driven. McKinley and Baltas knew from past operations that the Hells Angels corrupted cops, lawyers, prosecutors, secretaries—anyone with access to information. Sometimes information was passed on through carelessness, naiveté or friendship.

The Hells Angels tried twice to penetrate the FBI San Francisco office through two support staff. They did penetrate the FBI several months before Tait signed his contract through a new agent trainee whose boyfriend fed information to the club. The trainee, a lawyer, was allowed to resign to avoid being charged. She claimed she didn't know her boyfriend passed on the information she gave him. McKinley had no doubt Tait would have been killed if she had not been caught. The experience made him paranoid for the duration of Operation CACUS.

The Angels also sent girls and women to seduce young officers in the police academy in Los Angeles.

They pumped them for information while they pumped them sexually, and recorded conversations. San Francisco police officers also sold information to the Angels.

The Angels keep tabs on police frequencies. A man in a wheelchair monitors a bank of scanners for them 24 hours a day in the Bay Area. He doesn't let the machines scan automatically, but channel flips so he can locate new frequencies used by law enforcement other than those listed in government publications. Individual Angels keep scanners in their houses to alert them to transmitters anyone who enters their house might have concealed in their clothing.

For their part, even though CACUS agents trusted each other, they harbored a healthy wariness of one another. No one moved without consulting the other agents. Everyone knew what everyone else did. There was no room for mistakes or misunderstandings. There was one exception to this rule. McKinley and Marischen kept secrets from each other.

For Baltas, the move west was like going from cub scouts to the army. California Hells Angels took care of business. They were older, more mature, survivors. They experienced gang wars, wars with law enforcement and wars among themselves. They plugged into the drug business in the 1960s when Timothy Leary preached to America's youth to turn on, tune in, drop out. They fed the original hippies the stuff of dreams, cornered a large portion of the chemical drug market and ended up wealthier and more powerful than they ever wanted to be. Baltas reminded himself the Hells Angels may be bikers, but they are businessmen first.

Ted Baltas brought stability and sanity to the case. McKinley, driven and intense, brought inexhaustible drive to the investigation, but the air around him was like a brick wall. His ability to organize lent structure to the case, but he alienated people in the process. He had the assuredness but lacked the diplomacy to be more tolerant of other people's views. He was resentful of those who didn't commit themselves completely to a case.

Baltas, although no less hard a worker, was laid back. He was a joker who played tricks on people, and he knew when levity could defuse tension. He put people at ease. As well, the Hells Angels trusted Baltas. They knew him as the ATF's weapons man. He treated them fairly and professionally. They talked to him and never had a beef against him. On the other hand, the Angels hated McKinley. They thought he took Operation Roughrider too personally and let him know through the grapevine. Sonny Barger kept a copy of McKinley's affidavit in that case on his desk.

Tait flew to Kentucky late that month to pick up a new white with red and gold pinstripe Harley-Davidson Electra Glide FLHTC. Tait wore a full-face BMW helmet like Barger's, and since the Chief owned a Volvo, Tait rented one. McKinley felt the tiny gestures would ingratiate Tait with Barger and allow a rapport to develop between the men. The motorcycle, which Tait was to leave at Chico Manganiello's house in California, was also a status symbol crafted to indicate to the club that Tait had dope money to burn.

The motorcycle was only part of the profile developed for Tait. Special Agent Ted Baltas improvised on Marischen's airline scheme that made Tait attractive to the Hells Angels with his free plane tickets. Baltas created a fictitious flight attendant Tait met on a flight from Alaska to California. She immediately had to have him sexually and took him to the washroom where he pleased her as she had never been pleased. That started their relationship. When Tait told the story to Hells Angels, they replied, "Yeah, it happens to me all the time."

A fake employee package for the non-existent flight attendant was dummied up in case the Angels checked up on her. McKinley made her the black hole for the drugs Tait would buy from the Angels. Tait would tell sellers she supplied the airline industry and all his purchases went straight to her. McKinley's plan was more specific than Marischen would have liked, but then, Marischen was not told about it. McKinley and Marischen did not agree on how to handle Tait. Marischen didn't like to build legends that were easy to verify. He liked to leave them obscure and malleable to allow improvisation and make them snoop-proof. McKinley, on the other hand, was prepared to wrap his spy in more and more cloaks as the need arose. He liked a good scenario; the more complex, the better.

When McKinley made his first attempt to monitor a West Coast Officers' Meeting in May, he learned the hard way what Marischen already knew: a plan may look good on paper, but put a building in between you and the transmitter and you won't hear much. McKinley would have to experiment before he could locate a spot that would allow his receiver to capture Tait's transmission from inside the Oakland clubhouse.

The morning after the WesCOM, Tait met with McKinley and FBI agent Robert Barnes to be briefed on a drug buy that afternoon from J.R. Serrano. McKinley chose Serrano for Tait's first drug buy in Operation CACUS because Serrano had known Tait since a visit he made to Alaska four years before. Serrano was also the least sophisticated and security-conscious Hells Angel. He was what Tait called a patch user—he used the club to get laid, make contacts and impress people. Tait had an aversion to men who weren't repulsed by herpes, and called them slurpies.

The agents gave Tait $10,500 in $100 bills they photocopied to record serial numbers. The agreed purchase price for the half pound of cocaine was $10,400. McKinley parked 75 yards from Serrano's house in Daly City. Tait arrived shortly after noon. The gibberish of several police radio scanners that covered local, state and federal drug frequencies was the first sound to greet Tait as he walked into Serrano's house—the San Francisco Police Department drug squad, then the Daly City drug squad.

Tait's handlers had instructed him to turn off his transmitter before he entered so he wouldn't trigger a detection device. He turned it on once inside and was prepared to turn it off should one of the scanners tune in to its frequency.

SERRANO: Picked up the scanner just last week. That's Dawn. I picked up the TV, 25-inch stereo, electronic TV for $140.

TAIT: What, scratch-and-dent?

SERRANO: Yeah. I mean a pound for twelve-fifty or twelve.

TAIT: Oh, I just need half right now.

SERRANO: It's better than the one I had last time. Real good quality.

TAIT: Are we gonna be pressed for time?

SERRANO: Well, he's at the shop right now, so I don't know.

TAIT: 'Cause I got to be in Seattle this evening to meet my person there.

SERRANO: Well, we'll take you over by Dave's shop.

Serrano called the shop.

SERRANO: Hi, guy. You want me to stop over there or what? You're kidding me. Well, that's why I figured you're leaving right then. He just got here.

They watched a soap opera and talked about how complex electronics had become. Tait said he was happy cops in Alaska didn't have the technical gizmos cops in the continental U.S. had.

TAIT: It's 10-40, right?

SERRANO: Huh?

TAIT: Ten four?

SERRANO:	I guess so. I don't know. He just gave me the price and that was it. I used to get it for 500, you know, right off the top.
TAIT:	We all make money on it. Are we going to meet him somewhere?
SERRANO:	If you want to sit here, I'm gonna run out to his house.
TAIT:	Okay.
SERRANO:	Really fast.
TAIT:	Okay.
SERRANO:	Let's see, why don't we get that together.
TAIT:	Okay, here.

Tait counted out the money and Serrano left the house with a hand-held police radio-frequency scanner. About 40 minutes later he returned with the half pound of cocaine in a blue lunch bag he gave Tait.

Flushed with his first success, back in Anchorage Tait approached Hells Angel associate Thomas Deszo Vinczen at Fred's VW Repair to buy his Sten submachine gun and silencer. Again, the conversation was recorded. CACUS was finally under way.

Eight

TAIT DROVE TO SAN BERNARDINO for a party on Saturday, June 14. Then he drove to Ventura to socialize with Hells Angels there for a few days. He slipped away to meet with McKinley and Baltas to finalize plans for his real reason for being in Ventura.

Tait offered to drive Ventura chapter president George (Gus) Christie to San Francisco for the West Coast Officers' Meeting that Wednesday. He was to pump Christie about the enigmatic Ventura chapter. Christie ran a tight ship and little information about his members made the grapevine. McKinley and Baltas drove to Ventura to follow Tait's car back and monitor and record the conversation. The FBI car's air conditioner died halfway to Ventura. They rolled down the windows to lower the car's inside temperature to 110 degrees.

Tait and Christie left Ventura at noon. Christie suggested they take I-5, the quick route. Tait knew the agents had no air conditioner, so he "accidentally" took the cooler coastal scenic route.

McKinley drove while Baltas fiddled with the monitor, but they couldn't hear it with the windows down. They rolled them up and settled in for a seven-hour broil. The inside of the car heated up quickly, and soon both men were drenched in sweat. They never got more than four car lengths behind Tait.

Christie kicked back and listened to Tait's tales of
Alaska. The Hells Angels think they are men's men—the
toughest, bravest and strongest. The mystique of Alaska
is that of the last frontier. Tait never lacked for something to talk about. The Hells Angels gobbled up his
yarns of salmon fishing, bear hunts and ravenous bears
that ate humans. Just as people elsewhere in the U.S.
liked to hear about California, Californians liked to hear
about Alaska. Gus Christie was no different. He was a
martial-arts instructor and loved Tait's tales of wilderness danger. Some of them were so familiar to McKinley
and Baltas that they muttered them one line ahead of
Tait.

By the time they got to San Francisco, the agents'
car, littered with chip bags and pop bottles, stank of
sweat. The men were exhausted. And their job was only
half done.

Tait arrived at the San Francisco clubhouse in time
for the evening WesCOM. McKinley and Baltas monitored the signal from Tait's pager-transmitter. It was
weak; within minutes, it faded and they couldn't hear
anything.

Counter-surveillance was intense, as it always was in
San Francisco. J.R. Serrano cruised the area in his white
Mustang. McKinley and Baltas parked near the bus terminal. Serrano pulled up. They moved on. Serrano
checked out cars and pedestrians before he backed into a
parking slot that gave him a clear view of both streets
that led to the rear of the clubhouse. Four other San
Francisco Hells Angels with walkie-talkies and radio
scanners patrolled the streets up to four blocks from the
clubhouse.

Tait changed the battery in his transmitter in the
washroom, but the agents couldn't monitor the first part
of the proceedings because counter-surveillance forced
them to move farther and farther from the clubhouse to
find a secure site.

During the general discussion, a technique was suggested to identify law enforcement informants. Each

Hells Angels chapter was told to instruct its sergeant-at-arms to compile a dossier with photographs of everyone who hung around the chapter. Each sergeant-at-arms would then give a copy of the dossier to the West Coast or East Coast sergeant-at-arms, who would scan the files to identify anyone who associated with more than one chapter. Such a person was most likely a police informant and would be subjected to a detailed background check. The technique was designed to curb informants such as Vernon Hartung, who associated with several chapters across the U.S. during Operation Roughrider.

The usual business—anniversaries, arrests, expulsions, reprimands, rules and regulations, updated lists of Angels' addresses—dragged on. After half an hour, McKinley and Baltas finally found a spot from which they could monitor Tait's transmitter. They parked on Route 280, the raised multi-lane highway about half a mile from the clubhouse. The bus terminal sat in between. Every time a bus started up, static drowned out conversations on the monitor. A California Highway Patrol officer pulled up behind them because they were parked in the breakdown lane. He leaned through the driver's window—and jumped back.

"Whew! God! Do you guys stink!"

McKinley flashed his badge and explained they were on surveillance. He gladly left without asking questions, and they monitored the rest of the meeting without incident.

The important discussion of the evening focused on the war between the Hells Angels and the Outlaws Motorcycle Club and the attendance of both clubs at the Sturgis, South Dakota, run—the major event for outlaw motorcycle clubs. They considered peace talks with the Outlaws. Gus Christie, who had been in touch with the Outlaws, took the lead in the discussion.

"I think in a situation like this, the way I understand it, as to how out of control things get on the East Coast and the Canadians are just as bad. Last year at Sturgis, a couple of their members were marched out of town.

Now, should they ever run into a couple of our members, and the odds are different, like a couple of our members are going to go down right there. One of the reasons we wanted to initiate these talks was because we are for darn sure aren't going to be marched out of town. And we don't want to lose anybody else over this thing because it's been going on for a long time."

Christie asked if U.S. Hells Angels who sought to end the war with the Outlaws would interfere with the activities of Canadian chapters. Canadian Hells Angels replied that they wanted to discuss with their chapters the idea of ending the war. Christie said it would not hurt to continue to feel out the Outlaws for their position on peace. "My concern is to the club," he said. "I don't want to see us put ourselves any deeper financially or anybody in jail. That's my only concern."

One Hells Angel argued against ending the war. "There's a lot of people dead and a lot of people in prison. If we didn't feel that way. If we had half of our chapter taken out of prison and killed and stuff, I mean, go ahead and make a decision, and just shine on now."

Christie directed that everyone take the issue to their chapters and get a vote on it. The vote, he said, would only put the war on hold. "The reason I suggested saying put it on hold is because I've already talked with this guy on the phone a few times and he's . . . The guy's Taco"—Harry Joseph Bowman, national president of the Outlaws out of Detroit, Michigan. "The guy's real jerky. I know he's going to try to get real specific with me on the phone and I don't really want to get specific with him. But I felt like saying 'On hold,' that's pretty easy to understand."

The Angels decided that if Christie didn't hear from the Outlaws by Sunday night, after members reported to their chapters, he would call Taco and arrange to put the war on hold.

After spending a few days in California hanging around with Angels and invariably recording their conversations, whether they were about drugs, arms or the weather, Tait planned to ride to the U.S.A. Run in Stoner, Colorado, with a group of southern California Angels. At the Ventura clubhouse Saturday night, he met up with former vice-president Thomas Edward (Tommy) Heath, recently released from prison where he had served a sentence for explosives violations, James (Jim) Clark and vice-president David Ledesma (Dave) Ortega. They rode to Ortega's house, where Heath bought two grams of white powder "so as to stay up all night to work on the bike." Tait returned to the San Bernardino clubhouse at 10 p.m. to prepare to depart for the U.S.A. Run at midnight.

Tait and several other Hells Angels left for Colorado shortly after midnight the next day. Most of the bikers had a road stash of crank or cocaine hidden in a small compartment on their Harleys behind and below the seat and covered by a screwed-down chromed or black plastic fascia. They arrived in Flagstaff, Arizona, shortly before noon on Monday and checked in at the Canyon Springs Best Western Hotel for the night. They left the next morning at 10:00 and arrived in Stoner, Colorado, at 7:30 that night. Tait set up camp and went to bed.

The mood at the U.S.A. Run was subdued because Oakland Hells Angel Douglas Flynn (Doug the Thug) Orr had died of a heroin overdose in federal prison in Lewisburg, Pennsylvania, the previous Saturday. The huge tent Oakland Hells Angel Big Steve Brown had painted for the U.S.A. Run had a tribute to Orr airbrushed on its side, along with a tribute to Fu Griffin, who died in 1985. The painted tribute to Orr baffled CACUS agents. Little time had passed between Orr's death and the tent going up in Colorado, and much of that time was spent transporting the tent from California.

Most Angels did not arrive until Friday, August 1. Tait spent time with Oakland president Irish O'Farrell, who told him expenses for the run totaled $14,335 and he was still $5,000 short because several chapters had not paid their share. Tait gave O'Farrell $1,000 for the Anchorage chapter. O'Farrell told Tait he admired him and the way he did business.

The Colorado Bureau of Investigation stationed a mobile home near the entrance of the ski resort where the Hells Angels partied. Sonny Barger told cops it was a traffic hazard. They moved it, but not before Barger cut a pressure hose stretched across the road from the home. He figured the device triggered a camera.

The Hells Angels World Meeting was held Sunday afternoon. Only chapter officers could attend. Tait and several other Hells Angels complained that the French chapter had not learned to speak English as agreed the previous year. They discussed Rudolph Giuliani, U.S. attorney for the Southern District of New York, who wore a set of seized Hells Angels colors to make a drug buy and later at a press conference where he showed how easy it was to buy drugs in New York City. One Hells Angel commented that if Giuliani wasn't afraid to take on the Mafia, he wouldn't fear taking on the Hells Angels.

A Hells Angel from the Salem, Massachusetts, chapter reported that FBI informant Vernon Hartung would testify for the first time at an upcoming trial. Several Angels at the meeting made threats against Hartung and police officers. A New York City Hells Angel said the chapter feared that former president Sandy Alexander would cooperate with police.

Three motions tabled at the previous year's World Meeting were passed unanimously: "No cops or ex-cops in the club. No niggers in the club. No snitches in the club."

Tait's counsel and demeanor at the World Meeting earned him the respect of many Hells Angels. He came across as a solid, reliable and thoughtful Angel when he advised that war with the Outlaws wasn't good for business. His handlers, who wanted to curtail any violence that could upset their investigation, had primed him well.

Most Hells Angels left the run early to get to Oakland for Doug the Thug's funeral. Anchorage Hells

Angel J.C. Webb rode to Kentucky to visit his parents, whom he had not seen since the early 1980s when he fled the Outlaws. Webb quit that club because he didn't like the way members were forced to sell a certain amount of dope each week. His fellow Outlaws gave him half a week to sell the dope, then disguised themselves with ski masks, beat him and ripped him off for the cash and what was left of the dope. They beat him a week later because he didn't have the dope or the money.

Webb drove a tow truck for a year and a half before he hooked up with the Anchorage Hells Angels. Tait liked Webb, who was one of the sneakiest and quickest thieves he knew. Tait warned Webb before he left for Kentucky not to wear his colors while alone on the road and not to ride his motorcycle with Hells Angels decals around Outlaws. Then Tait rode to California with Sonny Barger and other Hells Angels.

Shortly after returning to Anchorage after the funeral, Tait received an emergency phone call from a fellow Anchorage member just before midnight. Someone had called a "Bonarue," the Anchorage chapter emergency code of unknown origin that meant get your ass to the clubhouse, be armed and expect trouble. The message spread rapidly through a phone tree and allowed Hells Angels to assemble troops within minutes to take care of business.

Tait paged McKinley in Oakland to break the news. He never called McKinley's house because the Hells Angels had access to telephone company records. (Likewise, McKinley always paged Tait. Tait's midnight pages were not unusual. He would put on his slippers and robe and hustle across the street to the nearest pay phone.) Tait was brief. Webb, he said, had been shot and killed outside a Kentucky bar. The triggerman was said to be an Outlaw.

McKinley recognized the specter of a biker war. The FBI had not planned for war. War meant deaths, and the bureau was bound by law not to allow people to die, even if it had to abort operations. McKinley stood in the phone booth in his robe and slippers and realized that this operation, into which he had sunk so much work and hope, might go nowhere. The case was not designed to investigate gang warfare, and Webb's killing threatened to become the tail that wagged the dog. His death would take Operation CACUS into uncharted territory.

McKinley told Tait to volunteer to travel to Kentucky to find out what happened, if chapter president Ed Hubert didn't order him to do so. After all, Tait was sergeant-at-arms. McKinley instructed him to fly through Oakland so they could plan security. Tait was going into an area where Outlaws had apparently killed a Hells Angel and would surely watch airports for Angels who would come to the funeral.

Tait didn't have to volunteer. At the emergency meeting, Hubert told him to get to Kentucky to scout for targets and claim Webb's body for the funeral. McKinley called Ted Baltas. Wars meant guns and explosives, and that was Baltas's bailiwick.

Tait met McKinley in Oakland the next day, and they flew to Louisville, Kentucky, and booked into the Galt House East, which promptly caught fire. They spent half the night helping elderly attendees of a black Baptist convention down the stairs. That night, Hells Angels from across the United States arrived in Louisville. Tait linked up with them the next day for Webb's wake.

McKinley tried to maintain surveillance. The local FBI office assigned Special Agent Kevin Wevodau to help him. Wevodau had been with the bureau for two and a half years, all in Louisville. McKinley, who was biased against young agents, was amazed such a young person would be assigned to a case that involved a top echelon informant. They operated under cover of being a photo-surveillance team and tried to monitor Tait's transmitter as he attended meetings. But the Hells Angels mounted vigorous counter-surveillance, directed not at cops but at Outlaws who could use the opportunity to attack a group of Hells Angels on their turf.

The Hells Angels were scattered throughout the area in several hotels. They got their act together that night and moved into the Best Western Motel in Shepherdsville for their final night in town before Webb's funeral. They posted guards around the building.

An Angel from Omaha handed Tait a handgun and told him to stand guard until relieved by a prospect in half an hour. Tait spoke aloud to McKinley over his transmitter as he stood next to the hotel.

"Tim, I know you're not going to like this, but this guy just gave me this gun and I'll give it back to him as soon as I get the information off it. Do you hear me?"

McKinley had parked his car in the shadows a quarter mile away. He flashed one of his turn signals.

"Oh, yeah. There you are."

McKinley flashed the signal again. Tait gave him the serial number off the gun and the model, make and caliber.

The Oakland chapter arrived en masse after midnight.

Ed Hubert, who told Webb's wife, Lori, earlier in the evening that the club was so organized "we could hide somebody forever if we wanted to," borrowed Tait's microcassette recorder to record four telephone calls he wanted to make about Webb's murder. McKinley wasn't pleased. The recorder was FBI equipment used to make redundant recordings of critical conversations and provided backup when agents couldn't get close enough with their receiver to pick up Tait's transmitter.

Tait walked with Fairbanks president Dennis (Bigfoot) Pailing from the funeral home to the Army-Navy Surplus store the next morning, where Pailing tooled up in case they ran into Outlaws. He bought camouflage field glasses, thin nylon cord, two Marine Corps-style K-Bar fighting knives, a bandanna and a pair of gloves.

Kentucky State Troopers stopped all Outlaws and caught a group of five bikers on their way to the funeral with a vehicle full of weapons. Police stretched a heavy security net around the funeral, with helicopters and snipers to ensure war didn't break out between the gangs.

McKinley and Wevodau ended up in the procession that left the Hardy Funeral Home after Webb's service. At one point, the van in front of them stopped and out jumped New York City Hells Angel Brendan Francis Manning, who McKinley had arrested in Operation Roughrider in 1985 on federal drug charges for which he was soon to go to trial. McKinley pulled his cap down to his ears and tilted the visor as the biker loped toward the car to ask directions. He would have been surprised to see an Oakland FBI agent in scenic Kentucky in a Hells Angels funeral procession.

Hells Angel counter-surveillance was brutal. Bikers scoured the area on foot and in cars. They kept in touch with walkie-talkies. When they suspected a van harbored a police surveillance team, they hopped out of their cars, cupped their hands to windows to see inside, yelled obscenities and rocked and kicked the van. In Kentucky, they got the wrong vehicles. McKinley foiled this type of surveillance in California by locking himself in the trunk of a car parked near a meeting Tait attended. It was a hot, sweaty way to monitor conversations, but he was never spotted.

The Hells Angels returned to the Best Western Motel after the funeral. They sat around as Hubert walked out of the shower clad in a small Best Western towel. He flapped the towel up as he passed Pailing, raised his leg and aimed his asshole at the Fairbanks president.

"Here Dennis, this one's for you."

What was supposed to be a fart turned out to be a violent spray of shit and gas that splattered Pailing, gagged onlookers and made one Angel bolt to the washroom to heave his lunch. Too much wine and late nights had loosened Hubert's innards.

Hubert called Tait to Cisco Valderrama's room that afternoon. Cisco charged a call on his calling card to the Oakland phone number of Sonny and Sharon Barger. It was his third call to that number that day. He spoke to Sharon and confirmed she would send a package to Webb's sister by express mail. Cisco told Tait it contained the portion of the El Paso Intelligence Center (EPIC) book on the Outlaws Motorcycle Club. The book is restricted to law enforcement and it is illegal for anyone else to possess it. The Hells Angels had obtained a copy and kept it along with other law enforcement manuals and documents in their intelligence and security files. Now they needed the information it contained: photographs and detailed descriptions and addresses of Outlaws in Kentucky.

That night, a dozen Hells Angels walked into Big Fred's Broken Spur bar to drink beer, show they weren't afraid to go into the bar where a brother had been killed and to find out what they could about Webb's killers.

Hubert and Valderrama talked to Terry Bittinger of the Kentucky Bikers Association, who had approached Hubert at the funeral and offered to help find members of the Outlaws club. They took Bittinger around the side of the building and asked Tait to secure the area and keep people away. Tait stood at the end of the sidewalk and watched. Valderrama got upset with the way Hubert questioned Terry.

"You're jamming him. Just back off. Back off."

Hubert got frustrated and went into the bar.

Valderrama offered Bittinger $5,000 for information on Outlaws before they returned to the bar.

Hubert called Big Fred the next day. Hubert had spoken to him briefly the previous night in an attempt to identify and find Webb's killers; now he wanted the nervous bar owner to tell him more. After wary hellos, Hubert got down to business and taped the conversation with Tait's recorder.

HUBERT:	I figure since I'm close I better, hey, those names, man, you got anything for me?
FRED:	Now, let me explain somethin' to

you, okay? . . . [Someone] told
me not to mess you around and
everythin' and I have no intention
of doin' that, all right?

HUBERT: All right.

FRED: When I got back here July the
seventh.

HUBERT: Huh?

FRED: I got back here July the seventh. I
just got out of the penitentiary . . .

HUBERT: Yeah. Right.

FRED: Like I told 'em, I'm at a halfway
house. They let me spend, go
home Saturday night.

HUBERT: Yeah.

FRED: All right? Now, I don't even
know where nobody lives. I've
not seen nobody.

HUBERT: Hey, all right, this name I got. I
got Cool Ray.

FRED: All right.

HUBERT: The right name?

FRED: Ah, yeah. I'd say it was.

HUBERT: And he is an OLer?

FRED: Right. But I don't know for sure,
okay?

HUBERT: You don't know for sure if he is?

FRED: It's just hearsay.

HUBERT: What about Blondie?

FRED: Blondie's Reaper.

HUBERT: Blondie's a Reaper?

FRED: Yep.

HUBERT: What about Marshall?

FRED: Well, that's pretty close, I'd say.

HUBERT: OL, huh?

FRED: (Sighs.)

HUBERT: Do you say so?

FRED: Yeah. That's what I hear. But I
don't know, okay?

HUBERT:	You don't know nothin' . . .
FRED:	I just—
HUBERT:	For sure.
FRED:	—don't want no trouble, man. I . . . My old lady scared to death, nervous as hell. She's about to have a nervous breakdown and she didn't ask for none of this.
HUBERT:	Yeah. I can dig it. I'd like to know . . .
FRED:	You going about all this the wrong way, I think.
HUBERT:	You think so, huh?
FRED:	You know what you wanna do? You need to come back in town about a month from now. Then you find somethin'. Like the bar. That's supposed to stay neutral grounds for everybody. Well, evidently it's not no more so I'm gonna put a thing up there: No Patches. I mean, I hate to do that. I wore a patch for 13 years.
HUBERT:	Again, you can't tell me if it was Reapers that done my brother?
FRED:	It wasn't. It wasn't.
HUBERT:	And you're pretty sure it's OLs?
FRED:	I wasn't there.
HUBERT:	But your old lady was. She seen 'em.
FRED:	But I say yes on the second thing.

Hubert then called Terry Bittinger, who implicated two Outlaws named Marshall (Marshall Howell Duncan) and Cool Ray (Leonard Wayne Mullen) but urged Hubert not to go after Big Fred's old lady. It didn't look as if anyone was going to say much.

Tait flew to Oakland later that day to attend church, where he knew Webb's killing would be discussed. McKinley and Baltas monitored the meeting from a plane that flew a tight circle over the clubhouse. McKinley, in the co-pilot seat, spent the evening with his face in a barf bag. Static drowned out parts of the meeting, during which the main speakers were Tait, James (Fuzzy) Neal, Sonny Barger, Mouldy Marvin Gilbert, Mike Lessard and Cisco Valderrama.

All the talk centered on how Webb had been set up.

VALDERRAMA: What happened is J.C. Webb he supposedly was set up by . . .

TAIT: Billy Bones.

VALDERRAMA: Billy Bones supposedly set up. Billy Bones had known J.C. for a long time before J.C. even went to Alaska. Went over to him and said that this guy Ray wanted to talk about some money he owed him. So he went to the bar, the Broken Spur.

J.C.'s old lady came back from horseback riding. I guess his mom dropped her off at the bar and she went into the bar. And she heard J.C. arguing with the guys. His back was to the wall like this and little Cool Ray being real bad. J.C. and he walked outside.

In the meantime, his old lady had forgot her helmet or J.C.'s helmet, I don't know which one it is. Walked in to get it and he come up, a piece on her and everybody else in the bar kinda ducked down. She just walked by 'em and didn't say nothing, got the helmet and walked back outside. He followed her outside and he's tell J.C. to take off his trophy.

Said take off your trophy and throw it on the ground. J.C. tells 'em, "Fuck you."

The guy tells him again. He didn't do it. The guy shot him. And he shot three times. He hit him once. J.C. is hit and then J.C. said, "Okay, man. I'm fuckin' leavin'."

And the guy says to him, "Take your fuckin' patch off, your fuckin' patch. Take your fuckin' patch off and throw it down."

J.C. looked, he got on his bike, started it up to leave. His old lady says, "Think you can make it?" Because he looked gray. "You think you can make it?" . . .

He said, "Yeah," passed out and he went down. Got back up, lifted his bike up and lifted it out of the street and went down again.

Now, on the people that did it, we're havin' a hard time tryin' to find out who did it. J.C.'s old lady, before the members had gotten there, they showed her some mug shots which she ID'd. The cops wouldn't give her any names, mug shots or anything . . . She looked on the back. There were witnesses on the back of the mug shot.

One of J.C.'s relatives had gotten a farmer guy, drove up to his house. The guy was on that paper. Three people. One of 'em was Leonard Wayne Mullen, the

other one was Marshall Howell
Duncan. How about Cool Ray. Is
he an OL, is he an Outlaw? Have
him say the same thing on the
tape. My idea for that—evidently
he offered $5,000 for it. I have no
intention [of paying it].

(Everyone laughs.)

VALDERRAMA: We have it on tape on pretext of
givin' him $5,000 [for informa-
tion] against the Outlaws. So
that's about where we stand. We
do believe it was Outlaws. Also we
believe that it was an isolated incident planned by the Outlaws . . .
I believe the argument
stemmed from something personal. I have no proof of that, but
I believe that some of the argument stemmed from his being a
Hells Angel though he used to be
an OL.
Back when he was an Outlaw,
according to the information I
have, he stole Cool Ray's motorcycle. But Cool Ray wanted it to
be stolen for the insurance. But
the insurance company wouldn't
pay off. Cool Ray didn't get anything and [he told J.C.] you owe
me some money. J.C. told him get
fucked, come and pick up this
fuckin' motorcycle.

BARGER: You gonna call up somebody?
VALDERRAMA: Do I wanna call 'em up?
BARGER: Call 'em collect.

(Everyone laughs.)

Sonny Barger's parcel to Ed Hubert arrived at the Louisville house of Debbie Mansfield, Webb's sister. She gave the package to Lori Webb and two Anchorage Hells Angels.

The agents realized that the Anchorage chapter bore the responsibility to avenge the death of a fellow member. This gave the FBI an unprecedented opportunity to study the gang wars and the Hells Angels' use of violence.

FBI brass recognized the implications of a biker gang war. Someone was going to die to pay for Webb's murder, yet the government could not let people die. McKinley was summoned several times to brief his superiors. They insisted that they needed to meet Tait. Ordinarily, supervisors never meet informants, but they had to determine for themselves whether Tait was stable enough to keep their asses out of the fire. Now that the case was going somewhere, they wanted to be associated with it.

The war between the Hells Angels and the Outlaws had started in 1974, when Sandy Alexander, president of the Angels New York City chapter, severely beat Outlaw Peter (Greased Lightning) Rogers for allegedly raping his wife. To save face, Rogers told the Outlaws he'd been beaten by a dozen Angels.

Until then, the two clubs had lived uneasily side by side, avoiding each other's turf. But from that one incident, acts of revenge on both sides escalated to murder, each one matched by another.

The first opportunity for vengeance came in April 1974. Albert (Oskie) Simmons had skipped out of the Hells Angels Lowell, Massachusetts, chapter in the early 1970s with the club's money. He drifted to Florida, where he hung around a motorcycle shop. He complied with a standing order from Sonny Barger that a member who quits the club in bad standing must remove the Death's Head tattoo and Hells Angels lettering from his

body. Simmons sat around the motorcycle shop and
blanked the letters out with a needle and ink. He covered the *H* and *E* and started on the two *L*s. Two Hells
Angels from Oskie's old chapter tracked him down to
check out his tattoo in mid-April 1974. Edward Thomas
(Riverboat) Riley and George F. (Whiskey George)
Hartman were not the type of men even a seasoned
biker wanted on his tail. They were both wanted for
murder.

Big Jim Nolan, president of the Outlaws tough South
Florida chapter, heard Angels were in the area. He called
a meeting to discuss what the club should do about the
presence in their territory of the maggots who beat
brother Greased Lightning. The Outlaws hung out at the
Pastime Bar the next day and waited for the Hells Angels
to show up at the nearby motorcycle shop to talk to
Simmons. Smiling Outlaws befriended the three men and
invited them to a piss-up at their clubhouse. The two visitors from Lowell explained they didn't wear their colors
out of respect for Outlaws turf. When enough wine and
beer was consumed, an outraged Outlaw argued he
shouldn't drink with scum. The rest of the members
agreed.

The Hells Angels were tied and loaded into a van by
four Outlaws: William (Gatemouth) Edson; Norman
(Spider) Riesinger, a visitor from the Chicago chapter;
Funky Tim Amis, who was later stabbed to death in
prison in 1980 when he refused to submit to sex; drove
the van; and Ralph (Lucifer) Yanotta, who carried a
sawed-off shotgun. They stopped at a flooded rockpit
near Andytown, north of Fort Lauderdale, and the three
Hells Angels were lined up at water's edge, arms tied
behind their backs with pink clothesline and eight concrete blocks tied to their legs.

"Do what you got to do" were one Angel's last
words.

Riesinger blew their brains out with a 12-gauge shotgun. The Outlaws sat in the grass afterwards to smoke
and drink beer.

About a week later, a passerby spotted a foot with a blue sock bobbing in the water. A diver pulled out the bloated, tattooed bodies.

Hells Angels Clarence (Addie or Butch) Crouch from the Cleveland chapter and Howie Weisbrod from the New York City chapter investigated the murder at Sandy Alexander's request. He feared police had killed the Angels to pit the club against the Outlaws. They returned to their respective chapters and blamed the Outlaws for the deaths. The Hells Angels East Coast Officers and representatives from all chapters met in Cleveland in 1974 to declare all-out war on the Outlaws.

The Hells Angels tried in 1977 to resolve the conflict. They sent Sandy Alexander and Oakland Hells Angels Sergey (Sir Gay) Walton and Gary Popkin to Durham, North Carolina, to have a sit-down with the Outlaws. Big Jim Nolan and friends didn't show.

The Hells Angels hit five separate Outlaws clubhouses from Charlotte, North Carolina, to Youngstown, Ohio, on July 4, 1979. The Youngstown clubhouse was hit with a LAWs rocket that lodged in the attic and did not detonate. Another clubhouse was machine-gunned. Some Angels chickened out and failed to attack their assigned clubhouse. The Charlotte clubhouse suffered the most casualties. The killers used silenced guns to kill the sentry on the front porch as he sat with a gun on his lap. The guard dogs were killed, as were three more Outlaws and a woman in the house. William (Mouse) Dronenberg, Randall Feazell, Leonard (Terrible Terry) Henderson, William Allen and Bridgette Benfield were riddled with bullets. Some Outlaws wear the tattoo "7-4-79" to remember.

Ted Baltas knew someone would die for Webb's murder and hoped Tait would be the first to know who. He was sergeant-at-arms for his chapter, he was a WesCOM representative and he attended all meetings. Baltas advised Tait to keep an eye on Mike Lessard of the Oakland

chapter. He had pleaded guilty in 1982 to transporting
an AK 47 and other guns to Sturgis, South Dakota, for
the Hells Angels. He did his time and was now back on
the streets. If he had been prepared to participate in a
retaliation against the Outlaws in 1982, he might do so
in 1986. Tait met Lessard when he visited Anchorage in
April of 1986.

Baltas had wanted Tait to take a weapons and explosives familiarization course early in the investigation, but
Tait couldn't fit it into his busy schedule. Now he had to
keep Tait in Oakland for a few days and have Bureau of
Alcohol, Tobacco and Firearms experts teach him how to
identify weapons and explosives, what constituted a violation so he could properly set up buys and how to handle the materials without killing himself or anyone else.
He wanted Tait to learn the terminology and current
black-market prices so he wouldn't look foolish and lose
respect among criminals if he paid too much for guns
and explosives. Paying too much would also allow
defense lawyers to cry entrapment.

Tait took a two-day explosives course and a day-
and-a-half firearms course. He went to the ATF laboratory on Treasure Island, where explosives enforcement
officer Jerry A. Taylor of the ATF Explosives Technology
Branch taught him about explosives and blasting caps
and how they were put together. Taylor spent hours in a
bunker with Tait where he showed him various types of
military ordnance he might encounter. Many explosives
on the black market are stolen from the military. Baltas
didn't want Tait to turn in Silly Putty he had been sold as
C-4 plastic explosive.

Firearms specialist Edward Peterson of the ATF
Forensic Laboratory taught Tait how to identify a
machine gun and silencers so he wouldn't be taken in by
con artists. Even ATF agents have been fooled by arms
dealers in the rush of a sale.

Baltas emphasized to Tait that he needed taped conversations with the people who sold the guns and explosives if
he were to convict them. He wanted Tait to encourage talk,

to find out where the guy got the explosives, to see if he could get more. He also wanted Tait to tell sellers he wanted the guns and explosives to kill Outlaws. This gave them the opportunity to back out of the sale if they didn't want any-one killed. It was good tradecraft on Baltas's part to cover all bases and undermine any defenses that the Angels might use in court.

Webb's killing was discussed again at the WesCOM in Oakland on August 21. Tait reported that J.C.'s memorial would be held in Anchorage the next day. Some of his ashes were buried in his father's grave, some were given to his wife, Lori, and the rest were poured into a motorcycle oil tank hung on the Anchorage club-house wall. Webb had wanted members to pour a spoon-ful of his ashes into their gas tanks and burn him through the engine, but nobody wanted to mess up their motors with grit. Tait said he would keep a container of Webb's ashes fastened to his motorcycle fork so Webb could ride on after death.

Tait and Anchorage Angel Dan McIntosh talked about J.C. Webb's murder after church on the day of the memorial. McIntosh, who was always on the lookout for an extra dollar, told Tait he had explosives to sell. Tait said he would like to see what he had. McIntosh took him to his house trailer at the rear of the clubhouse lot. As they reached the porch, McIntosh reached down and moved two plastic milk crates that covered a dog-food bag. From the bag he removed a Samsonite briefcase secured with two strips of duct tape. They entered the trailer and McIntosh opened the briefcase to show his wares, which he said Tait could have for $500. Tait said he would also need blasting caps. McIntosh said he had them. He also had more explosives buried in the Matanuska-Susitna Valley.

Tait showed up at McIntosh's trailer a few days later to buy the explosives. They talked carefully because McIntosh had a "citizen" houseguest. Tait asked if McIntosh had looked up the price of the "motorcycle parts." McIntosh said $225, which was what he paid for the C-4 in the briefcase of explosives. They walked to the second trailer on the lot, which McIntosh used as a workshop. Tait asked McIntosh if he could draw a diagram on how to wire a bomb to a car, which McIntosh did readily.

Tait took the briefcase and fishing-rod tube to the undercover apartment where Ken Marischen and ATF agent Ron Tarrington were waiting. Tarrington opened the suitcase. The trio joked about the contents, which included two sticks of Dupont Tovex 220, one block of C-4, one white phosphorus smoke grenade, one half-block of TNT, one Kinepak Boulder Buster and two sticks of Atlas 40 percent gelatin dynamite.

"Oh, shit," Tarrington said. "I'm starting to get a headache."

"Now, what does that mean?" Marischen asked. He looked into the briefcase, but didn't know much about explosives. He saw lumps and tubes.

"I get a headache every time I'm around nitro," Tarrington said.

"Nitro what?" the inquisitive Marischen asked.

"Nitroglycerin."

"Holy mackerel, are you kidding? We're sitting on a load of nitroglycerin here?"

"Yeah."

Tait showed an uncharacteristic lack of curiosity. "Well, I'll see ya. I'm out of here. I done my job. See you guys around." He trod lightly out the door with a grin.

Marischen and Tarrington delivered the explosives to the military's Fort Richardson Explosive Ordnance Division for storage; the dynamite, which had leaked and was unstable, had to be destroyed.

Tait and Hubert drove to the Isaak Walton Shooting Range in Birchwood, Alaska one day in late August to sight in their hunting rifles. En route, they talked about killing Outlaws and citizens in Kentucky to retaliate for Webb's murder. Hubert said he wanted to put together three two-man hit teams. He suggested himself, Tait, Dennis Pailing, Pee Wee Protzman and Russ Hagel. He wanted Protzman to live in Kentucky for a couple of months to scout targets. He could live off his credit cards and the club would reimburse him. Hubert said he wanted to take down two citizens in Kentucky whom he believed had set Webb up: Mark (Meatloaf) Loving, the hang-around they ran off in 1985, and Billy Bones. Bones had called J.C. and asked him to meet at Big Fred's Broken Spur bar. Hubert said he wanted to borrow the Oakland chapter's EPIC manual on the Outlaw Motorcycle Club to pick out clubhouses in Chicago, Louisville and Houston that could be hit simultaneously.

"I'd like to use a car bomb to blow up Big Fred's bar," he said.

Tait told him it would take too much explosive. Hubert replied that the Fairbanks chapter had a lot of explosives, especially C-4, that they promised to make available for retaliation.

The Anchorage and Fairbanks chapters met at the Anchorage clubhouse that night for their State of Alaska officers' meeting. Tait was sitting with Pee Wee Protzman when Hubert walked up and looked menacingly at Tait.

"FBI, huh?"

Tait didn't know what to say. He slowly slipped his hand into his coat to draw his gun and kill everyone in the room. He had a Browning Hi Power 9-mm pistol in a shoulder holster and a snub-nosed .38 caliber revolver tucked in his waistband.

Hubert directed his next statement at Protzman. "Yeah. They were just at my house questioning me. The FBI wants to know what's in the package. We're not going to tell them what's in it."

Tait was so shaken he went to the washroom to check that he was all right.

FBI agents had approached Hubert in his front yard to ask about a package sent to Lori Webb. Hubert told them the package was received by Webb's sister and was picked up by Protzman, Hagel and Lori Webb. Hubert told Tait to warn Sonny Barger about the heat because his Oakland address was on the package, which was the one that contained the EPIC manual on the Outlaws.

The FBI rented Tait a condominium on Muldoon Road in August 1986 to enhance his profile as a high roller and to create a trap where Hells Angels could be recorded as they planned or carried out crimes. Jim Hill, the FBI technician, crawled into the condo's attic and wired three microphones into the ceiling. He linked them to the garbage disposal switch after he disconnected the machine. Tait flipped the switch to activate the microphones, two of which transmitted to a reel-to-reel tape recorder in a secure room in the FBI office.

Tait kept his house trailer on Fireweed Road equipped with power and a telephone in case he needed a crash pad. But Brenda found out he spent some of his days there to unwind and followed him to harass him.

Ed Hubert took extraordinary security precautions for his meeting to discuss retaliation against the Outlaws. He wouldn't even tell Tait where it would be held. He only volunteered it was south of Anchorage. Marischen couldn't plan surveillance and had to fly by the seat of his pants. He would cover the ground in his car and three agents would try to follow the bikers in a light aircraft equipped with a receiver tuned to Tait's secret transmitter. Agents John Jansen, Billy Andrews and Jim Hill were ready for a hairy night.

Marischen parked his car a block from the clubhouse at 7:00 the night of the meeting, Friday, September 5. The bikers planned to leave after church. The shuffle of feet was all he heard over the receiver hidden in his glove compartment. The plane circled tightly overhead to stay within the cone of transmission. Marischen made a mental note to find a backup for the transmitter. Too many important conversations were being lost.

When church began, Hubert reported that members would be assessed $100 in three months to establish a permanent defense fund. At the end of the meeting, he referred to "a situation we have on hand,

I've got in my mind that I haven't told anybody. I won't
say where we're going because they might follow.
Those of you that don't want to get involved don't have
to be. We've got a place picked out and haven't told
anybody about it."

The Angels waited outside the clubhouse for Hubert's
wife, Fran, to deliver a propane lantern. Tait and Arnold
(Animal) Hibbits got into a red Ford Ranchero pickup
driven by William (Gypsy) Spearman. Monty Elliott rode
in Russ Hagel's car. Dirty Dave Gonzales and another
Angel rode in the Ryder rented truck driven by Tom
Joiner. Hubert, Sleazy Ric Rickleman, Pee Wee Protzman,
Happy Jack Cottrill, Michael Hurn, Paul Edward Boyce Jr.
and Rick Fabel rode behind the caravan on their motorcycles.

Two Harleys blew away from the clubhouse at 9:15.
Marischen didn't know if they were part of the entourage
or had been excluded from the meeting. He let them go.
By then, darkness hid the clubhouse from the agents in
the air. Marischen drove past at 9:25. He needed to know
if the truck was still there. It was, and bikers milled
around it. Two more Harleys blasted down the street five
minutes later. He let them go too. They rode out a little
way, turned around and came back. They had cleaned
themselves from any possible tails and established a
security perimeter. Marischen was relieved he hadn't followed them.

The procession filed out of the compound at 9:34.
Marischen lost them at the first intersection—he caught
a red light after the bikers turned left. They made the
next light, but Marischen was boxed in by cars and the
median, and the light turned. He raced, but couldn't find
them. Neither could the agents in the plane.

Marischen took a chance. He took his best shot and
tore down New Seward Highway. It was dark; no houses,
no lights. All of a sudden, he nearly flattened a motorcycle that crossed the road. The caravan had pulled over to
the shoulder of the road and turned off all lights. Hubert
had trouble finding his destination in the dark.

Marischen couldn't stop for three-quarters of a mile on the straight road. He squealed to a stop at the first bend and turned around. He doused the lights and called the plane. Then he flickered his lights and jerked the car around until the pilot found him. The pilot had problems of his own: New Seward Highway runs along the glide path for jets coming into Anchorage International Airport. Half the circle the plane had to make to stay over the bikers put it in the glide path.

Marischen headed back toward the bikers. He transmitted constantly to the plane so the pilot could set up over the site to eavesdrop. He passed prospect Rick Fabel, who guarded the site. Then he noticed the truck had gone into a canyon. Hangaround Paul Boyce stood guard farther down the road. Marischen couldn't stop. The pilot took his coordinates and circled the truck. The receiver was silent. Marischen parked five minutes down the road. His receiver stayed silent.

The Angels observed strict security precautions in the canyon. Hubert rode in first on his motorcycle and checked the site. The truck followed. The Angels milled around while Pee Wee Protzman searched the back of the truck for wires. They climbed into the truck and closed the doors.

"Everybody knows why we're here—to maintain security," Hubert said. "We're going to have a few more meetings like this." He told them that Oakland Angels talked about leveling Big Fred's bar to prevent it from becoming a shrine for Outlaws. Hagel reported that he and Protzman ran into Sonny Barger at Expo in Vancouver, British Columbia, immediately after Webb's death. They quoted Barger as having said, "I don't want to beat a dead man, but he died like a Hells Angel and it's time to start killing them again."

Hubert said he talked to Hells Angels in Kentucky who said they had no automatic weapons or silencers. The Omaha chapter offered two cold cars, which could not be traced back to the Hells Angels if used in a killing. Hubert said they probably wouldn't get the Outlaws who killed Webb, but would go after Outlaws officers in Houston, Chicago, Detroit and Milwaukee. He wanted to retaliate after the heat died down and asked that Angels with "little stashes" of guns and explosives turn them over to the club. Hagel said he was worried the Outlaws might travel to Alaska to retaliate and proposed that the Angels travel in pairs and start a 24-hour watch on the clubhouse.

The meeting lasted 20 minutes. Several Hells Angels stood outside the truck afterward, looked into the dark sky and discussed the possibility of being overheard by monitors on weather balloons. At 10:33, half an hour after they parked in the canyon, the bikers drove off. Tait paged Marischen to be debriefed.

Tait attended the West Coast Officers' Meeting at the Oakland clubhouse in late September. Barger reported that the Oakland chapter had elected new officers: president—Sonny Barger; vice-president—Cisco Valderrama; secretary—Big Steve Brown; treasurer—Michael Malve; sergeant-at-arms—Samuel Botchvaroff; corporate officer—Flash Gordon Grow.

Barger explained that corporate officer was a new position. The Hells Angels had spent thousands of dollars to incorporate, and Fu Griffin had watched over the corporation until his death. Since then, the Hells Angels had not taken care of corporate business. Barger announced that Irish O'Farrell would step down as board president and each chapter must report next month who its representative on the corporate board would be. They, in turn, would elect four corporate officers. One of the first issues for the board to discuss, he said, was whether it should issue licenses for members to sell items that bore the Hells Angels Motorcycle Club logo. He complained that many items were being sold in the name of the club for which the corporation did not receive its share of money. Barger's concern could be labeled the great T-shirt debate. Many hours at many meetings were spent debating the value of selling T-shirts with the Hells Angels name or logo. T-shirts with logos could not be sold to people who were not club members. It appeared that the motorcycle club was on the verge of becoming a clothing franchise. To protect the corporation, licenses had to be issued to chapters that wanted to sell T-shirts and other items. Barger said, "Our job now is to protect those guys by making them get their permits. Everybody has got to get this through their heads. We love ourselves. We think we're great. Businesses are scared to death of us. Businesses don't want our name on a lot of things. Established businesses, especially motorcycle businesses. We've got to be able to control what our own members do before we even think about working with somebody outside."

Tait had told his handlers he would approach Barger later that night at a party at the Sacramento clubhouse at 3405 9th Avenue to celebrate the 10-year anniversary of Frisco John Stevens and the five-year anniversary of Mark Perry. McKinley sought the help of Roger Davis and Del Rowley in the FBI's Sacramento office. He also enlisted the aid of Sacramento police officer Bert Sousa, who had hounded the Hells Angels for decades with the same zeal, persistence and deadly professionalism with which he flew combat helicopters for the U.S. Army in Thailand and elsewhere. Sousa knew every porch step worn thin by the fat ass of some lazy Hells Angel who sat there all day with a finger up his nose.

Tait's handlers asked Sousa to find a safe spot from which to monitor Tait's conversations, and he set them up two houses away from the clubhouse. The clubhouse had been willed to Edward (Lonesome) Rajotte, one of the original Sacramento Hells Angels, by his grandfather. A couple of Hells Angels registered the house in their name after Lonesome was killed. Sousa once found a prospect asleep outside the clubhouse while on guard duty during a party. He sauntered into the building with a couple of police officers.

"Hey," Sousa told the surprised Angels. "Your prospect's out here asleep."

They stripped the prospect of his patch.

Security was not lax the night of September 27. Tait and Barger talked without worry.

TAIT: The other day we got some visits
                  by the FBI. They came and they
                  were lookin' for the people who
                  received the package up there in
                  Kentucky and they subpoenaed
                  the gal at that house there and
                  her husband—J.C.'s sister and her
                  husband and his brother-in-law—
                  to the grand jury there and they
                  admitted that they got a package
                  and they—dumb fucks—said that
                  they didn't open it because they
                  weren't in the habit of opening
                  other people's mail. They come
                  up to us there in Anchorage. And
                  they went to J.C.'s wife and asked
                  her who the package was to. It's
                  like they're grasping for straws.
                  She said: "Well, hey, I don't know
                  shit, man. I was under the influ-
                  ence of downers because I was in
                  so much stress and I didn't know
                  what the hell to do."
                      And then they went to Eddie
                  and jammed him the same thing,
                  but they put it to him like Lori
                  was the one who received the
                  package. I had to tell you to make
                  sure you knew about it in case it
                  came back.

BARGER: Well, I'm not even sure in whose
                  name we sent it, but it was either
                  mine or Sharon's name. And we
                  sent it through legitimate things
                  so there's a record of it.

TAIT:	Yeah. I know. The way they worded it was: "We got a teletype from Louisville. The FBI office in Louisville to the FBI office in Anchorage. And they asked us to come over here and ask you who sent the package. Who got it?" 'Cause it came through American Express. Some express delivery service or somethin'.
BARGER:	Yeah.
TAIT:	What we think is they're just tryin' to put some heat on us up there. Like they've been drivin' around all of our houses and checkin' everythin' out. We think they're grasping for straws. Tryin' to put somethin' together. I just wanted to make sure that you knew about it.
BARGER:	We sent to his wife, didn't we? In her name.
TAIT:	No, to his sister.
BARGER:	To his sister?
TAIT:	Debbie or somethin' like that.
BARGER:	Okay, she didn't open it?
TAIT:	She didn't open it.
BARGER:	Then there's really no problems.
TAIT:	Yeah.
BARGER:	Ya. I don't know what they're talkin' about.
TAIT:	Well, that's the same way we played it off up there. We didn't know what package. We didn't know what the fuck they were talkin' about.
BARGER:	We sent 'em some sympathy cards.
TAIT:	Yeah.

Hells Angels label their motorcycles and other possessions with decals.

Anchorage Hells Angels deliberately misspelled Tait's top rocker when he became a full-fledged member. Tait misspelled Angels on club literature.

Tait, in white cap at left, mingles outside funeral home at Oakland Hells Angel James (Fu) Griffin's funeral in July 1985.

(FBI Photograph)

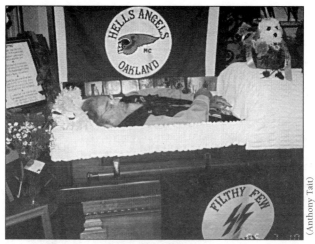

Fu Griffin decked out in Hells Angels' finest.

(Anthony Tait)

Sonny Barger, his hand resting on a shovel (*left*),
watches Oakland Hells Angel Deacon Proudfoot shovel
dirt on Griffin's coffin.

(Anthony Tait)

Tait plays with kids at the 1986 USA Run in Stoner, Colorado.

(Anthony Tait)

Oakland Hells Angel Sonny Barger hams it up at the 1986 USA Run in Stoner, Colorado.

Alaska Hells Angels in front of Big Fred's Broken Spur
bar in Kentucky, where an Outlaw killed Anchorage
member J.C. Webb in August 1986.
Big Fred, center, doesn't look too happy.

Tait outside the Oakland Hells Angels clubhouse,
a former dance studio.

Tait gained the confidence of Oakland Hells Angel Chico Manganiello and bought enough methamphetamine from the underground chemist to send him to jail for 40 years.

Oakland Hells Angel Kenny Owen is one of the world's best methamphetamine cookers. His product is 100 percent pure.

(FBI Photograph)

Surveillance photo of Tait leaving Kenny Owen's house with two pounds of methamphetamine in a paper bag. Owen got 41 years for the deal.

(FBI Photograph)

Tait bought this pound of methamphetamine from Oakland Hells Angel Werner Sohm.

FBI agent Ken Marischen had Tait wear a fake cast to avoid transporting drugs to the Hells Angels USA Run in the summer of 1987.

Tait married Anchorage prostitute Brenda Fowler in 1984. She continued to turn tricks during their many break-ups.

BARGER:	You know, overnight service so it'd get there by the time of the funeral. That's the only thing I know that went up there.
TAIT:	Excellent.
BARGER:	That's the only thing I can say.
TAIT:	Well, we think they might just come back on us a few more times. Several other people at home wanted me to give this to you and get that book with the names and addresses.
BARGER:	Whenever you want 'em, then just send somebody down.
TAIT:	Okay. Well, I'll be here until the middle of next week.

Tait took Barger up on his offer to provide the EPIC manual to the Anchorage chapter and showed up at his Golf Links Road home a couple of nights later. Tait kept his transmitter turned off until he had scanned Barger's house for electronic counter-surveillance equipment. They talked in Barger's study while his rottweilers sniffed and panted around them. Barger introduced the two dogs as Heidi and Eubar. The name Eubar was a cross between Eugene and Barbara, friends from Ohio.

BARGER:	They never bite unless you're trying to hurt them or they're told. Well, what can I do for ya?
TAIT:	Well, we wanted to put together some addresses in that thing besides the Tennessee and Kentucky thing.
BARGER:	Ah, which ones?
TAIT:	The ones in South Carolina, Illinois and Oklahoma. And the outlying areas. We wanna kinda build up the thing to where we're

gonna have one or two people a month out visitin' East Coast charters and they're gonna be ridin' around and takin' a look and see if all this stuff's still current.

BARGER: Okay. Everything I got's a year old.

TAIT: That's probably still real good, though. Do you have a photostatic copier?

BARGER: Ya, but it's one page at a time. What I should do is loan you the book and let you get it copied. That way, you can get it back to me, buddy.

TAIT: Okay.

BARGER: But what I would really appreciate is that you don't let anybody else have it.

TAIT: Oh, no. This is just for us at home. I'm state security.

BARGER: But I mean other charters or anything. Nobody has got these.

TAIT: Okay.

BARGER: It's out of that El Paso Information Center. And when they find out who's got it, they're gonna start askin' questions. About why we got it. How we got it.

TAIT: I can understand that.

BARGER: Here's the way it works. A bunch of this is just all bullshit, background. And then it goes into charters, mailing addresses. And then it lists them all, alphabetically. Then it goes into charters and like who's in 'em. And what their nicknames are. Then from charters it goes to true names, nicknames and then it goes nicknames and true names. Then alphabetically, by last name. Name and photograph. When I made my copy of this, I took it down on Lakeshore. And they have a machine there that you can run yourself. When I was using the machine, jammed a couple of times. And I had to call the guy over? The guy looked at me, said, "What are these? The bad guys?" And I just said, "All depends on which side you're on." And the guy never said another word. Just try not to lose it. We have one other copy stashed away. What I usually do if anybody wants anything, I give 'em what they need out of it. I never really give 'em the whole thing, but you're probably gonna end up needin' the whole thing.

Barger discussed the 10 percent discount demanded by Hells Angels from Harley-Davidson motorcycle dealers in the Bay Area. He referred to the legitimate business Bob Dron Harley-Davidson Motorcycles in Oakland.

BARGER: I told him, "We're not going to have a Harley-Davidson dealer in Oakland that doesn't work on our bikes. If you don't want to do it, we're going to have another dealer in there that will." He said, "Let's not get into blow by blow."

"And that's not a threat, Bob." I said, "We'll put you out of busi-

ness. We'll get a dealer in there
that wants the business. It's all
the bottom line."

I said, "I'll be down to talk to
you tomorrow and talk to your
service manager because he's the
one that said it."

And I said, "I don't care where
we bought the bike. If we bring it
to you for service, and then
there's a warranty problem, you
will fix it or you won't be the
dealer in Oakland."

Tait mentioned he was probably in Hells Angel Howie
Weisbrod's house while it was bugged during Operation
Roughrider.

BARGER: Yeah. I read where I'm on oral
           tapes. That'll be good, 'cause I
           remember what we were talkin'
           about there. Fuck them mother-
           fuckin' feds if they had to tape
           me. I don't care. No-good sono-
           fabitches followin' me will give a
           crook a chance to get away.

They talked about Outlaws recently arrested in Florida
in connection with the 1974 slaying of three Hells
Angels that led to the war between the clubs. Barger
described how they were killed and how the faces were
so disfigured by shotgun blasts they had to be identified
through fingerprints. He showed Tait a photograph of
Riverboat Riley.

BARGER: I'll show you here why they
           couldn't verify them. That's RB
           [Riverboat]. Shot right through
           the side of the head with a shot-

gun. They tied 'em up and RB was shot in the leg with a smaller-caliber gun, like a .22. They tied 'em up and then shotgunned 'em in the head and then threw 'em in an abandoned quarry with cinderblocks tied to 'em. But they didn't gut 'em and . . .

TAIT: Yeah. The gas. One cinderblock ain't gonna hold nobody down.

Tait returned the EPIC book to Barger the next day. Barger was at a motorcycle shop, so Tait made small talk with Sharon. She promised him he would receive a puppy from Heidi's next litter.

The Webb murder wasn't the only one on Tait's mind that fall. Billy Grondalski had fled the Vallejo chapter after his wife filed for divorce. He regretted the pain he had caused his family during his two years as a Hells Angel. He loaded his tow truck and drove north to Fort Bragg with his wife, Patricia, their five-year-old daughter, Dallas, and his 17-year-old stepson, Jeremy. They lived in a trailer at Westport-Union Landing state beach just outside Fort Bragg. Bikers harassed them. He rented a house in September that a local woodsman had just bought at an estate auction.

About a week later, two Vallejo Hells Angels walked into the house with guns drawn. One killer shot Grondalski in the mouth with a .45-caliber bullet. He turned and shot Patricia through the head. The second killer shot the stepson in the face. The first killer turned to the girl and shot her in the chest, then stabbed her five times in the throat. She died with a toy clutched in her arms. The two Hells Angels then torched the house. Grondalski was too charred for the coroner to find the bullet hole in his head. An x-ray located the bullet.

The Grondalski killing served many times to motivate Tait to continue his role when he felt like giving up. Though he could countenance most of the Angels' criminal activities, including murder, the thought of murdered children enraged him. Another Hells Angel murder of children served the same purpose. He was reminded of it every time he attended a West Coast Officers' Meeting and sat near the man suspected in a slaughter in Oregon.

Margo Compton tired of being beaten by her husband in the mid-1970s and sought protection from the Hells Angels. Her guardian was Angel Odis (Buck) Garrett of California's Nomads chapter, then based in Vallejo. He assured Compton she was in good hands, pumped her full of drugs and made her work as a prostitute in the Love Nest massage parlor in San Francisco to pay off his protection fee. Garrett ran the parlor with Flash Gordon Grow, president of the San Francisco chapter.

A customer raped and beat Compton in 1976. She wanted out, but Garrett said she owed him $4,000 for protection and methamphetamine. Compton violated the Hells Angels code: she told police that four women who worked in the Love Nest had to pay the Angels 40 percent of their earnings. Two San Francisco vice officers protected the business for money and sex, she said.

Local and state police promised to protect Compton, who testified against Garrett and his associates on prostitution charges. Compton was relocated to the Oregon village of Laurelwood with her twin six-year-old daughters, Sylvia and Sandra. The 25-year-old woman avoided neighbors and kept her daughters in the house as she spent the winter of 1976 writing a book about her life with the Hells Angels—with names, places and incidents.

Compton and her daughters started a new life with the Oregon spring. The kids made friends and she let the word slip out that she was on the run from the Angels. Compton sat in her cottage with Gary Selsar, a 19-year-old coast guard, on August 7, 1977, two weeks before she had to testify again. The twins were asleep, face down in their beds. Two men walked in. Compton was shot once behind the ear with a .22-caliber pistol. Three more shots were fired. The men left four bodies and Compton's .357 Magnum revolver behind.

Compton never had a chance: the Angels had intercepted letters she wrote to relatives in Vallejo and sent the hit men to the return address.

Nine

TAIT LEFT ANCHORAGE IN EARLY OCTOBER 1986 for a one-month stay in Europe. McKinley listed Tait as officially being on holiday because he planned to visit family. But he also intended to fraternize with Hells Angels in Switzerland, Austria, Germany, Denmark, Holland and England.

Brenda Fowler had always sought refuge with John Jones when she and Tait occasionally split up. He died in the fall of 1986, and Brenda realized she couldn't just bail out anymore. Tait thought she had become "a decent old lady, staying at home and minding her own shit, taking care of everything that's supposed to be done at the house." Come October, she started to piss him off again. This coincided with Tait's trip to Europe.

"Fine. Fuck it," he told her. "You think that everything's so bad here, why don't you go live with your mother."

"All right."

Tait had been set up. He reacted as Brenda wanted him to. Marischen had realized back in March, when Brenda learned Tait was an FBI informant, that he had to get the woman out of town. She was a security risk. When would Tait slap her hard enough to make her finger him to the Hells Angels? Marischen felt like Atlas as he tried to support an undercover operation on his shoulders while it threatened to slip off on the tears of his informants. He repeated one comment during their talks: "You can make it easier on him, Brenda."

He meant she could get out of town. She said she loved Tait, but then she didn't really know if she did. She complained that Tait and the FBI put her in a position that forced her to withhold information from the Hells Angels. She would be a target once they found out about Tait. She didn't ask to become an informant's girlfriend. She knew her man was a spy. She escorted him to Angels functions and backstopped him—supported his cover stories. She ferreted out information from the guys' girlfriends. She flirted with the boys. She kept her ears open for any indication they suspected him. Brenda Fowler was an informant's old lady and that's as good as being a rat. She was so freaked out by the pressure that Marischen was sure she'd confide to a dancer friend while they did coke. He offered to relocate her near her mother in Aurora, Colorado. Brenda never turned down free money. She was a prostitute by nature and a professional prostitute.

Marischen paid Brenda's plane ticket and gave her $3,300 to leave Anchorage on November 10. He wanted her to leave earlier, but she stayed on. He didn't know she had a court date on November 7 for a prostitution charge on which she was convicted. The relocation money was the most cash she received from the bureau. She was paid several hundred dollars for information in 1985 and got $400 in July 1986 to move after she hurt herself in a hit-and-run accident.

Marischen knew he could not break contact with Brenda. He often appealed to her not to blow the case. He asked her to be patient because the investigation was nearly over. He kept her hanging on to the hope Tait gave her that they would get together when the case ended.

Marischen knew the phone calls of the previous 18 months would continue for more than a year. She would continue to ask the same questions: "How much longer is this going to go on? You've got to tell me when this is going to go down because I'm going to be at risk myself. I have to look out for myself. I didn't have a say in this thing. I was put in the middle without ever having made a decision to be put in the middle."

Marischen wouldn't even hint at a date. But he promised she would know the day after the case went overt.

Tait returned to his Anchorage condo on November 12 to find Brenda gone. He called Marischen. "Hey, you know where Brenda is? She's gone. All her shit is gone. She left a pile of shit here."

"No, I don't know what happened."

An hour and a half later, Marischen called Tait and said he wanted to talk to him about something.

Tait confronted Marischen as he walked in the door. "What do we need to talk about? You mean you want to talk about Brenda."

"Yeah. I gave her some money so that she could leave."

"How much money did you give her?"

"A few thousand bucks."

"Why didn't you ask me?"

"It wasn't your decision."

"Yeah. Fuck you. It was more my decision. More than any other decision, this is my decision. You're messing around in my shit and I don't like that. I think we ought to fucking box about it."

"Well, if you don't think we're doing this the right way, let's just shut this case down."

"It's too big for you to shut down."

"I can shut this thing down right now."

"I don't think so. This thing is bigger than both of us. It will eat us. There's too many other things that have happened. There's too much shit going on. You can't shut it down."

But Marischen's bluff worked. He took away from Tait the only leverage the informant held over the agent: the case. He threatened to shut it down before Tait did,

which would have put him in a subservient position to
his informant. Tait would have gained control and used
the threat repeatedly to get his way. Tait, whose ego
hung on the investigation, walked out of the apartment a
victor, thinking the case was too big to shut down, that
he was too important. For his part, Marischen was
relieved to finally get Brenda out of the picture.

Tait underwent his second polygraph examination
that month. This time it was administered by Special
Agent Joseph E. Gersky, who worked out of the Las
Vegas field office. Tait also passed his first unannounced
urinalysis that day. Gersky's report of the polygraph test
was forwarded to Larry Nelson by the director of the FBI.
It greatly exaggerated the use to which Tait's information
was put, to impress the bureaucracy.

This source has worked in an undercover capacity
for the FBI since January of 1985 . . . and has furnished information which has resulted in the
seizure of automatic weapons, the arrests of individuals for illegal drug trafficking, murder, robbery
and numerous other offenses. To date, his information has been of immense value.

Early in 1985, he was given an FBI polygraph
exam where the principal issue was to determine if
he was a "plant" or double agent. He reportedly did
not show "deception" at that time. The FBI and the
San Francisco Drug Task Force requested that
he undergo an updated polygraph exam to clarify
the following issues:

1. Has he kept any of the drugs from the drug
deals he set up for the FBI.
2. Has he used any drugs for personal use during
the past six months.
3. Has he deliberately furnished any false information to the FBI.
4. Has he told anyone he was working for the FBI.

The source denied all the above issues except
issue #4. He admitted that he had confided his job

with the FBI to several immediate family members, and to his girlfriend. He volunteered to take the polygraph exam.

The following relevant questions were utilized on this examination:

A) Regarding the drug deals you've made for the FBI, have you kept any of the drugs? No.

B) Besides your family and Brenda, have you told anyone else you work for the FBI? No.

C) During the past six months, have you taken any illegal drugs? No.

D) Have you deliberately furnished important false criminal information to Agent Marischen? No.

It is the examiner's opinion that the source showed deception to question B. During the post-test interview he admitted there were several other persons to whom he had confided his relationship to the FBI. He named Anchorage Police officers Ron Becker, Mike Cargel and Larry Robinette (who has since become deceased), as well as the mother of his child, Tina Thrasher, as those persons.

The source was given an additional polygraph exam utilizing the following relevant questions:

E) Are you withholding from me the name of any-one who knows you work for the FBI? No.

F) Are you still withholding the name of anyone you told about working for the FBI? No.

It is the examiner's opinion that the source was now being truthful and was not withholding any important information.

After his holiday, Tait heard talk he would be brought up at church. His fellow chapter members wanted to vent years of jealous anger that Tait traveled freely far and wide. They resented his friendship with powerful Hells Angels in California and chapter presidents in foreign countries. They envied his luxurious lifestyle. They hated the way he always got the best-looking women.

Tait was fearful as he walked into Anchorage church

on Friday, November 21. He expected to fight that night and didn't wear his transmitter in case it broke open. He needn't have been scared. Anchorage Hells Angels had enough courage to talk behind Tait's back but little guts to confront him.

Conversation that night centered around taxi driver Royal Hull, with whom Anchorage Hells Angels were extremely upset. Hull wrote sexually explicit letters to Sonny Barger that involved fantasies about Hull and Barger and his wife, Sharon. The Chief was not amused. Fairbanks chapter president Dennis Pailing read a copy of the 20-page single-spaced letter, a copy of which Barger had given him. In it, Hull invited Barger and Sharon to Anchorage. He told Barger he could fuck his girlfriend and would like a threesome with the Bargers. Hull said he would like to see Barger's balls slap off his old lady's ass. He said he'd like to lick and suck her pussy after Barger had come in her. It would be the greatest thing in the world, he said, to eat the sperm of the Hells Angels leader.

The Hells Angels agreed to take care of Royal Hull sometime.

Otherwise, it was business as usual. Tait was still traveling between Anchorage and California constantly, buying crank and weapons and recording every transaction. For the moment, the furor over Webb's murder seemed to have died down, and Tait was once again involved in the minutiae of daily life in the Angels. He attended the West Coast Officers' Meeting at the Oakland clubhouse in late November.

There, the San Jose chapter requested that Hells Angels who visited their area with a patch let the chapter know. The San Jose Hells Angels were unsuccessful in their attempts to track down a "bozo" who ran around their area and told people he was a Hells Angel.

Sonny Barger said he had offered years ago to record meetings so all motions could be transcribed as presented and passed around. His suggestion had been voted down. Barger said, "We got to get one thing straight with everybody: what goes on in this room is 100 percent legal. We don't talk about illegal things here. Because if you're doing anything illegal, I don't want to know about it 'cause it's not club business."

He noted that club minutes introduced at the RICO trials proved they did nothing illegal. So it was not wrong to keep notes.

He said that anyone was welcome to drop by his house and read his minutes from past meetings. Many of his notes were destroyed in 1979 when he was jailed because people were scared. However, his notes from the 1960s to 1986 were complete except for a few years. Barger emphasized he would not let anyone copy the notes because he once gave a copy to every chapter on a Saturday and they appeared in the *San Francisco Chronicle* on Sunday. He suggested that chapter presidents and vice-presidents drop by the Oakland clubhouse one weekend to go through old minutes and clean up their by-laws. A current and valid set of rules could then be drafted and distributed.

In bureaucratic rapture, Barger also told Hells Angel Al Joseph Hogan of the Salem, Massachusetts, chapter to discuss at the next East Coast Officers' Meeting something "we've done out here and it's something you guys are gonna have to do back there so that you don't run into more problems." He said the West Coast was in the process of setting up a corporation board with one member from each chapter.

Tait reported that the Anchorage chapter suit against the Crazy Horse Saloon for failure to serve Hells Angels—namely, Tait—who wore colors was delayed while the lawyer for the bar defended a murder suspect. (This was one of dozens of such suits brought by Angels across the continent.)

One Hells Angel tabled a motion that the club no longer sell Hells Angels items such as posters, cigarette lighters and stickers to the public. "The main reason I brought up this motion," he said, "is because every month we're in here arguing for hours about these items and stuff pertaining to them. I figure if we don't sell them, we aren't making no money on them anyway. All it is, is opening up loopholes for us to get busted [for income unaccounted for]. All we do is argue about it. If we don't have them to sell, we ain't going to argue, we ain't gonna have loopholes to get busted on."

The Hells Angels officers discussed a British Columbia member who some Angels had heard, but had not confirmed, was black, which would disqualify him from membership. The man they talked about had been a Satan's Angel well respected by fellow bikers. They kept him as a member in 1983 when they became Hells Angels. Hells Angels from Cleveland and Oakland threatened to kill the man if he showed up at a run in the U.S. The B.C. Hells Angels, who put brotherhood ahead of the club's racist bent, supported their brother Angel and hid him from fanatics. They continued to deny publicly and to the club they had a black member. San Fernando Valley Hells Angels obtained a vial of sickle-cell anemia to inject into the British Columbia Angel. They agreed to keep him in the club if he lived.

The question of allowing blacks into the Hells Angels was also raised by the Windsor, England, chapter for consideration at the World Meeting. The chapter made its request in letters sent to chapters worldwide.

Brothers,

We the Windsor Charter, are going to ask for a decision on one of our brothers, at a coming world meeting, the brother in Question is a member of our club, and has been for seven years. As you know we have only held a charter since December 1984. Although we have been a Hells Angel club for twenty two years.

We are now very proud to be part of the brotherhood, and can now ask the brotherhood for support, and ask that you take this letter to your next meeting, with views on an answer for us in the world meeting.

John Mickleson was born in London, and lived there all his life. Johns mother is Danish, and white, John is coloured outwardly but inwardly is a Hells Angel, some of the charters in England say he is a nigger and that is a world rule. So John can not be a Hells Angel, we say John is a Hells Angel and we would like your support on our brother.

John Prospected for six months with the rest of my charter before going to jail, and in that six months wore like the rest of us a red and white bottom rocker, whilst in jail we were told as a prospect charter, John could not be a member of our club, now we are in a position where John is still in the jail, be we can now argue his right to stay a member of our charter, and to exercise his right to wear a Hells Angel patch.

We ask, that you give your support in this matter, but respect the decision your charter makes.

The writer included an address for John Mickleson at Wormwood Scrubs prison for anyone who cared to write to him.

On November 30, Oakland secretary Steve Brown called church to order, and Sonny Barger, who always minded club business, brought up the first item of new business. He said a woman called Moleen, who visited the clubhouse on Thanksgiving, had split up with Greg and wasn't welcome in the clubhouse any more. He mentioned her younger sister Nancy and what he called a serious problem. "What we've got to stop doing is to let these . . . that letting the minors . . . with drugs. I mean, we can't let that happen." He said the Hells Angels could get into a lot of trouble if a minor left the clubhouse drunk or high and got into an accident.

Tait reported on problems with the Rio de Janeiro chapter, which had accepted money from the European Defense Fund and at least one American Angel without explaining what had been done with it, and had not been

helpful when a fugitive Swiss Hells Angel fled to Rio.
Barger interrupted the discussion.

"When we give people money, we give them money.
We don't ask them about it afterwards. I don't know
where they're coming from, but if they got some kind of
a case going and somebody donates money for that case
when they're doin' what they told us they needed the
money to do, we don't ask questions. It goes that way
and the case is over with. That's happened here and
nobody's ever asked questions. There was a judge back
east that got convicted of accepting some of that and he
died in prison without saying a word. Think there's a lot
of us could do the same thing. And so there are certain
things you don't talk about."

Barger was referring to Judge James McGettrick of the
Cuyahoga County Court of Common Pleas in Ohio. The
judge got drunk in a bar in early 1984 several months after
he directed a verdict of acquittal in the capital-murder trial
of a Cleveland Hells Angel who had killed three people
when he bombed what he wrongly believed was an
Outlaw's house. A ragged-looking agent with the Bureau
of Alcohol, Tobacco and Firearms who had worked on
the case sat with the drunken judge without introducing
himself.

"Thanks for what you did for us on the Angels trial."

"Yeah, I never got all the money I was supposed to
get out of that," said the judge, who, missing the sarcas-
tic tone, mistook the agent for an Angel associate.

The agent set up a sting in April 1984. The FBI
watched him pay the judge $5,000 in the video-equipped
men's room of the bar. McGettrick was convicted of
three counts of bribery, for fixing two murder cases
against Hells Angels, and was sentenced to four years in
jail. He died of a heart attack behind bars.

Although the bribe money was traced back to the
president of the Cleveland chapter, the Hells Angel
whose acquittal was bought could not be retried because
jeopardy had attached to the case.

Judge McGettrick was not the only bencher in Ohio

paid off by the Hells Angels. A Cleveland Angel bragged to member Dave (Gorilla) Harwood in 1984 about McGettrick's bribe. "How about that judge in Cleveland? They're saying we bribed a judge. Wait till they find out about the other two judges we bribed."

On a special trip east in December, Tait had dinner with Gary Allen Wolf in a small shopping mall. The previous day, Wolf had taken Tait to see chapter vice-president Matthew F. Zanoskar, who said the Cleveland chapter wanted to be notified before the Anchorage chapter took action in their area in the Webb murder because they had to face retaliation from Outlaws. Tait and Wolf were joined by Hells Angels Donnie Mahovlic and Kenny Yates. They didn't talk business until they sat in Tait's rental car afterwards.

"I guess you guys know why I'm here," Tait said. He talked about the Kentucky problem as ordered by his chapter president, Ed Hubert. Yates said the Cleveland chapter didn't have any explosives or guns to give Alaska. He added that it was best for Alaska to take care of business, but they should notify Cleveland. All three Cleveland Hells Angels said they didn't want to see another "Fourth of July thing" against the Outlaws.

It took until December 1986 for Marischen to iron out the bugs in the receiver. He also stumbled across a piece of equipment that made recording much easier. Marischen traveled to Cleveland with Tait. He visited the local FBI office, where Stuart Shoff, the agent who handled the case in that city, listened to his tales of woe about the transmitter and receiver.

"I've got a guy downstairs who's a wiz. Why don't we give him a crack at these things and see what he can do for us?"

The technician, Charlie Redrup, rigged up two small recorders in series so Marischen could record seven continuous hours of conversation without changing tapes. Marischen decided to carry extra batteries and recorders instead of extra tapes. He would rather plug in and unplug tape recorders than fumble with tapes in a cold, dark car. The technician also showed Marischen how to wire the recorder into a rental car so Tait could pull up to wherever he was going, start the recorder and hop out. It would never again be difficult to get the receiver within range of the transmitter, even if it were in a basement.

Marischen also visited the FBI's technical unit in Quantico, Virginia, on the same trip to have his transmitter repaired, because he didn't have the luxury of waiting while it was shipped back and forth. He sat around and shot the bull with six technicians. They desperately needed feedback from people in the field. Marischen made friends as he described day-to-day problems with the recording equipment and limits to the transmitter's range. They offered him a miniature recorder for Tait to wear. Marischen turned it on and it made a loud hiss.

"You gotta be shitting me. I can't use this thing. First of all, there's an awful lot of hugging and kissing going on and body pounding. I can't have anything that's a bulge where a bulge shouldn't be."

These were the same guys who had sent him the weighted baseball cap.

Marischen noticed a technician hunched over something at the back of the shop and went to have a look. The man was at work on a tiny recorder, a Panasonic microcassette recorder that was not yet available to the public. It was the smallest recorder Marischen had ever seen. Tait had briefly used a Sony recorder, but its microphone wasn't sensitive enough to pick up conversations. Marischen desperately needed a backup system.

"Isn't this the cat's meow?" the technician said. "This is the greatest thing."

The recorder had no playback capability but came equipped with a playback unit that plugged into it. It also had a detachable microphone. That was great for Marischen's purpose. The Hells Angels suggested years before that officers carry tape recorders in case they got stopped by police so they could catch any incriminating cops on tape. There was nothing suspicious about a Hells Angel with a tape recorder in his pocket; many Angels carried them. Since the unit had no playback capability, anyone who suspected Tait would have to find a machine to listen to the tape. This would buy precious time to get out of the situation.

"This is outstanding," Marischen said. "You could put it almost anyplace."

There were 10 recorders on the desk.

"I can't give that to you," the technician said. "We're not giving them out. We're still working on them. What division are you from?"

"Anchorage."

"You might get them in a couple of years. We've got an allocation going out to the major divisions that have operations."

"I want two of them and I want them now. Who do I speak to? I'm not jumping on you here. I need you to give me a little instruction on them and I need to walk out with them today. I need them where I'm going."

"I can't do that, but you can see my unit chief."

Marischen walked into the unit chief's office, and walked out with two recorders.

The first went right into Tait's pocket. Several weeks later, Tait looked down at his shirt pocket during a meeting. The red light on the recorder shone through the cloth. He nearly shit himself. He went to the washroom and wrapped it with $100 bills. That night he painted nail polish over the light.

Tait visited Ed Hubert at home and briefed him on his trip east.

HUBERT:	Did you go to Cleveland?
TAIT:	Yeah. We got some questions from Cleveland.
HUBERT:	What's Cleveland wanna know?
TAIT:	If we're sittin' on our asses and forgettin' about this, or we're gonna press on with it. And I

said, "Hey, don't worry about it, man, things are in the making. Anchorage is takin' care of things. Don't get excited about it." . . . I said, it's not somethin' that's been forgotten. Time has to settle to let things cool down. You just don't jump on the bandwagon with a fuckin' big flag and say, "Hey, we're takin' care of this thing." That's just between you and me, though.

HUBERT: Just between me and you that Cleveland wanted to know what we were doin'?

TAIT: They wanted to know what we're doin' because a) they got people racin' in their territory all the time. And b) they had four charters that surround them within a 50-mile radius. And they really didn't know what our status was. Whether we're just gonna ignore it and pretend it never fuckin' happened, or we're goin' on it.

The two men went on to discuss strategies—maybe shooting at Outlaws on the road from an overpass—along with possible cooperation from Angels elsewhere. Over the next few days, Tait visited Dan McIntosh to see what explosives he could get and contacted the Fairbanks chapter to see what they had.

Tait answered the phone one night in early January 1987. Brenda wanted back into his arms. Tait leaned over the counter at the travel agency in the Captain Cook Hotel the next day and reserved a flight from Denver for Brenda Fowler and two cats. He thought of Marischen's reaction.

"This is my life, not yours," he thought. "If it's going

to get fucked up, I'm going to fuck it up. You're not fucking it up."

Tait attended the West Coast Officers' Meeting at the Oakland clubhouse in the new year. There was all the usual business and updating, until Sonny Barger spoke about the increased publicity the Outlaws were getting. He cited an article in the latest *Easyriders* magazine on an Outlaws party in Chicago and several other newspaper and magazine stories about them. "It looks like with these guys doing all of this stuff, there may be a change in their leadership," Barger said. "Because they are dead set—Stairway Harry, and Taco, who took over from Harry, and Harry took over from Mellon—and all three of these guys are dead set against publicity. And now, in the last few months, big-time publicity on these guys. But they're agreeing to it. So it's either a change in leadership or through one reason or another, a change in policy. Maybe we ought to start looking into it, about why."

The subject of race came up when the San Fernando Valley representative questioned whether the club enforced its rule that only white males are accepted as members. "Is there, or is there not, a nigger in the club in Vancouver?"

Barger replied there was a rule about members being white, but it was formulated after the Vancouver Hells Angel joined the club. He said he had assumed the man was Polynesian until he heard his nickname was Buckwheat. He asked if the man was a "nigger." The man then changed his nickname from Buckwheat to Detroit, which was no different. Barger said that Detroit is also a "nigger-type name" and he might as well call himself Watermelon. (The black Angel later changed his name to The Cuban.)

Barger said he didn't hate all "niggers" and got along well with some in Oakland. He said the East Bay Dragons, a black motorcycle club in Oakland, recently celebrated its twenty-fifth year and the Oakland chapter gave the club a plaque. He said they were the only black motorcycle club in the world to receive a 25-year anniversary plaque from the Oakland Hells Angels.

Tait passed around photographs of the two Outlaws involved in "that Kentucky thing." The photographs were from a television news report. Tait said the club had a problem with J.C.'s wife, Lori. He asked that she be black-balled from the club and not allowed to visit other chapters. Barger asked what the problem was.

Tait said she complained that an Anchorage Hells Angel had tried to rape her after J.C. was dead. She told other old ladies and the member's old lady found out. No one asked what the Anchorage chapter was doing to avenge Webb's murder.

The subject then moved from murder to merchandise. The officers discussed yet again whether East Coast chapters could sell T-shirts. The East Coast representative argued that they badly needed money and the sale of T-shirts was a good way to raise funds. Barger was against this, as an organizational rule prohibited the sale of T-shirts and other items without club approval.

After more digressions, New York City Hells Angel Brendan Manning reported on the status of the prosecution of Quebec Hells Angels who slaughtered five members of their North chapter at a party in 1985 and dumped the bodies in the St. Lawrence Seaway.

"Well, speaking of murders," said Barger. "While we're at it, what might make a lot of people feel pretty good: there's an unconfirmed rumor we're trying to get confirmed, is that Sergey [Walton] received multiple stab wounds in a prison in New Mexico last week."

Barger changed the subject to expansionism and the Hells Angels' plan to take over all territory from California to Alaska and from British Columbia to Nova Scotia in Canada to keep out rival gangs. "We definitely need charters in Oregon and Washington. The people who come around us are gonna be the people who make these charters. And we definitely got to close that gap. Because whether anybody likes it or not, the Bandits are up there and the OLs are up there all the time."

Barger also worried about the many Hells Angels who became police informants. He was certain the feds were preparing a national conspiracy case against the club. "They've got about eight or nine guys now who were all officers at one time or another. And they're not gonna pay them for five, six, seven years for nothing."

Another Hells Angel agreed. "They got a whole bunch of info on us from those motherfuckers."

Tait took Chico Manganiello sweet rolls and milk at the Hells Angel's request when he visited him at home the next morning. For weeks Tait had been trying to arrange a big buy with Manganiello, and today was the day. Manganiello showed Tait his new colors.

MANGANIELLO:	I got another fuckin' whole patch, man.
TAIT:	Wow. That's brand new.
MANGANIELLO:	Well, it's not new.
TAIT:	Looking good. Scotchgard it yet?
MANGANIELLO:	Huh? Naw, I never Scotchgarded one yet.
TAIT:	Oh, yeah. The dough's in here.
MANGANIELLO:	Huh?
TAIT:	The dough's in here.

Tait pulled out a bank bag that contained $12,000. He put it on the table. Manganiello removed the kick panels under some kitchen cabinets and pulled out a clear plastic bag that contained one pound of crank, 94 percent pure. Tait put it in his coat pocket in the next room. As he left, he got directions to Manganiello's Portola lab, which he was to visit soon.

Special Agents Ted Baltas and Jay Colvin followed Tait to the Hyatt Regency Hotel in downtown Oakland, where he gave them the crank and a map that showed how to get to Manganiello's lab in Portola. Colvin and Tim McKinley photographed the bag. They noted the handwritten "81-4" on its side; the number 81 is Hells Angels code for *HA*. They took the crank out of the bag and weighed it—474.9 grams.

Tait drove to Sonny Barger's house in Oakland two days later. They talked for three minutes about breeding Barger's rottweilers, then got down to business.

TAIT: Well, would you like to consider coming up to Alaska to talk to a few people up there? Some people are uncertain about what's happening.

BARGER: In which area?

TAIT: In Kentucky.

BARGER: I'm a little unsure myself.

TAIT: Yeah. We've got [some who'd like to] throw it out the back door and forget about it, so to speak. But they're not really the key people in the club up there. They were what I consider pretty much the slackers. I discussed it with him, as security officer in Anchorage. All the state officers we got together and you're the boss. We look to you for guidance. Talk to us so I can figure out what the hell we've gotta do.

BARGER: I think if you can let it go one for one, for that shit's not gonna live long.

TAIT: Yeah. Yeah.

BARGER: It doesn't matter which one.

TAIT: Sure, I understand that.

BARGER: You're not going to get the guys that did it.

TAIT: I know. We know that. Yeah, that's up already. People understand that they're probably gone

to Canada. Or if not, done by
their own people already. We got
a couple people, they're for taking
the thing right to 'em and doing
every one of 'em in the entire
nation.

BARGER: You can't do it this way.

TAIT: Yeah. None of the guys got a stick
in the fire and stir all this shit up
and we come down here to do
something and we go home and
it's left on the people in that general area to deal with them. The
way I look at it is we're a pretty
new charter. I wouldn't wanna
fucking stir up a bunch of shit. I
feel like I'm doing all the legwork
by myself and I don't want to
have everybody pointing the finger at me later on saying, "Hey,
you're the bastard that's responsible for all this problem."

The conversation drifted to politics—what to do about
setting up chapters in the Northwest, and the perennial
debate about T-shirts—and ended with Barger mention-
ing that his dog Heidi might be pregnant, and Tait would
get a puppy from the litter.

Later, Jay Colvin and Ted Baltas removed the recording of the conversation from the tape recorder hidden in
the trunk of Tait's rental car.

By early January 1987, Tim McKinley felt the pressure of
the long hours the CACUS investigation required him to
work. Most of McKinley's time was taken up with paperwork that should have been handled by an accountant.
McKinley fired off a memo to the special agent in charge
of the San Francisco office on January 13.

SUBJECT: CACUS
ACTION: REQUEST FOR CLARIFICATION OF COM-
MITMENT OF PERSONAL [sic] TO CAP-
TIONED INVESTIGATION

On 01/12/87, SA McKinley and co-case agent Jay E. Colvin were advised that SA Colvin was to be detailed to surveillance duty in connection with that investigation entitled [BLANKED OUT]. As represented to SAs McKinley and Colvin, the duration of assignment would be from one to three weeks. Additionally, SA Carlos Villar, also previously assigned to assist with the CACUS investigation, was detailed to the [BLANKED OUT] investigation for some thirty + days.

For the past several months, SA McKinley has reported that staffing of the captioned investigation ranged from barely adequate to grossly inadequate. SA McKinley reported that a backlog of some sixty hours of critical recorded conversations essential to the progress of the captioned investigation existed. Additional logical investigation, preparation of necessary affidavits, briefing communications to the SAC and FBIHQ, as well as briefing of OCDE [Presidential Organized Crime Drug Enforcement Task Force] Coordinating Attorney Stephen Graham, were being substantially delayed. At that time SSA Lusby advised that SA Colvin would be detailed full-time to the captioned matter with SAs Robert D. Barnes and Carlos Villar detailed on a part-time basis.

It is the purpose of this memorandum to advise that the anticipated results of the captioned investigation as briefed to SAC Held and ASAC Mawn on 01/06/87 cannot be met without adequate staffing. The anticipated statistical accomplishments cannot be realized. Most seriously, the captioned investigation cannot proceed to maintain an adequate response capability if the various murder conspiracies reach an imminent stage.

While McKinley was trying to rustle up staff, Tait was applying for money from Alaska's Permanent Fund, as he had in past years. The money, available to all Alaskans, is a type of public welfare. Tait took his money wherever he could. In 1987, he wrote on the application form that he was employed by Alaska Pioneer Tile. Two Hells Angels counter-signed. On his 1986 application, he wrote he was employed as a carpenter by the Hells Angels Motorcycle Club of Alaska. He wasn't. It was counter-signed by club president Ed Hubert and treasurer/vice-president Pee Wee Protzman. On his 1983 application, he said he worked for Rickleman's Spenard Wrecking. He didn't.

Tait attended the East Coast Officers' Meeting in February at the Charleston chapter compound in Summerville, South Carolina. That night, Tait sat with Durham, North Carolina, president Lawrence Dean (Chitlin) Lenihan in his van outside the clubhouse to discuss retaliation against the Outlaws. Lenihan was prepared to give Tait some plastic explosives and sell him a LAWS rocket. Tait then struck up a conversation with Horace Anderson (Country) Powell of the Charleston chapter, who had four Uzis as well as explosives.

Ed Hubert instructed Tait to attend the weekly church of the Fulton County, Kentucky, chapter. Tait asked what they wanted to do about Webb's killing. The members wanted to talk to the Outlaws before they took action.

They discussed the "paperwork" from Oakland, which identified Outlaws and gave their addresses. Tait asked if they had explosives or automatic weapons to contribute to the Anchorage chapter to use against the Outlaws. They didn't. Hells Angel John Robert Curry wrote "300" on the piece of paper on which Tait had written "plastic or automatic weapons." He later explained in Tait's car that he had 300 percussion-type blasting caps.

Hubert and Pee Wee Protzman, who had been in the area for a few days, directed Tait the next day to a house outside Louisville to reconnoiter and photograph the building where they believed the parents of one of Webb's killers lived. They wanted to murder the parents of Leonard Wayne Mullen to lure him into the open where he could be shot.

Tait warned his handlers a couple of days later about the plot against Mullen's parents. McKinley asked the FBI's Louisville office for a background check on the parents of both Outlaws and on the people in the house Tait was directed to photograph.

The following week the Louisville office teletyped McKinley and Marischen that the Angels had the wrong address for the home of one Outlaw's parents. The elderly people who lived there had no connections to the Outlaws.

Tait returned to Alaska. He discussed the murder conspiracy with his handlers. They could control it only if Tait were aware of all plans made to retaliate against the Outlaws. The FBI feared plans made without Tait's knowledge left them out of control and could jeopardize the case. The handlers suggested to Tait that he subtly manipulate the conspiracy by lying to the Hells Angels. The agents wanted breathing space. They asked Tait to tell Angels that Sonny Barger suggested nothing be done until after the U.S.A. Run in Eureka Springs, Arkansas, in July and early August. That would allow all Hells Angels to get home safely. The lie was a calculated risk. If word got back to Barger, it most likely would be in the form of praise about his concern for the safety of club members.

Tait started his manipulation back home in Anchorage when Russ Hagel visited his condominium.

TAIT: East Coast claims it's their back yard.

HAGEL: Right. I'm afraid it's their back yard, too. I don't want anybody to say, hey, I've done this. Come on, man. I'm gonna be right up front

with ya, brother. I'll back any
Hells Angel in anything. But I'm
not naive enough that I could
trust the man. I have to spend
time with people before I can.
They're real naive.

TAIT: Yeah. They are.

HAGEL: People have enemies just everywhere. And even personal ene-
mies. It doesn't have to be
club-oriented type thing. That's
why I want to make sure when
it's done, 'cause I'm not stepping
on nobody's toes. But I also want
to make sure that it's not any
fuckin' conglomeration of three
fuckin' people dying in a matter
of fuckin' month and a half.

TAIT: Yeah. It was suggested that give it
some time and perhaps U.S.A. Let
everybody get home and take care
of whatever we can take care of.
Ralph [Sonny], he was interested
in Chicago, Milwaukee. You
lookin' for some other people?

HAGEL: Uh-huh.

TAIT: You lookin' for some other club
member? Yeah. It wouldn't be too
hard.

HAGEL: Hey, I'd love to get my hands on
the one person. But in all reality, I
don't think we're ever gonna see
that one person ever again.

TAIT: Yeah.

HAGEL: Unless by chance we run across
'em. And the one person, there's
two people involved. Hey, but
one was trying to stop it, man.
The other flipped out and did

whatever he had to do. Now, you know it could end right there as far as I'm concerned.

TAIT: Yeah.

HAGEL: That guy could go out of my life and merrily and live happily ever after. And in the beginning of all this shit here, years and years ago, if those who were initially involved could have just taken care of doing it. Ongoing. People dying every year on both sides of the fence.

TAIT: Yeah.

HAGEL: What it comes down to, I don't care if it's him or not.

Most of the Anchorage chapter met at Tait's wired condominium that same evening to discuss retaliation against the Outlaws. Prospect Rick Fabel was posted outside the door to guard Tait, Tom (T.J.) Joiner, Happy Jack Cottrill, Michael Hurn, Gypsy Spearman, Ed Hubert, Russ Hagel, Sleazy Ric Rickleman and Pee Wee Protzman.

HUBERT: From now on we don't yell. We talk low. I know where to start this story at. Everybody knows that was at the last meeting what we decided.

HAGEL: After-dinner bitters, okay.

HELLS ANGEL: What do they do for ya?

JOINER: Cleans your palate and settles your stomach.

SPEARMAN: Settles your stomach.

HUBERT: That's okay, but what we decided was last time didn't pan out for us. I have pictures over at the house. I didn't bring 'em. I showed 'em at church and other people live there now on those addresses that we came up with. I'm trying to decide a solution or some kind of satisfaction actually for ourselves.

PROTZMAN: What was the general feeling of the people on the East Coast about what exactly what kind of satisfaction they're gonna want to have?

TAIT: South Carolina, they're willing to go along with what we want. North Carolina . . .

HUBERT: Whatever it might be?

TAIT: Yeah. They're pretty—

HUBERT: They haven't got any opinion either way, though.

TAIT: No, but when I went, when I got to Kentucky—

HUBERT: Steamers.

JOINER: It got hot.

(They laugh at the fart.)

HAGEL: That spoke for itself.

(They continue to laugh.)

SPEARMAN: No shit.

TAIT: When I got to Kentucky they said, "Well, we want the West Coast. We want Irish [O'Farrell] to call them in Milwaukee and find out whether it's an isolated

	incident, this or that."
HAGEL:	Why did they want Irish to call?
TAIT:	Because they thought Irish was still the power out there.
HUBERT:	Yeah, Irish talked to Taco [Harry Bowman] before. Taco was their fuckin', uh . . . What is he? The president?
TAIT:	Yeah, he's the national president.
HUBERT:	National president of 'em.
JOINER:	Oh, of the Outlaws, right?
HUBERT:	Sonny says fuck callin' anybody. That's like if we did it to them and then we call and tell 'em, "We're sorry." Is that gonna fuckin' do anything?
PROTZMAN:	Yeah, I think we already hashed that out months ago—
HUBERT:	Yeah, right.
PROTZMAN:	—that phase of the fuckin' thing.
HUBERT:	Big Gary says Joanie told him, Joanie was the bartender that was tending bar that night. Huh. Fuckin', this guy's running around here bragging about fuckin' going and getting these other two guys and gettin' 'em back to the bar.
SPEARMAN:	Yeah.
HUBERT:	But the issue is these people. No other issue and the two people, they've been maybe sighted on east coast Canada. I'd like to send somebody back to the east coast of Canada to fuckin' visit for a while. Pee Wee was talking about it. I

don't know if he's still interested, but I'd like to see the club fuckin' buy him a ticket, a round-trip ticket over to fuckin' wherever we got the people on the street. I don't know if it's gonna do us any good, to tell you the truth.

PROTZMAN: The only thing it'd do is, if one of us personally got, went there, I don't think us personally could fuckin' probably really get around and find too awful much out but we could make it well understood to the people on the street who exactly we are looking for.

HUBERT: Yeah. We need to fuckin', and we can't find 'em, we need to fuckin' look for 'em or we need to pick an alternate. We got a brother that's already spent money out of his own pocket, like about twenty-five hundred, to pick us up a car, that's not traceable though.

HAGEL: It's more than twenty-five hundred. Tony told me the other day that it was ten grand of his own money.

HUBERT: Well, I don't know.

TAIT: That's just one particular thing I've bought.

HUBERT: I don't know all that he's bought. You know we talked about maybe gettin' somethin' that shoots, comin' from the shoulder.

SPEARMAN: Yeah.

HUBERT: Do we want to spend money on something like that? Do we want to fuckin' think about Detroit? Do we want to think about anything else besides Kentucky? Go ahead, Russell.

HAGEL: I think anything you decided to do, I think we ought to do it in a place where it wouldn't necessarily reflect back on just Hells Angels might have done it.

JOINER: Exactly.

HUBERT: That's what Sonny said. Sonny said—I talked to Tony about it—Sonny said, "Hey, they got skirmishes going on with the Pagans, they got skirmishes goin' on with the Galloping Gooses. They've got skirmishes goin' on with all kinds of fuckin' little clubs over there."

After the U.S.A. Run? We can fuckin' drive by in that car and fuckin' do a clubhouse and hopefully we can pick off people in it.

JOINER: Yeah.

HUBERT: You know it's all up for fuckin' for us to decide.

PROTZMAN: One thing I'd like to add, I think we should fuckin' put into consideration here on this whole thing that I hate to see us gettin' to the point to where we completely deplete our funds and we still haven't done nothin' and then somethin' does happen and fuck then we need some money to help somebody that did something after the fact. In other words, let's not fuckin' blow the whole fuckin' wad fuckin' in preparation and then not have nothin' when it comes time to fuckin' to do somethin' . . .

HUBERT: . . . What I believe, look at a place in Michigan or look at a place in fuckin' Florida or Texas or wherever. I got the paperwork, you know what, wherever we can decipher that their national place is at, that's the place I'd like to go to.

TAIT: Okay, we already got that ascertained and we're talkin' the Great Lakes area is where their fuckin' headquarters is.

HUBERT: Power is.

HAGEL: And that's all, and doing somethin' in the Great Lakes area. The last thing I want to see happenin' is any Hells Angels suffer from what we're doin' and standin' up for our brother. In other words, I don't want to put Kentucky in jeopardy. I don't want to put South Carolina in jeopardy.

HUBERT: And they all said let's go to war.

HAGEL: Well, it was more West Coast let's go to war. The East Coast, the East Coast was more on the lines, why call war.

TAIT: Yeah, why call it a war?

HAGEL: When does it stop?

TAIT: That's the general consensus of

the East Coast is they never buried the hatchet. They're keepin' on doing what they've been doin' all along. Except, OLs have enough enemies that they've made on their own to where they can expect retaliation from anybody at any time. And it was said to me that "Hey, if ya do it, don't get caught. Fuckin' do whatever the fuck you fuckin' want. If you want to snipe two for one, five for one."

Kentucky said fifty for one. That's what got me on that one is how they felt about it. But they wanted contact made. The Chief said, "Fuckin' no way, man. Why should we call them and fuckin' talk to them on the phone? It's like a snivel and then have them fuckin' snub us on the fuckin' phone."

JOINER: If it happened, how do we know who we're gettin' a hold of anyhow on the fuckin' phone?

PROTZMAN: If they wanted to talk, they'd be talkin'. They're the ones who should be fuckin' calling here to talk.

HUBERT: They ought to be blowin' up our ass tryin' to be our fuckin' friend, man. Russell, go ahead.

HAGEL: . . . Fuckin' with these people down south is gonna put our brothers in jeopardy down south and I'm in favor of up north where there's all kinds of bike clubs and no tellin' who the fuck was doin' what. That's where they're gonna be most relaxed is in their back fuckin' yard. Their own fuckin' place. 'Cause they're in control there 'cause just like we're relaxed and we're in control here in Alaska. We're so fuckin' relaxed up here, if they came in on a fuckin' airplane, they could wipe out 90 percent of this fuckin' club today before anybody knew what the fuck was happenin'. So that tells us maybe they're relaxed in their fuckin' home too.

SPEARMAN: Maybe.

HUBERT: I don't know about 90 percent, but they could take 50 probably.

PROTZMAN: They could get everybody that's home. The only ones they couldn't get is the ones they can't find that day.

HAGEL: Yeah. I hear ya there . . .

HUBERT: . . . Let's decide what we wanna fuckin' do to 'em and start puttin' the wheels in fuckin' motion. We don't want to do it until after the U.S.A. Run.

HAGEL: . . . How far do you want to go? What do ya want?

PROTZMAN: Do we want to do like the whole clubhouse and start a major war? Or do we fuckin' just hit this guy or this guy and whoever's available? Or the two people that were directly responsible? That's what we got to decide. Now, if we're gonna get that [LAWs] unit, we're talkin' about goin' fuckin' all out. Complete fuckin'. And then we better get a whole bunch of 'em. It's gonna continue after we're done fuckin' pullin' the first trigger.

HUBERT: I suggest we don't do fuckin' nothin', man. We'll probably get some shapes and do this or we can fuckin' get a few people here, you don't think it's gonna continue? I'm sayin' let's try to wait and see when the fuckin' [Outlaws] meetin' is and the fuckin' high people in this area. Go by there and blam! And fuckin' we got half the fuckin' top brass in the fuckin' organization. Or are we just gonna piddle around and plunk, plunk, plunk, and they're gonna plunk, plunk, plunk?

PROTZMAN: Well, that's what's been goin' on for years. Maybe it's time to change.

HAGEL: I'd love to see all the officers in one fuckin' building and us fuckin' throw a couple fuckin' rockets.

SPEARMAN: What's a rocket go for?

TAIT: Fifteen hundred, two thousand bucks, fifteen hundred.

SPEARMAN: What's that training unit go for?

TAIT: A few hundred.

HAGEL: That's all we need, myself included. I don't know how many other people have been in the fuckin' military. Is there any real need to have to fuckin' go train? I have the fuckin' qualifications, go fuckin' do it. Then there's no record of us going out and training and doin' this shit. Just say the possibility that they might fuckin' catch on that we're fuckin' training.

HUBERT: I think we all ought to fuckin' go play these war games out here with the colored darts and learn how to fuckin' survive and learn a few things myself. You got a bunch of people up here, a few people that have been in the service, and you got a bunch of street fighters in the rest of the people.

They don't have no real fuckin' idea how to kill somebody like this. They just keep beatin' and beatin' and beatin' 'em until they can't fuckin' move. But it'd be nice for us to fuckin' learn a few things if we're gonna fuckin' go on like this. I don't see no other way if this happened. It's been goin' on for years and it's gonna continue to go on. Let's make a devastating blow . . .

Ten

By FEBRUARY 1987, Anthony Tait had collected intelligence on the Hells Angels at a rate that outstripped the FBI's analytical capabilities. CACUS case agents busily directed Tait and had no time to collate or analyze the information. Analysts in the bureau's Washington headquarters took more than six months to process information. Tim McKinley explained the situation to his superiors, who decided to go outside the agency for help. Richard W. Held, special agent in charge of the San Francisco Division of the FBI's Oakland Resident Agency, asked Bert Jensen, director of the Western States Information Network, or WSIN, in Sacramento for help.

In his letter, Held wrote: "It is presently anticipated that the covert phase of the investigation will continue for another three to six months. Thus far, some thirty plus prosecutable charges exist. Massive amounts of intelligence pertaining to criminal activities of members of the Hells Angels Motorcycle Club throughout the western United States have thus far been collected."

In less than a week, Jensen agreed to help, and assigned analyst Karen Sanderson to the case.

WSIN is a narcotic-intelligence system little known outside law enforcement agencies in the five western states where it operates: California, Oregon, Washington, Alaska and Hawaii. Similar agencies exist across the U.S.

It is funded by the U.S. Department of Justice to promote the exchange of narcotic intelligence information. It provides a central repository of information on narcotic traffickers from more than 625 agencies and supplies analysts who identify narcotic-trafficking organizations and help to convict traffickers as well as coordinate multi-jurisdictional investigations.

WSIN shares information through a narcotics-intelligence file set up on a pointer system. Member agencies submit to WSIN's computer the names of people or organizations under investigation. If a member of another agency inquires about a name and gets a "hit," the person is directed to whomever originally submitted the information.

Few agencies and task forces share information on active investigations. But those that do would rather deal with one person in a central repository than with hundreds of people in local, state and federal agencies in their area. Inquiries are made to WSIN on toll-free lines and callers are patched through to the people they need to speak to in other agencies at no cost. WSIN also supplies specialized investigative equipment to agencies that can't afford to keep abreast of technology. This includes radios, cameras and night scopes.

McKinley had asked Karen Sanderson to work on the case before their respective agencies exchanged letters. He called her in early February and asked if she'd like to get involved in a sensitive case on the Hells Angels. What he didn't tell her was that Tait and Ken Marischen, out of fear that case security would be breached, were vehemently opposed to letting another person in on the operation. But McKinley knew that there was no point collecting information if you couldn't keep track of what you had.

Sanderson sat across from McKinley in his Oakland office.

"I've known you for a long time," he told her, "and I've seen the kind of work you can do. I think it would be really valuable in this kind of a case." He put a photograph of his informant on the table.

"Oh, Anthony Tait," Sanderson said.

McKinley was so proud that he had so far kept CACUS watertight and the name of his informant secret that he couldn't suppress his surprise. "How did you know that?"

It was a dumb question. He wanted Sanderson in the operation because he knew her to be the best motorcycle-gang analyst in California, if not the entire United States. She knew her bikers.

"Well, I thought he looked out of place when I saw him at [Hells Angel] Fu Griffin's funeral and I knew who he was."

Sanderson had known about Anthony Tait since his days as a prospect for the Brothers Motorcycle Club. She had his mug shot in her files and knew he was arrested in Monterey in January 1982. She had an extensive background in criminal analysis and learned much from her husband Bill Sanderson, who was head of California's Bureau of Organized Crime and Criminal Intelligence.

Sanderson went to work at WSIN in 1982 and was assigned to motorcycle gangs and clandestine drug labs. She found law enforcement agencies did not document the Hells Angels or other outlaw motorcycle gangs. The El Paso Intelligence Center, whose manual Sonny Barger had sent to Kentucky, published a book of biker mug shots that listed addresses and criminal records, but no one kept detailed records on what bikers were doing.

Part of this negligence stemmed from the fact that cops focus on particular cases in their areas and don't have time or resources to grasp the broader picture. There also wasn't any established means to keep track of detailed information on bikers. Most important, law enforcement had taken a severe beating at the hands of bikers in the previous four years. There were allegations that police planted evidence during a raid on the Outsiders clubhouse in Portland, Oregon. And two lengthy and well-publicized RICO cases against the Hells Angels in California from 1979 to early 1981 flopped miserably because prosecutors were ill prepared and used poor tactics and discreditable witnesses who had committed worse crimes than the defendants. People were reluctant in the early 1980s to work bikers, especially the Hells Angels, who had the financial clout to hire ball-breaking lawyers.

Sanderson's greatest asset in 1982 was her naiveté about this problem. She made charts and graphs and applied link analysis—which ties people and events together—for the first time to the Hells Angels. She mapped out chapters, membership and associates, and linked chapters and members with circles and lines that highlighted the flow of power and business dealings within the gang.

Then she did something not often done in law enforcement intelligence circles. The information she used in her analysis had been fed to WSIN piecemeal by police officers, and they had never got anything back for their efforts. Now, Sanderson sent out copies of her chart for feedback. For the first time, police officers saw someone cared about their information and did something with it. She got more feedback than she anticipated.

Much of the information she worked from was dated. John Dixon, head of biker intelligence for the Oakland Police Department, told her it was a great start, but "this guy's been dead for 28 years. And this guy's out of the club." So Sanderson updated her chart. She put her name and WSIN's on it, and police officers now had a repository for information—a contact they could send information to who would give it back when they needed it. Sanderson quickly grasped that intelligence is like trading baseball cards. People won't give you information if you have nothing to trade.

In 1983, the FBI was forbidden to have direct contact with WSIN. The federal agency has always felt superior to state and local and even other federal agencies, even though local and state agencies generate the bulk of criminal information. Tim McKinley heard of Sanderson's chart and wanted it. The FBI knew little about bikers and McKinley had spent four years trying to bring the bureau up to speed. To circumvent interagency politics, he called Dave Tresmontan at the California State Bureau of Narcotic Enforcement and asked him to ask Sanderson for a copy of the chart.

McKinley and Sanderson started a professional friendship. She had information he needed and she was the means by which he could get information to the street cops. Sanderson became a go-between from the top to the bottom of the intelligence pyramid.

Sanderson's role in the intelligence community was a prime reason McKinley inducted her into CACUS. He not only wanted her to keep track of the intelligence Tait gathered, he wanted her to keep her eyes and ears open while she attended intelligence meetings in WSIN's five member states—in other words, to act as a counter-intelligence agent. He wanted her to keep tabs on what others heard about the Hells Angels, whether there was talk about an informant inside the gang and whether anyone talked about Tony Tait. The FBI did not send representatives to these meetings of local and state police and wasn't always invited.

Sanderson's primary task for CACUS was to organize the mound of reports filed by agents and feed the information back to them so they could keep tabs on what was up in other areas. Marischen was so busy in Alaska he couldn't spend hours on the phone with McKinley and Baltas going over every detail of Tait's activities in California. And they in turn knew little of what he did in Alaska. They couldn't manage the case properly if they didn't have the big picture. Not that the investigation wasn't clear-cut. It was. They looked at five distinct violations: murder conspiracy, conspiracy to manufacture and distribute narcotics, conspiracy to manufacture and distribute weapons and explosive devices, theft of government property and the interstate transportation of drugs, weapons, explosives and stolen government property.

Because she knew what investigators in other jurisdictions worked on, Sanderson read through CACUS

material and looked for information that would help
them. She laundered the information and passed it on as
quickly as she could. Minutes from officers' meetings
and churches that Tait obtained were distributed so
police officers knew what the Hells Angels were up to.

To ensure security, Sanderson worked on a disk she
locked away at night. No information was entered on the
WSIN computer's hard drive. Printed reports were
locked up. As an extra precaution, the names of all Hells
Angels involved in the investigation that were already in
the agency's computer were flagged so that information
on them would not be released to any member agency
that inquired. All inquiries were recorded and forwarded
to CACUS case agents who checked for security leaks.
The office itself was staffed 24 hours a day and protected
with a high-tech alarm system. WSIN has never been
robbed, despite large sums of money paid by many criminals to uncover grand jury information it keeps.

Sanderson was well aware that investigators couldn't
be too cautious around the Hells Angels. When she was
in charge of the Northern California Motorcycle Gang
Investigators Association in 1987, she chaired a meeting
of 16 investigators where she passed out copies of the latest U.S. Marshals Service book on outlaw motorcycle
gangs. When the meeting ended, she noticed her copy
was gone. One of the 16 people in the room had stolen it.

"Who has my book?"

No one answered. She gave the signed roster of
everyone at the meeting to McKinley. One week later,
Hells Angel John Makoto (Fuki) Fukushima, who had
just transferred from San Francisco to Oakland, showed
the book at Oakland church.

The Hells Angels cleverly obtained law enforcement
information. Nomads Hells Angel Odis (Buck) Garrett
bought advertising space in the California Narcotics
Officers Association magazine, and the association gave
him a free subscription. The magazine was a dope
dealer's dream. Garrett copied and distributed to other
Hells Angels articles on the latest surveillance equipment

and ways to hide cameras. The magazine also had a
bounty of photographs of successful narcs, even one of
U.S. Marshal Budd Johnson, which the Hells Angels circulated on a wanted poster.

Tait was busy with matters other than the revenge for
Webb's murder. Anchorage Hells Angels lawyer Shawn
Holliday filed Tait's affidavit in the Crazy Horse Saloon
discrimination lawsuit in March.

Tim McKinley's burden of investigative work and
paperwork was considerably increased that month when
FBI headquarters in Washington started to question
CACUS expense vouchers he worked on until 4:00 in the
morning. It seemed bureaucrats changed accounting procedures as often as they did underwear. They returned
McKinley's vouchers for October and November 1986
with a request for actual receipts.

McKinley wasn't the only case agent hassled by
bureaucracy. The two supervisors who overlooked the
case in Washington—Byron Sage and Tom Owens—were
transferred and replaced by people who knew nothing
about Operation CACUS. They came in mid-stream and
didn't see the big picture. They dealt with supervisory
decisions as they arose. They had no idea what the case
was about and no confidence that it would continue.
These were the people Marischen regularly dealt with.
Rather than make decisions they were paid to make, the
new supervisors worried that their careers would go
down the tube if the case messed up—so they wouldn't
make decisions. That way, they wouldn't be responsible
if the decisions proved wrong. Marischen felt that the
bureau put more obstacles in his way than the Hells
Angels did.

The Anchorage chapter held its second major retaliation meeting at Ed Hubert's house early in March to go
through the EPIC manual and pick potential targets.
Most Anchorage members were present: Tait, Russ
Hagel, Tom Joiner, Ed Hubert, Happy Jack Cottrill, Pee

Wee Protzman and several others.

TAIT:	Oh, this motherfucker's dead.
HUBERT:	Yeah, some of 'em are.
COTTRILL:	Take 'em and put 'em in the portfolios for different areas and when we go in that area, have that portfolio to study before we leave.
TAIT:	Sort of break it down by charter?
COTTRILL:	Yeah.
HUBERT:	Here's a former president, the Chattanooga president . . .
COTTRILL:	That's a good fuckin' picture. He's a hunchback and he's awful, awful dark.
TAIT:	You gotta remember that when we copied this, we just did it on a standard fuckin' copier.
COTTRILL:	I understand. That was my sense of humor.
TAIT:	Oh.
COTTRILL:	I was making a joke.
TAIT:	Oh. If the picture wasn't light when I started out with it, you know, it . . .
JOINER:	It don't get no lighter.
TAIT:	Yeah. Yeah.
COTTRILL:	Okay, okay, you guys. Don't pick on me.
HUBERT:	There's a Kentucky Outlaw.
TAIT:	A real handsome bastard.
HUBERT:	Aren't they? There's the president of the Detroit chapter.
JOINER:	Is he a nigger?
PROTZMAN:	Has anybody heard of any niggers being Outlaws? I went in and had fuckin' lab work done on me—nigger lab technician.

They were givin' me chest x-rays, right? They found some scrap metal in me. So he got talkin' about it, man. He's a nigger, right? And he goes on to tell how he used to ride motorcycles and how his brother got shot in the shoulder two or three years ago with a shotgun ridin'. He's all right now, but he's still ridin' and all. That's why I was askin' if there's any niggers in their club. His brother woulda had to been a nigger.

HUBERT: Fat Sam. Caucasian male was born in '52, he's five-six and 300 pounds.

TAIT: Holy shit.

HUBERT: Now you're talkin' about a real fat man. I don't care how much hair he cut off. This guy is fat.

COTTRILL: How long since he seen his dick?

TAIT: Hey, in the mirror every day.

HUBERT: I know I don't have to say this, but we get busted with this it's a felony. So if somebody catches you, sees you, that's a felony of havin' the stuff. All this paperwork there.

Tait's fellow Angels in Anchorage continued to be jealous of his jet-set lifestyle and plotted behind his back to clip his wings. Tait attended the monthly West Coast Officers' Meetings in California, a place that the snow-bound members of the Anchorage chapter would rather be at that time of year. They forgot that Tait supposedly paid for the trips with his own money rather than dip into the club treasury. Anchorage and Fairbanks members persuaded Ed Hubert to curb Tait's travel, and Fairbanks chapter president Dennis Pailing attended the March WesCOM in Tait's place.

While the Hells Angels struggled with in-house battles, McKinley continued to be swamped by the ever-changing tides of bureaucracy: the accounting unit had a problem with how Tait was paid. McKinley placed several frustrated phone calls to FBI headquarters, reminding senior special agents of the bureau-approved employment contract.

Ed Hubert told Tait that he and the other chapter members had kidnapped and beaten Royal Hull, the cabbie who had been writing letters about sexual fantasies to Sonny Barger. They put in a personal call for Hull's cab to pick up a fare at the Tradewinds Bar, and one Angel had Hull drive him to the clubhouse. A Hells Angel pulled in behind him at the compound and they dragged Hull into the building. They took his 50,000-volt stun gun and zapped him 50 or 60 times until the battery was dead. They beat him with sawed-off baseball bats and pool cues. They held his hands flat on a large tree stump, in which they had fastened a ring bolt to handcuff people, and smashed them. Blood flicked off the clubs onto the walls, ceiling and floor.

Hull cried out, "I don't know what I did to piss you guys off, but I'm real sorry."

They put Hull in his cab, drove him away and left him in the parked car. Two days later, Hull bought two AK-47 Assault rifles at a gun show.

The FBI battle of the vouchers intensified to the point where McKinley believed the mindless bureaucrats were putting Tait's life at risk. He detailed his ongoing headache in a memo to a senior special agent assigned to the case, Tom Lusby. In it he wrote: "I reiterate that these original receipts largely identify [Tait] . . . and thus the mailing of them constitutes an unwarranted and unnecessary risk to the life of [Tait] as well as risk compromising the case unnecessarily." He also printed out that the receipts constituted evidence in the case and should be kept secure in his hands.

Tait called several East Coast Hells Angels to talk about the murder conspiracy. His first call was to Durham president Chitlin Lenihan.

"How's everything looking?" Tait asked in a coded conversation about armaments.

"Pretty good."

Tait called Charleston member Country Powell, who said he'd talk to Tait at the Oakland chapter's thirtieth anniversary party or at the next East Coast Officers' Meeting.

"I'll be at both," Tait said.

Tait called Cleveland Hells Angel Gary Wolf at a pay phone used by Cleveland Angels to "take care of business." FBI Special Agent Kenneth Riolo of the Cleveland Division observed Wolf in the phone booth as he picked up the phone on the first ring.

"Is that you?" Wolf asked.

"This is me."

They talked about the weather and Wolf described a run-in 15 Cleveland Hells Angels had with 70 members of the Pagans Motorcycle Club at a local bike show. Tait brought up the retaliation against the Outlaws.

"Down there [in Louisville]," Wolf replied. "Should be taken care of down there. That's where it should happen."

"This is what we have in mind."

Tait asked if Wolf had "anything" available. Wolf said he had not worked on that angle but would look around. Tait said he wanted "snap on" or "Mac" tools—submachine guns.

"I understand what you mean."

Wolf told Tait he would see him at the East Coast Officers' Meeting in Lowell, Massachusetts in a couple of weeks' time. Tait told him he might stop in Cleveland on his way through.

Ed Hubert called yet another meeting of the Anchorage chapter at his house. Again there was a lot of talk about retaliation but no firm decisions were made.

Hubert told Tait how chapter members beat Royal Hull.

HUBERT:	You missed a good one. We had a good one. There was blood all over the walls and the lockers.
TAIT:	There still is.
HELLS ANGEL:	I think we ought to have a designated beating area. He bled well.
HUBERT:	Somebody took a boot to him. He's got to have ribs busted. I stomped dead on his hand. Then hit it with a baseball bat. Jack was on top of him punching him in the head. He walked away, too. He never went out once.

The FBI voucher saga continued through late March with another McKinley memo to Tom Lusby along with a thick bundle of vouchers and receipts. "You might be interested to know that this took three full days to produce, largely because most of the receipts were already mounted by me. Again, I must request an SAA or accounting clerk take over this burden. It is now entirely unreasonable to continue as we have been."

Ed Hubert called Tait at his condo one night in April. The Anchorage president was panic-stricken. "Hey, man, I don't know what's going on, but Sonny's trying to get hold of you. He's called here. He's called Pee Wee's. You need to call Pee Wee and find out what's going on."

Tait called Barger immediately. "Hey, Chief, what's up?"

"I got bad news for you."

"What's wrong?"

"Your dog's dead."

"What happened?"

Barger explained he had not installed a railing in the dog pen to prevent Heidi from crushing her puppies. Tait's pick of the litter, promised to him by Sharon, had been smothered.

"Ah, man. That's too bad. I'm sorry to hear it. Well, do you have any left?"

"All I have left is the runt."

"Well, I'm not averse to having runts. In fact, I think they're better dogs most of the time."

"You're right. The little one's the first one that walked, the first one that ate by itself, the first one that did anything by itself."

"Okay, the runt sounds cool."

Four days later, a frantic Hubert called Tait. "Man, Sonny's looking for you again. What the fuck's going on?"

Tait called Barger from Hubert's house. "Hey, Chief, what's happening?"

"Man, I hate to tell you this. Your dog's leg is broken."

"What the hell happened?

"Her mother layed down on her and broke her leg. We got her in a doctor right now. She's had steel pins put in her and she's got a bandage and cast on."

"Let me know what the bill is and I'll take care of it."

"Don't worry about it. Everything's all done."

Hubert couldn't believe that his sergeant-at-arms was on such friendly terms with Sonny Barger. Hubert was afraid of all California Hells Angels, and especially those in Oakland. "Was that Sonny calling you wanting to talk to you like that?"

"Yeah. No big deal."

"What's this? You getting a dog from him?"

"Yeah, he's giving me one of his rotty pups."

"Man, I'd like to get one of them."

"Well, it's too late now. All of them are gone. The first one I got was crushed, so he gave me another one out of the litter, which I'm fortunate, I'm lucky to get that dog."

Tim Bobitt was a cop slated for early achievement and rapid promotion in the California law enforcement community. He was tall and big, yet docile as a teddy bear. He was quiet and softspoken, and used lapses in conversation to assess what he heard and formulate a solid response. He didn't step on anyone's toes, yet was always ahead of the pack. Bobitt was a rare mix of politician and street cop who devoted his life to fighting crime. He started his career as a patrol cop in Richmond, California, but quickly headed to where the action was: the California Department of Justice, Bureau of Narcotic Enforcement, BNE for short. Bobitt ran the Hells Angels hard as a street cop in Richmond, and he continued to hound them in BNE. He worked in the bureau's San Jose office in 1987 for supervisor Dave Tresmontan, who worked many Hells Angels cases with the FBI. Tresmontan was involved in one case his employees knew nothing about: Operation CACUS.

Special Agent Bobitt tried to gain expertise on the Hells Angels. He started to work the San Jose chapter, whose associates ran a sophisticated drug lab. Bobitt tried to find out who financed the operation. His leg-work took him to San Francisco and Oakland. Tresmontan took note of the work and played match-maker. He knew enough about CACUS to want BNE in on the action.

He told Bobitt about McKinley, his expertise in investigating Hells Angels, his experience in Operation Roughrider and other cases aimed at individual Hells Angels. Then Tresmontan told McKinley that Bobitt would like to meet him to discuss Hells Angels and pick his brain to get ideas for his investigation against the San Jose chapter.

In mid-April, Tresmontan drove Bobitt to Oakland to meet McKinley, whom he described to the junior agent as the FBI legend of biker investigation. Indeed, the Hells Angels had been heard in wiretaps describing how McKinley should be skinned alive and interrogated about his investigations into their activities. Bobitt was as excited as a little boy about to meet a baseball legend.

Bobitt described his work to McKinley. Fifteen minutes into the conversation, McKinley interjected.

"I have a proposal for you."

"What's that?"

McKinley lifted a piece of brown butcher paper that covered an analytical chart drafted by Karen Sanderson. It was an investigation-analysis link chart that tied together people and events with lines, circles and squares. In the middle of the mass of colors, Bobitt noticed the letters TE, which stand for top echelon—as high as an informant could go in FBI nomenclature—followed by a number. McKinley gave him a rundown on CACUS.

Bobitt's jaw dropped. He was handed a gift. He had thought the Hells Angels would be impossible to penetrate after Operation Roughrider. McKinley invited BNE into the case. He said CACUS was about to become very active in California as Tait rose through the Hells Angels and befriended members who manufactured and sold drugs. McKinley wanted BNE to take care of the dope end of the operation.

He didn't explain that he and several other FBI agents who helped on surveillance were overworked, or that the FBI didn't have ready access to funds to take advantage of opportunities to make spur-of-the-moment drug buys. As case administrator, McKinley had to devise ways to ensure the success and survival of CACUS. BNE agents were drug-buy and surveillance experts. BNE also had seemingly inexhaustible funds to take drugs off the streets. McKinley cut BNE in on a major case that would give it needed publicity. BNE brought security—physical and financial—to his operation.

"We'll get back to you," Bobitt said before he left. However proud, elated and enthused he was by the offer and that McKinley trusted him with sensitive information, Bobitt wanted to assess the situation, write the proper memos to his supervisors to explain what BNE could gain from CACUS and determine ways to succeed.

Tim Bobitt always aimed to win. Ironically, McKinley was impressed with Bobitt's size and calm demeanor. If he had known Bobitt was only 27 years old when he walked into his office, McKinley never would have told him about the case.

Bobitt outlined in a memorandum to his supervisor the manpower and money he needed, and two weeks later he was transferred to San Francisco. McKinley gave him four four-inch-thick binders that contained all CACUS reports. Bobitt read them over and over.

BNE took unusual steps to ensure secrecy in the case. Normally, reports and vouchers—just about all paperwork, in fact—went through several hands to be cleared, from Bobitt to his supervisor to his boss in Sacramento in the Administrative Support Division. But BNE recognized that too many eyes could get Tait killed, so reports were sealed and held. No information was put on the statewide computer. Bobitt submitted expense vouchers to his supervisor who initialed them, sealed them and locked them in a safe. He carried them to Sacramento once a month and sat face to face with the person who cleared them. They were sealed again and locked up. BNE would not unseal vouchers and other paperwork until the case ended.

Bobitt was assigned full-time to CACUS, and the case was run on a need-to-know basis. He was given a backup partner who was told little. Another seven BNE agents to be used on surveillance were told nothing, and they were professional enough not to ask. Bobitt was familiar with the Hells Angels' record of violence toward witnesses and the near-mystical ability they have to reach out through violence, corruption, bribery, fear and coercion to manipulate people and gain information. There was no way BNE would allow this to happen.

Tait called Hells Angel Waylon Timothy Hicks of the Fulton, Kentucky, chapter on Tuesday, April 28, to tell him that Outlaw Cool Ray Mullen had surrendered to Louisville police at 3 a.m. that day.

Tait sent Brenda away again in early May to live in

Colorado.

Tait visited Monty Elliott at home to discuss the purchase of two ounces of cocaine and 100 Valium tablets. Tait picked up one of Elliott's guns.

TAIT:	Does this work?
ELLIOTT:	Almost as good as this.
TAIT:	What is it? Thirty-rounder?
ELLIOTT:	Yeah.
TAIT:	This is a John Wayne special.
ELLIOTT:	It's a Rambo special. You don't run out.

Elliott slipped a videotape of the Phil Donahue show about Hells Angels into his VCR. Tait looked at a jar of Valium tablets.

TAIT:	Holy shit! That's a bunch of 'em. You going to sell a hundred of 'em? How much do you want for a hundred? I'll take a hundred. Yeah, Halcion. That's what it is, sleeping pills. I'll tell you what. I'll take a hundred of these guys. That's what's in here, huh? And a couple of oh-zees. I'll pick it all up on Wednesday.
ELLIOTT:	Take . . . with you.
TAIT:	That's all right. I don't have any money on me. Only maybe a hundred dollars. You want to use my credit card, huh? We're still talking about eighteen [$1,800]? That way I know how much I'm looking at.

Tait returned to Elliott's house the next evening and they went upstairs to Elliott's office. "I wanted two oh-zees and a hundred Valium, okay?" Tait reminded him.

"Eighteen an ounce and a buck and a quarter for Valium."

Elliott took from a desk drawer a bag that contained four ounces of cocaine in rock form. He measured two ounces on an electronic scale with an LED readout. Tait paid him $3,600 for the coke and $125 for the Valium. Elliott took a $100 bill and showed Tait that it weighed one gram.

Tenacious FBI bureaucrats in Washington who scoured CACUS expense vouchers returned them again in May with queries about questionable expenses. Expensive man-hours in Oakland and San Francisco were spent to resolve problems that never should have existed. McKinley's calendar entry for Thursday, May 7, 1987, summarized the latest scuffle and showed how FBI supervisors can be enticed to fudge paperwork in a classic cops-and-donuts case.

> Conference with SSA Lusby in presence of Lyndell Morgan and partially in presence of SA Wyneken re how to handle problem of SA Colvin's vehicle on UC [undercover] voucher and also in regard how to handle coffee and donuts arranged by SSA Lusby which generated receipt with FBI on it.
>
> SSA Lusby offered no answers re rental of SA Colvin's vehicle after being advised it is imperative to the case.
>
> SSA Lusby suggested altering receipt to remove FBI from appearing on receipt re coffee and donut purchase he arranged.
>
> SSA Lusby declined to call FBIHQ in presence of SA Wyneken re identifying alternatives to these problems.
>
> McKinley pointed out that failure to resolve these problems would result in UC vouchers being rejected at FBIHQ and would further delay submission of UC vouchers as well as causing them to be

repeatedly re-done.

Colvin's vehicle was a beat-up Toyota pickup with fiber-glass camper. The Hells Angels would never suspect it was a surveillance vehicle, and the fiberglass shell allowed the receiver to pick up Tait's transmitter.

Hells Angels on the road are required to attend weekly church at the nearest chapter in the area they are in, and Tait attended Daly City church at the house of president Jerald Emmett Caldwell in early May. Daly City members were concerned that the chapter that owned the Hells Angels trademark—Oakland—would use the copyright to pull patches and impose its authority on the club.

On Saturday, May 9, Tim Bobitt met McKinley in his Oakland office at sunrise. Tait was in town and the agents would cover the West Coast Officers' Meeting. Bobitt would finally get a ringside seat. He wanted to show McKinley he could handle the investigation, but he also felt like a kid in a candy store.

McKinley described Tait's abilities and mindset on the drive to the Oakland Hyatt Regency where Tait was staying. "He's more than an operator. He's a Hells Angel." The agents took an elevator to the club floor of the hotel. Tait stayed on club floors for security reasons: access to the floors was controlled by a special elevator key given to patrons.

Bobitt stood behind McKinley at the door to Tait's room. A tired-looking man with short brown hair and a clean-cut mustache answered the knock. He was still wet from a shower and wore a bathrobe. Tait looked over McKinley's shoulder. His eyes widened when he saw the big bearded man. He looked at McKinley.

"Let us in," McKinley said.

Bobitt was mesmerized by what he saw. Tait's lug-gage was spread out. Hells Angels colors hung in the closet. Three Hells Angels T-shirts lay on the bed. A gold Hells Angels belt buckle caught his eye. The colors meant a lot to Bobitt. Every time he stopped a Hells Angel, he knew the colors meant trouble. It was their badge in the underworld. He couldn't believe he was involved in the case.

The agents and Tait had coffee and planned the morning. Tait was reserved with Bobitt. Bobitt was reserved with Tait. The agents left and parked their surveillance camera around the corner from the Oakland clubhouse an hour before Tait arrived.

"These things last three or four hours," McKinley briefed Bobitt. "You have a receiver on and hear a squelch. When he starts to arrive, you hear the transmitter fading in stronger and stronger. In receiving distance, you would hear him: radio music and him talking to us."

Bobitt had never listened to a WesCOM and expected it to be a heavy tribunal. The meeting started at 10:00. At 10:15, the transmitter was still quiet. At 10:40, McKinley packed up for the day. The transmitter was broken.

Tait reported later what was discussed at the meeting. Bobby (Dirt) England announced he would get married in the Oakland clubhouse on June 6. A motion was tabled to expel from the club any member who injected drugs, regardless of whether he was alive or dead. Oakland Hells Angel James Frank (Guinea) Colucci was going through the out-takes of the Hells Angels movie *Angels Forever, Forever Angels* and had already burned half of the footage. The Vancouver chapter reported that the Rebels were a hangaround club, with 43 members in four chapters in Moose Jaw, Saskatchewan, and Calgary and Edmonton in Alberta.

Barger approached Tait when the meeting ended and invited him home to see his dog. Tait said he'd pick it up Monday. Tait had lunch with Fuki Fukushima, who told him he had many Motorola walkie-talkies stolen from movie sets. Fuki also said he was moving to Oakland from San Francisco that month.

Tait drove to Barger's house on Monday to pick up his rottweiller puppy, which he named Gretchen. Barger gave him a phony receipt for $450. Barger told Tait he was proud to have him in the club because he was clean-

cut, took care of business, put the club first and foremost
and went places and did things that he need not do but
did so for the club. He told Tait he was what the Hells
Angel of the '90s was about. "You're everything a Hells
Angel should be." McKinley roared with laughter in the
surveillance van across the street. "Yeah. An FBI agent."

He shut up quickly and turned down the volume on
the receiver as Sharon Barger walked Heidi and Eubar
past the van.

McKinley knew he would spend more than $3,000
to board the dog with a professional trainer while Tait
was on the road. He didn't want anything to happen to
the animal. He wanted to keep Tait in Barger's good
books.

Former Oakland Hells Angel Terry Dalton, expelled
in April 1986 after 15 years in the club, was arrested in
May for assault with a deadly weapon, felon in possession of a concealable firearm and receiving stolen property. FBI Special Agents Jay Colvin and Robert Barnes
interviewed him to gather information that would help
direct Operation CACUS. To establish his bona fides,
Dalton told them 10 things about the Hells Angels that
an outsider would not know. Dalton also said one of the
Vallejo Hells Angels who killed Billy Grondalski and his
wife and children was Gerald Butch Lester, whose case is
still before the courts.

Although the voucher saga took up an inordinate
amount of McKinley's time and energy, he managed to
inject humor in the situation in a memorandum to
Senior Special Agent Keith Berry, resident agent in
Hayward.

As discussed in our telcal of 05/22/87, the FBIHQ
green airtel you require was mis-directed. A copy
thereof is attached here. It is a poor copy but the
date and amount ($20,000) can be made out.

Inasmuch as FBIHQ does not have a copy of the
greenie either (we tried to get one), I submit that
rightfully the funds now belong to me. I will see

that they are removed from the trial balance of the
direct funding. (Just kidding).

U.S. attorneys and FBI agents from all areas where Hells
Angels were being investigated, including ATF Special
Agent Ted Baltas, Karen Sanderson of WSIN and Steve
Graham, head of the Presidential Organized Crime Drug
Enforcement Task Force, met in Santa Rosa on May 27
and 28 to discuss Operation CACUS. Sanderson had had
access to all CACUS reports since February and drew
charts that hung on the wall. An FBI agent asked, "How
do we know we can trust her?"

"I've known her for four years," McKinley replied.
"I've given her information. I've tested her. She's never
given anyone anything. I personally believe I can trust
her."

Sanderson wasn't deterred by the doubts. She listened to the agents talk about all the information they
got from this guy inside the Hells Angels. Steve Graham,
whose job it was to guide Operation CACUS through
legal quagmires, argued vehemently against prosecuting
the Hells Angels on the murder conspiracy charge under
the Racketeer Influenced and Corrupt Organizations
(RICO) statute, which was drafted to combat traditional
organized crime. The statute requires prosecutors to
prove a gang operates as a criminal organization and
shares profits among its members. The Hells Angels
Motorcycle Club is structured, under the advice of
lawyers, to avoid RICO prosecutions, the law they most
fear.

The Hells Angels are truthful when they say they are
not a criminal organization. Rather, they are an organization of criminals. They go out of their way to maintain a
barrier between the Hells Angels as a club and the Hells
Angels as a business. Criminal matters are discussed
among members of many cliques within the gang.
Whereas individual Hells Angels have been convicted of
criminal offenses committed through use of fear, intimidation and connections generated by membership in the

gang, the club itself has yet to be prosecuted successfully.

The only attempt to prosecute the Hells Angels Motorcycle Club under the RICO statute was a dismal and embarrassing failure by a group of ill-prepared prosecutors. In June 1979 the government charged 32 people, including most of the Oakland chapter and Sonny Barger and his wife, Sharon, with violating the statute. The indictment, the most comprehensive ever compiled against the gang until then, alleged that the Hells Angels dealt in drugs, weapons and death.

"The cornerstone of this illegal drug enterprise was the large-scale manufacture and mass distribution of methamphetamine, also known as speed and crank," U.S. Attorney G. William Hunter said.

"The club's by-laws clearly spell out that members will engage in distribution of drugs of a specified quantity and quality in order to remain members," Jerome Jenson, regional director of the Drug Enforcement Administration, said.

"Federal sources" told newspapers the case against the gang was "airtight." Barger's bail was set at $1-million.

Sonny Barger led the Hells Angels through their wildest and toughest times as chapters became involved in multi-million-dollar operations and embarked on a course of success that any corporate executive would envy.

"I can tell you why they want to get rid of the Hells Angels," Barger said in San Francisco county jail in 1979. "First of all, we're a virtual army. We're all across the country, and now we're in foreign countries also. And they have no idea how many of us there are. We have money, many allies that are outlaw bikers that are not Hells Angels that would probably do anything we asked them to if something happened. Like a revolution, or anything like that.

"They know we're basically the most probably well-armed people in the United States. We've never took a political stance on anything other than that one time on the VDC [the Vietnam War protest march in California in October 1965] and at that time I thought we were right, but I've done 180 degrees on that since. And I think that scares the authorities—this untold number of people that really have no fear of dying for what they believe in. And they're armed."

Barger accused the government of being against the Hells Angels ever since the club started. "They tried to paint us as rowdies, you know. We're sort of against society, or whatever, just drink beer and tough guys that didn't get along with anybody. And when that didn't work, it changed to marijuana-smoking-crazed, you know. And when that didn't work, then it became drug dealing . . . They needed something to go after that's visible. And we're a highly visible group."

He added that while the government feared and hated Hells Angels, the public loved the wild ones. "I think we probably stand for what the majority of people would like to be . . . Maybe they have a vision that at least once they'd like to just get on a motorcycle and roar down the street and somebody would sneer at them and they'd punch them in the nose."

Four months into the trial of 18 Hells Angels—half of those charged—Judge Conti harshly criticized prosecutors for their poor witnesses and threatened to throw the case out of court. "It's a big waste of time to listen to witnesses like this. If this was solely the evidence, I would grant an acquittal."

The jury began deliberations after eight months of testimony by more than a hundred prosecution witnesses who accused the Hells Angels of threatening and murdering to protect a lucrative speed, heroin, LSD and cocaine business. The defense argued that individual Angels committed crimes without gang support or endorsement. Barger told the court he used and sold heroin and other drugs during the 1960s, and such matters were his "personal affair," not those of the club. He swayed the jury.

Judge Conti declared a mistrial in July 1980 after the jury announced it couldn't reach a verdict on 32 of 44 charges against 18 defendants.

Sonny Barger's bail was dropped to $100,000 and he was a free man after spending 14 months in jail. The government dropped charges against him and his wife "in the interest of justice."

Undaunted prosecuting attorneys restructured their case against 11 Hells Angels and were back in court in October. A federal district judge declared a mistrial in February 1981 when a jury failed to reach a verdict. The government dismissed all charges the next day.

Jurors in both trials were bothered by attempts to convict an organization. They were also disturbed that prosecution witnesses were granted immunity for serious crimes in return for testimony. One former Hells Angel was given $54,000 and immunity for six murders.

"They let these people off, people who committed more crimes than the people they were trying. I felt I just couldn't believe them," said William Aylward, a juror who voted for acquittal.

Government lawyers estimated the cost of trying to convict the club was somewhere between $4-million and $7-million. Defense lawyers pegged the price tag at $10-million to $20-million.

As she listened to Graham and McKinley duel over whether the Hells Angels should be prosecuted under the RICO statute in San Francisco, Sanderson felt she must speak up. "I just don't understand this. For the first time since I've been working motorcycle gangs, you guys have someone who's inside the Hells Angels who's actually a member of the Hells Angels. We've been saying that these guys are a Racketeer Influenced and Corrupt Organization that's self-perpetuating; that they're organized crime. If we can't prove this with someone inside giving us information, then we ought to stop saying it."

Graham looked long at Sanderson. "Karen, you just don't understand juries in San Francisco."

Graham spoke from experience. He knew he could

prosecute drug charges against individual Hells Angels in San Francisco, but the gang was an integral and sacrosanct part of the city's anything-goes culture. Few San Franciscans would bad-mouth the Hells Angels, let alone convict a legend. California is the land of fruits and nuts and San Francisco got a double scoop.

Steve Graham was hired as a staff attorney for the Presidential Organized Crime Drug Enforcement Task Force in 1983. When the task force coordinator for the northwest region returned to private practice in 1986, Graham got the job and responsibility for Operation CACUS. The task force is a separately funded and organized arm of the Department of Justice under the supervision of the U.S. Attorney in San Francisco. Graham had a staff of 10 lawyers in San Francisco who worked drug cases in the northern district of California. He was also responsible for seven other districts, in California, Oregon, Washington, Alaska, Hawaii and Guam. Graham coordinated all drug investigations in these areas. Because he had the authority to approve or disapprove investigations, he prevented agents from tripping over each other. Graham was one of the few people who had the big picture. Nothing happened without him knowing.

He handled the legal end of Operation CACUS for the agents and gave them counsel. He coordinated contacts with other regions. He imposed an absolute need-to-know on the operation, and even people in his office were kept in the dark until several weeks before CACUS went overt and they needed to prepare warrants and other legal paperwork.

One of Graham's most important tasks was to ensure that the four key investigators acted legally and did nothing to jeopardize the investigation. He didn't want anyone taking action that would impede tactics and strategy for litigation.

Graham was adamant that all charges be acted on individually. There would be no RICO fiasco in this investigation. Graham was too familiar with the court history of the Hells Angels, whose trials had turned into successes for the Hells Angels because dozens of lawyers and defendants made them unwieldy. Graham saw CACUS was a solid investigation with high-quality evidence and a witness beyond reproach, and he didn't want to risk that for a chance to prosecute the Hells Angels Motorcycle Club, though he thought the case could be won. He preferred to send as many individuals to jail as possible.

McKinley wouldn't back down. He wanted to take down entire chapters, if not the whole club. Graham understood, and sympathized with McKinley's desire. After all, the Hells Angels always did their time and slipped right back into the club when they got out of prison. If the club could be eliminated, the Hells Angels would lose their power base. Graham also wanted to see the Oakland chapter wiped out. Its members set the pace for the whole club's criminal activities. It had the best drug manufacturers and, according to former members who testified against the club, many killers. Graham overruled McKinley, but suggested he try for a RICO prosecution against the club once individual CACUS cases were dealt with.

By the end of the meeting in Santa Rosa, Sanderson's performance and charts had put to rest all doubts anyone had about her.

"You know," an FBI agent told her, "it would take us six months to a year to get a product back from headquarters. That's why they went outside the FBI for analysis."

Kentucky U.S. Attorney Cleve Gambill volunteered to prosecute the murder conspiracy case against the Hells Angels in Louisville. The jury there was more likely to be conservative and God-fearing rather than flaky and Angel-fearing. Jury polls in Louisville show the favorite television shows are *Andy Griffith* and *Donahue*; the favorite book is the Bible. These people were not likely to be impressed by shows of bravado by defendants or spectators. All drug, weapon and explosive charges against individual Hells Angels would be prosecuted in the jurisdictions where the charges were laid.

Attendees at the meeting then tried to fix a price for
the EPIC manual Barger mailed to Kentucky and later
supplied to Tait. If the value could be set over $100,
Barger's actions could be prosecuted as a felony. They
asked Wade Gardner, who prepared the EPIC manual,
and polled a cross-section of law enforcement officials. A
California Attorney General's report stated someone
offered to pay $50,000 for information in the depart-
ment's files about the Hells Angels. During the RICO trials from 1979 to 1981, the Hells Angels paid $100,000 for
police reports on the gang stamped "Confidential,"
"Secret" and "For official eyes only" and sent copies to all
chapters. The meeting decided to go after Barger big time.

Early in June, Marischen instructed Tait to call Hells
Angel William (Mr. Bill) Coldren to ask if he had
obtained explosives from the "guy up north" so Tait
could pick them up at the South Run in Hartsville, South
Carolina, mid-month. He had not.

Tim Bobitt monitored his first West Coast Officers'
Meeting on Saturday, June 6. The WesCOM was at the
San Francisco clubhouse, south of the Bay Bridge and up
from the water. It was a foggy, miserable day. The agents
got to their perch atop an abandoned building at 7:30
a.m., three and a half hours before the meeting was to
start. They couldn't chance being seen on the street later
in the morning. The agents put their gear in bags and pretended to be workmen; Bobitt was scruffy enough. They
trudged up flight after flight of stairs, exited through a
small storage shed onto the gravel roof, braced the door
to prevent surprises and set up the receiver. They shivered while they waited for the sun to burn off the fog.

The donuts provided by the San Francisco chapter
were inferior as usual. But something happened before
the meeting to take Tait's mind off donuts. The
WesCOM sergeant-at-arms, Chicago Joe Scotella from
Richmond, said he would step down and told Tait the

job was his if he wanted it. Tait was nominated and acclaimed. Two and a half years after signing on as an FBI informant, Tait was one of the top four Hells Angels officers on the West Coast—a position that would open countless doors and give him access to the club's most closely held secrets.

Tait drank coffee in the clubhouse. He knew the agents were miserable on the roof. In a style that had become his trademark, he walked to a quiet corner and talked to them over the transmitter. "Boy, it sure is cold and wet out there, isn't it? I'm sitting here and it's nice and warm and I've got some coffee. I've got a nice donut here."

Halfway through the meeting, the agents heard a door open and close. Then they heard a tinkle.

"Ahhhh, this feels good. I'm going back to have a cup of coffee. It's nice and toasty and warm in here."

It was near impossible to piss on the roof, since the wall around the edge was only three feet high.

Back in the clubhouse, a motion was tabled to ensure Hells Angels could party with abandon while on the road. It seems that brotherhood among the Hells Angels does not come from the heart, but is a fickle creature prodded along with carrots and sticks.

As Hells Angels, we pride ourselves in the fact that we are self-reliant as a group and can depend on one another—no matter what the circumstances. This fact, which is the cornerstone of our brotherhood, is all the more important when it is needed to provide protection from outside influences.

Never is this more evident than when we are on a run. The purpose of these gatherings is to relax with one another, exchange ideas and be ourselves, in an environment void of criticism and safe from external threat. Traditionally, the "gate watches" have allowed us these safe environments and without them any manner of adverse situations could, and would, occur.

Therefore, since these "gate watches" are impera-

tive to our safety, and failure to stand a watch as
scheduled is contrary to our basic code of self-
reliance, the following is herewith proposed:

PROPOSAL . . .
1. A gate watch list must be prominently posted by
   host charter at the onset of each run.
2. It is the responsibility of each charter to know
   when and where they are scheduled to pull a
   watch.
3. If any charter fails to report for their watch as
   originally scheduled, or to make prior arrangements to switch with another charter, that a fine
   of $500 be levied by California, to be paid to the
   California treasury at the following OM.

Oakland Hells Angel Bobby England got married in the
Oakland clubhouse that afternoon. Tait told England his
gift to the couple was a videotape of the wedding and
reception. His handlers equipped him with a video camera in which the On light was disconnected to allow Tait
to surreptitiously tape the party. This allowed him to
interview people and tape them doing coke.

Tait left the reception at 10:30 and returned to his
Hyatt Regency room. Tim Bobitt and Jay Colvin followed
him. They waited for Tait to settle in before going up to
visit and discuss the afternoon's events. It was not common practice. They usually phoned Tait first to say they
were coming up. But it was late, they were tired from a
long surveillance and they knew where most Hells
Angels were. They were also curious about the wild wedding. Bobitt called the room. Tait told him to come up
and he'd give him the videotapes.

Bobitt and Colvin entered the elevator and pressed
the button for the twentieth floor. The elevator stopped
on the seventh, the door opened—and their hearts leapt
to their throats. Bobby England, in Hells Angels colors
and stinking drunk, stood before them. He glared at the
two men in the elevator. Bobitt had never seen England

and didn't know who he was. He thought the game was up and the guy was on his way to kill Tait. "This is it," Bobitt thought. "Show your hand. We're going to shoot it out."

England stepped in and went to press the button for Tait's floor. The button was already lit. The agents didn't budge. The elevator went up. When the door opened, the agents went right, England went left. England, it turned out, had booked the honeymoon suite on Tait's floor.

At Oakland church the next evening, Sonny Barger was upset with the kind of women some Hells Angels brought to parties. He talked about a woman named Cathy who stayed with various members and stole Hells Angels T-shirts. Barger said she was "touched up" by Richmond Hells Angels. "We, as a club, are really, really getting fucking loose with bringing women to the clubhouse and to members' houses," he said. "Especially women. You get out. You start having a good time. You pick up a fucking cunt and, believe you me, what I'm worried about more than stealing is bringing a cop.

"But at any rate, it's lucky this one was a thief and not a cop. Whenever the police get enough [sense] to send a woman in without a man with her, we're all gonna be in prison."

Barger talked about San Bernardino Hells Angel Aristeo (Mexican Art) Carbajal, who thought he might soon be arrested. "There's a guy from another charter in the United States that would rather not be seen by certain people out there. And he hasn't been for quite a while. And we need to take up a collection to help him keep from being seen, and we need $1,000. I think you know who I'm talking about. The guy got jacked up by the cops the other day and got away."

A week later, Tait rented a car at the Paducah, Kentucky, airport and drove to Fulton, where he planned to get the percussion blasting caps John Curry had offered during Fulton church. He called Curry from a pay phone and was invited to his house, half a mile

from the clubhouse. Tait talked to Ken Marischen and
Kevin Wevodau over his transmitter as he drove to
Curry's house.

TAIT:	Pulling onto 924 West. Atop the second hill across from the church. Across the street from the church. There's supposed to be John Curry's house. There's the Baptist church, Crutchfield Missionary Baptist Church.
CURRY:	How ya doin' brother?
TAIT:	Good to see ya.
CURRY:	Good to see you, too. Come on in. Warm out, isn't it?
TAIT:	Yeah. I just listenin' to the radio. Said it was gonna get down to 72 degrees today.
CURRY:	The other night when I talked to you, you said you talked to some people back home and they told you what's kinda goin' on out here.
TAIT:	Yeah.
CURRY:	About the heat.
TAIT:	Yeah. With Richmond.
CURRY:	I didn't want to say too much even over that other number. I might be able to help you out a little bit. I bought some things here. Just in case you need something right now. That's Missy and Tommy's boy.
TAIT:	Oh, yeah?
CURRY:	Their little boy. I got two of mine runnin' around here, too. Went to a water slide yesterday. I come off one of the slides and it pulled my shorts down. And I couldn't get

> my feet down underneath me. I
> was tryin' to get my shorts up. It
> like to drowned me.

They walked out to Tait's car.

TAIT: Watch out when you get ready to
sit down 'cause I left my knife on
the seat there somewhere.

CURRY: There it is. Yeah, I brought up
some of them coupling caps.
Couple packs of them. And trip
flares. The main thing everybody
was concerned about if anything
was gonna go, they wanted to
make sure that, the ones that I
talked to, wanted to make sure
that nothing was goin' on before,
you know . . .

TAIT: No. Nothin's gonna happen
before U.S.A. Run. As a matter of
fact, it'll be more than a month
afterwards. Is this the clubhouse
right there?

CURRY: Yeah. If I can help you with what
we talked about before. I can get
you the booby traps if you want
real military-issue booby traps.

TAIT: Next ECOM's gonna be in July.
Think we could have it all
squared away by then? What I
wanna do is take it from here up
to where I got a bunch of other
stuff stashed. It's up north.

CURRY: So you don't want what I got right
now, buddy?

TAIT: Yeah. I'll take what you got.

Tait pulled to the side of the road a few minutes

from Curry's house and checked the blasting caps he was given during the three-mile drive to ensure they wouldn't blow up in the car. He drove back to Paducah and handed them over to the FBI.

Eleven

On Wednesday, June 17, Mike Lessard from Oakland told Tait in code that he had explosives.

LESSARD: We kind of miss you down here. Are you scared to come down and party or what? I can hear your knees sound like castanets right over the phone.

TAIT: You're right. That's exactly right.

LESSARD: Don't be so scarce.

TAIT: Okay, you got it. I'll try to come down there real quick.

LESSARD: Like when?

TAIT: The next couple of days or something?

LESSARD: If you're not scared.

TAIT: If I'm not scared.

They both laughed.

Tait made plans with ATF Special Agent Ted Baltas, who would monitor the explosives deal, and then called Tim McKinley to inform him he'd be in Oakland. McKinley ordered him to fly first class to get some sleep.

"Think about how that's going to look in court," Tait replied.

"Fine, think about how your body's going to look in a body bag. You're no good to us unless you're rested. Take a first-class flight, get your butt rested and get down here."

Tait met Lessard at the Oakland Airport Hilton the day after their phone call. They had lunch in the hotel restaurant, then got into Lessard's black Chevy pickup and drove to the back of the building to Tait's parked car.

TAIT:	Okay. You brought me a couple of pounds of green sausage?
LESSARD:	Yeah.
TAIT:	And you got caps?
LESSARD:	Two caps. Listen, there's an extra bag on the seat right there. Usually it's always recommended to double cap it with two loaves or two pounds. That's not enough insurance for me. Can you wait about seven days or so? I'll get this cash. I'll get you some more caps or whatever you want.
TAIT:	Sure, sure. I've got to go to Europe the middle of next week. I'll be back down for the next OM.
LESSARD:	Okay, that's fine. See, like I ordered about 25 pounds.
TAIT:	Twenty-five pounds?
LESSARD:	Yeah. And probably about 25 pounds and about 60 caps.

Once alone, Tait talked to his handlers. "Okay, fellows.

Let's get the fuck out of here. If you can see this big red handkerchief that I've got here, it's got the caps. One in my shirt pocket here. I'm going to be turning off the Panasonic now."

Lessard had cut all but one of the dateshift codes off the commercial grade Touex plastic explosive he gave Tait so it could not be traced. All explosives are coded to help track makers, sellers and buyers. He also sprayed and wiped the explosives with Armorall to remove his fingerprints.

A week later, Special Agent in Charge Jerome Smith of the California Bureau of Narcotic Enforcement, along with Special Agent Supervisor Mike Harman and Special Agent Tim Bobitt, met with the FBI's Assistant Special Agent in Charge Barry Mawn and Special Agent McKinley in San Francisco to sign a formal agreement between the two agencies in regards to BNE's role and participation in Operation CACUS.

The BNE would provide one full-time special agent plus more special agents as needed for surveillance and execution of search and arrest warrants. The FBI would provide one or more special agents who would gather evidence, provide security for Tait and assist in surveillance. The FBI would be primarily responsible for expenses, including funds for Tait to purchase narcotics, though BNE might provide some supplemental funding when requested.

The agents who handled CACUS used every opportunity to gain insight into the Hells Angels and their criminal enterprises and to seek new avenues to approach and ensnare them. While Tait pursued the social circuit of active and upwardly mobile Hells Angels, the agents picked the brains of jailed members who informed on the club. Tait was not told about all these debriefing sessions or the information they garnered. The agents learned facts Tait would not have known and he could have jeopardized the case had he let them slip during a conversation.

Hells Angel informants are a relatively new phenomenon. They were virtually unheard of until the 1980s. Informants are a direct result of the increased violence among Hells Angels as a greater number of members began to import, manufacture and distribute drugs. Aggressive Hells Angels started to drive away and kill off those who weren't good for business—those who didn't generate money for them. Greed slowly supplanted the brotherhood that bound the men who first formed the Hells Angels. By the mid-1980s, the embraces and hugs, once demonstrations of brotherly love, became ways to check if someone wore a bodypack transmitter or recorder.

As the Hells Angels instilled fear even among longstanding and violent members, rejected Angels turned to law enforcement for protection and vengeance. They traded their knowledge for the promise of safety. They knew that the sooner they rolled after being arrested, the more valuable their information was because it was current and useful.

The Hells Angels held their World Run in Haarlem, Holland, from June 21 to 27. Their World Meeting was held on June 26. Tait was there.

It was politics as usual. The Amsterdam chapter brought up the Rio de Janeiro chapter for missing three World Meetings in a row. The issue could cost the Rio chapter its charter. Hells Angel officers complained that Rio Hells Angels constantly asked for money to solve problems rather than show initiative and take care of them on their own. The officers wanted the begging to stop. Amsterdam asked where the money went from the European Defense Fund. Switzerland said it went to the right place.

The Kent, England, chapter warned anyone who planned to attend the Kent Bike Show to watch out for the Road Rats Motorcycle Club, which caused problems for Hells Angels. The West Coast, England, chapter reported that no more "Free the Angels" T-shirts would be given to non-members, as the U.S.A. trademark registration did not apply to England and unprotected use of club logos could lead to their loss.

The Vienna chapter reported that a member was kicked out in bad standing at the World Run after he stole T-shirts and drugs from the concession trailer at the run site. The Hamburg chapter warned that it still had problems with the Supreme Court, which had banned neo-Nazi groups, and asked Hells Angels who traveled to Germany to do so incognito. They also asked visitors to prove membership with photos and telephone numbers.

The Copenhagen chapter reported that it had completed a documentary about the club after five years of work. Copies were made available to members. The Armagh, Ireland, chapter thanked everyone who attended its party and said the problem of the Halloween rapes had been resolved. The Halifax, Canada, chapter tabled a motion that required all Hells Angels to own Harley-Davidsons within three years.

The World Run was a mix of drugs, broads and shooting and knife-throwing competitions. Dozens of Hells Angels failed to hit a pop can at 20 yards with a Rossi .22-caliber rifle fitted with a Parker-Hale silencer. When Tait picked up the gun, he noticed it lacked the leaf that held up the rear sight, so the bullets whizzed high above the target. He aimed well below the can and smacked it into the air. The Angels thought him a master marksman and word of his abilities quickly spread.

Meanwhile, the agents discussed strategies for drug buys. At one point, Bobitt wanted to go into the case as an undercover agent. That way, he could drive Tait around. But Bobitt was known in the Bay Area, so they discussed getting an agent from somewhere else. They decided the case moved so smoothly and quickly that a new face would stall the operation while the agent established his credentials with the Hells Angels, who had just gone through Operation Roughrider and were on their guard against undercover agents.

The agents devised ways to make their drug buys watertight. They knew defense lawyers would look for any crack in the operation to stick their legal pry bars into, so they planned to have all drug buys witnessed by agents and had to be careful that surveillance vehicles were not spotted. The Hells Angels were wary of narcs, but they let their defenses down when they dealt with each other. The agents would record all buys through Tait's transmitter and his pocket microcassette recorder. They would photograph and videotape buys and Tait going into and coming out of buildings. They would search Tait before he went in to make a buy to ensure he didn't have drugs on him, so defense lawyers couldn't allege that Tait didn't buy drugs from their clients but merely pulled them from his pocket when he left their houses. They would search Tait's car to ensure no drugs were hidden in it to curtail similar defense strategies. They would take a statement from Tait immediately after a buy. They didn't want to give defense lawyers the opportunity to create doubt in jurors' minds.

Then they developed a general strategy for Tait's drug buys. Crank was much cheaper in California than farther north, so his profit margin was bigger. If questioned why he bought from several Hells Angels, Tait could say he picked up what he could while he could.

The agents crafted a way to present Tait to the club as a street-smart and successful drug dealer. His image was shaped slowly to give him the ambience of a man who did something below board and reaped the benefits. Tait wore his own heavy gold-nugget jewelry all the time. He gave gifts unique to Alaska to prominent Hells Angels—polar-bear teeth. The Angels are the underworld's boy scouts; they like to plaster their colors with pins and badges. Tait got a lot of bounce from his Death's Head lapel pin carved out of ivory. When the Hells Angels had a party at a restaurant, Tait ordered three entrees and sampled from each one. Then he'd buy two or three bottles of wine for the party. The only kind of unemployed people with that kind of money are drug dealers. The drug cookers and dealers in the Hells Angels took notice. Here was a man they would like as a customer. They knew him to keep his mouth shut. They knew him to respect their secrecy and not pry into their business. Because they considered Tait reliable, they told him what they did.

Tait's security was paramount on drug buys. The agents were constantly vigilant for anything that could compromise him. They were in such a constant state of awareness that they worried when they saw the same people twice in the course of an afternoon. They took turns watching each other's backs. Bobitt knew McKinley had a family and a shaky marriage to keep together, so he volunteered for weekend operations. But it was difficult to keep McKinley the workaholic away.

The agents and Tait had three or four cars at drug buys, including surveillance cars and chase cars to follow Tait to and from the buy site.

To maintain security, Tait and the agents met in secret places. No one wanted to be seen with Tait. The world gets small at times and the odds were high of someone in the Bay Area recognizing Tait and the same person together. An agent would stop in an indoor parking lot and Tait would hop into his car. They would drive to another city to talk in a motel or public place while two other agents carried out counter-surveillance. BNE brought in nine other agents to help watch Tait during buys. They weren't told he was an informant; they thought it was routine surveillance of a bad guy.

McKinley was experienced with electronic surveillance and knew how easily Hells Angels could get access to phone records. The agents and Tait used only public phones and pagers. They flew on separate planes because the Hells Angels regularly gained access to airline computers to check passenger lists and flight schedules.

Sometimes after a drug buy, the agents and Tait would go to a restaurant. They scouted the place out before they entered and had a cover story that they were friends in case they ran into someone they knew. Hells

Angels must inform the chapter in any city they visit that they are in town. When the agents and Tait said they were "hot," it meant the Hells Angels knew he was around. If they were "cold," then he had not told the Hells Angels where he was. Despite their precautions, they were always wary that someone was watching. They feared most the one element they could not plan for: the unknown.

The agents and Tait grew close as they worked long hours. They lost friends. McKinley's family life suffered. Baltas was dumped on by his superiors, who wanted quick results. But their devotion to secrecy was so deeply ingrained that they shrugged off the complaints and abandonments by friends and buried themselves in the case.

The weekend beginning Friday, July 10, was profitable for Tait and his handlers. By Friday night, Tait had already bought two pounds of crank from Hells Angels. The agents had determined that Tait could contact Oakland Hells Angel Werner (Krusi) Sohm at his house and arrange to buy a pound of crank that night or the next day. Sohm was an easygoing guy, more like a kid in a man's body. He loved to build and race motorcycles, drink and pick up women. He was a happy-go-lucky slob who drag-raced under the auspices of the Hells Angels all over California. Sohm built a prototype motor mount on which a motorcycle could be fastened to test its engine. He first made it out of wood, then metal. He sold the patent to Harley-Davidson.

McKinley and BNE agent Thomas Moore searched Tait and his car for drugs at 10:30. They checked the transmitter broadcast to the receiver/recorder in McKinley's car. BNE supervisor Mike Harman gave Tait $13,000 to buy the crank. McKinley and Moore took up their surveillance post near Sohm's house at 10:50. Ten minutes later, Harman followed Tait to Sohm's house and drove by as Tait pulled in.

Tait was greeted by Sohm's wife, Inga. After small talk, Tait told Sohm he wanted to buy a pound of crank. Sohm told him he was cooking crank but didn't have any available. Sohm said he hated to cook crank because every time he did, it took two years off his life. When he cooked, he assembled his lab and made 100 pounds before he tore it down and moved it. The lab was stored in five or six storage lockers in a 300-mile radius. His laboratory equipment was stainless steel and supplied by a friend of Oakland Hells Angel Big Steve Brown.

Sohm said he knew two guys who just might have a few pounds lying around. They drove to Big Steve Brown's house to look for a pound of crank or a man called Roy who might have some. They returned to Sohm's house empty-handed and Sohm promised he'd find some. He told Tait to call him at 11:00 the next morning to set up the deal. Tait drove away at 12:30 a.m. to the designated spot where he met his handlers and turned over the money. Tait returned to his hotel room to shower and relax. The agents scrambled to secure the day's tape recordings and prepare surveillance for the next buy.

Tait called Sohm at 11 a.m. on Saturday and was invited over. McKinley and Bobitt parked their beat-up surveillance camper near Sohm's house at 11:30 and waited. Tait and his car were once again searched for drugs. Harman once again gave him $13,000 in buy money. Then, with BNE Special Agent Robert Nishiyama, he followed Tait to Sohm's house to ensure he didn't stop along the way.

Tait and Sohm chatted. Inga made breakfast and they watched TV.

Tait asked, "You think this guy'll be here soon?"

"Yeah," Sohm said.

They talked about Tait's visit to Holland for the World Run.

TAIT:	Pee Wee was really upset while we were over there.
SOHM:	Why?

TAIT: 'Cause he said it wasn't like he
             was breaking any laws when he
             went and bought a bag of crank
             over the fuckin' counter. He said
             it just bummed him out. It wasn't
             like he was doin' somethin' ille-
             gal. It was like it was okay and
             what was the big deal about doin'
             it if it's okay? He was really
             bummed out and that was the
             whole deal. That's one of the rea-
             sons he likes to do drugs, 'cause
             it's against the law.

SOHM: They have good crank over there
             too. That was my main thing.
             Teach somebody.

By 1:00 it was so hot in the van that Bobitt stripped to
his soggy T-shirt. McKinley dripped sweat. His eyes
bugged out and his hair was a mess. They listened to Tait
laugh and eat and drink and have a good time. The
agents expected Tait to leave when the deal didn't go
down quickly. And just when they expected or hoped
Tait would leave, he got asked to lunch and accepted.
Then they settled in to watch the Indy 500. It was
European hospitality at its best—nothing rushed and a
lot of talk. Bobitt swore. McKinley got desperate and
looked at his partner.

"Tim, I'm so sorry. I'm so sorry I got you into this."
"Let's just go in there and get him," said Bobitt.
Tait and Sohm continued to watch television.

TAIT: Well, why don't you call that bas-
             tard and make sure he didn't get
             back to sleep.

SOHM: He's on the way. No answer no
             more.

TAIT: Ahhh. Goot, goot. I'm just gonna
             give him ten, what the hell.

SOHM: The guy'll get a slap in the face.

TAIT: Yeah, for makin' me wait so long.

Tait counted out the money.

TAIT: Goddamn. What's that American shit doing? Probably took that broad right home and decided to hump her there one time.

SOHM: Probably go to the hot tub in between.

TAIT: Fuck that hot tub. I'd take a goddamn chainsaw to that motherfucker, man. That's what I told I might do with our hot tub at the clubhouse in Anchorage. We got a big hot tub in there.

SOHM: You got a hot tub at your clubhouse?

TAIT: Eight-hundred gallon.

SOHM: Yeah?

TAIT: Yeah.

SOHM: Must be party, huh?

TAIT: Oh, man. Jesus Christ. They get a bunch of broads over there and they got this game they play called diving for dildoes. They got a box of fuckin' 30 or 40 dildoes underneath it. Underneath the bunk there. They got 'em floatin' around in that thing. I told them, "You keep it clean or I'll come in here with a fuckin' chainsaw and chainsaw this son of a bitch up."

I went in there one day, there's fuckin' shit floatin' all around. There's some cigarette butts in it, man. I said, "Fuck you guys, man."

SOHM: Fuckin' AIDS floatin' in there.
TAIT: Yeah. A herpe pit.

Sohm left the house for 10 minutes and returned with a book of recipes for the crank chemist. He gave Tait copies. By the end of the Indianapolis 500, Sohm said the deal would take another hour and a half. Tait had another iced tea and sandwich. Sohm drove away at 4:30 in his red jogging suit with the letters "AFFA" (Angels Forever, Forever Angels) on the sleeve and returned with a plastic bag of crank.

"Here's twelve," Tait said. "You want me to count it for you?"

"No. You want a coffee can or something to put it in?"

"For this? You got another zip-lock bag?"

Sohm counted his cut—$500—out of the money Tait gave him and placed it on his desk. He pocketed the rest. Tait walked out of the house and into his car. "Holy shit. Okay, listen. He was real suspicious about the fuckin' van. You might as well stay in position for a while. He's getting ready to leave and go to the shop to work."

As the chase team followed Tait to his hotel, McKinley and Bobitt raced to the nearest store. They didn't care about Tait—they thought they were going to die. They were soaked with sweat and dehydrated. They jumped out of the van and Bobitt fought McKinley to get in the door. They ran to the refrigerator at the back of the store. McKinley grabbed three jugs of water.

"You pay for them." He ran out the door with the jugs.

Bobitt struggled to get his hand into his wet pocket. He pulled out some soggy bills, threw them on the counter and ran out. He got frightened when he saw McKinley, who had poured water down his throat and over his head. He could barely talk. If his eyes were opened any wider, they would have rolled out of their sockets. He shook his head and looked at Bobitt.

"This is the closest I've ever come to dying."

"Leave it to the FBI. You can't take a few hours of surveillance."

They drove to the hotel where Tait greeted them as he coolly sipped a soda. "I had a lovely afternoon."

Bobitt grabbed Tait by the neck and shook him. They would never again be reserved with each other. Bobitt and McKinley posed for a photograph with Tait and the pound of crank he had bought from Sohm.

Rumblings spread through the East Coast that Tait pushed several Hells Angels and chapters hard to assemble what seemed to be a lot of explosives. East Coast chapters said they didn't mind if Anchorage took care of business, but they didn't want it done in their back yard. More and more, the Hells Angels have become the suburbanites of the underworld. They say everyone is free to do anything, but somewhere else. Tait picked up the dissension and talked to several Hells Angels before and after the East Coast Officers' Meeting hosted by the Salem chapter in Lynn, Massachusetts, in July. The day before, he had approached Dale L. Matheny, sergeant-at-arms of the Fulton County, Kentucky, chapter, and tried to quell some of the rumors that circulated about his arms-gathering expeditions.

Tait then flew into San Francisco, where he visited Oakland Hells Angel Mike Lessard at home and made arrangements to buy a bomb and explosives from him. Lessard said he would sell part of the explosives to Tait and give the rest as his contribution to the plot to kill Outlaws.

Tait then visited Oakland Hells Angel Mark Perry under the pretext of looking for another member. Perry is believed to have killed at least five people. They talked in Perry's back yard, where he had two cedar rounds nailed back to back, which he used as a knife- and axe-throwing target. Vehicle camouflage was rigged over the back yard between the garage and the house—Perry called it his "anti-helicopter net." He told Tait he wanted to be involved in the retaliation on the Outlaws.

"Yeah, I want to get in on it. I've got all kinds of weapons."

Perry said he heard Tait looked for a pound of crank the last time he was in Oakland and wondered if he found what he wanted. Tait said he had not and asked where Perry got his information. Perry said, "From the fat man." Tait had told Big Al Perryman before the ECOM he wanted a pound of crank.

"I can probably help you out," Perry said. "I don't do this with very many people, but I trust you. I know you are a shaker and a mover." He offered to sell Tait the crank for $12,000 on August 5, when Tait next visited Oakland.

The Alaska Hells Angels hit the road in late July to attend the U.S.A. Run in Eureka Springs, Arkansas. Members asked Tait to go through Oakland, where he would pick up his Harley. Tait felt he was going to be asked to transport crank and coke to the run, since the West Coast always supplied the party favors for East Coast mopes. Tait told Marischen. They decided he could not mule drugs for the Hells Angels or risk an arrest. Marischen took Tait to Dr. Bill Tomlinson, a discreet man who was a friend of FBI Special Agent Jim Hill. They asked Tomlinson to make Tait look like he was injured when a car rammed his rental car. Tomlinson put a cast on Tait's left arm and an air splint on his ankle. They considered hiding the transmitter in Tait's cast, but decided it would receive too much attention from Hells Angels who wanted to sign it. Tomlinson also wanted to mould the cast around the .38-caliber revolver. Tait refused. He did not want to have an accidental discharge while he scratched his head.

Tait visited Brenda in Colorado for three days on his way to Arkansas. They planned to get together once the case ended. Marischen never learned that she spent four months in Anchorage that year. Tait never told him, and Marischen stayed away from the condominium for security reasons.

The first day of the U.S.A. Run, Tait noticed that Hells Angel Dale Matheny of the Fulton County, Kentucky, chapter, met with three members of the Fairbanks chapter: president Dennis Pailing, Randy Rocheleau and Jeffrey Lynn Esley. He suspected they compared notes and discussed Tait's attempts to buy weapons and explosives from the Fulton chapter.

Tait didn't use his pager-transmitter because the run site made it impossible for agents to get near with a receiver. And it was so hot he could only wear a T-shirt, which would not hide his microcassette recorder.

Tait shared a room with Monty Elliott at the Ramada Inn during the run. Tait's new cast impeded hand movement, so he asked Elliott to help him trim it back.

"I do this all the time," Elliott said. He told Tait he paid $5,000 a pound for crank from a supplier in Nevada. The drug—shipped in solid one-pound blocks that Elliott sliced with a cheese grater—was muled to Anchorage in fiberglass arm casts flown up in the luggage of "big-titted Kimi." Elliott distributed the crank to three other Angels. The crank was so pure that even though Elliott cut it, the distributors cut it again before they sold it. Elliott said he had two kilos of cocaine buried near Anchorage and asked Tait if he wanted to buy some. Tait told him he had more than enough, but said he would consider his offer of partnership in a multi-pound deal.

Hells Angels from Alaska, Kentucky and North and South Carolina had several more meetings to which Tait was not invited. His own chapter members would not tell him what was discussed. Tait walked into a room where Alaska Hells Angels talked to East Coast Angels. The conversation stopped and did not resume until he left.

Some Hells Angels approached Sonny Barger. They wanted to know why Tait put so much effort into buying weapons and explosives from them. They felt Tait bypassed the system. He traveled and bought stuff without authorization. He didn't clear his actions with anyone. A lot of questions were being asked about Anthony Tait.

Sonny Barger asked Tait if he planned to go to the annual run in Sturgis, South Dakota, or return to Alaska. Tait said he was going to Alaska. Barger asked when he would next be in California. Tait told him not until the August 22 West Coast Officers' Meeting. Barger said he wanted to see Tait next time he was in California. Tait was worried.

Marischen was the first to learn that something was amiss when an extremely concerned Tait called him from Eureka Springs.

"I'm in deep shit. I think it's going to go bad."

"Get your ass on a plane and get your ass back here and we'll discuss it. Just play cool now."

Tait itched as he sat in Anchorage church on Friday, August 14. He couldn't just take off the cast. He had to keep up the charade and put up with itches and skin rot. He hacked away at the plaster and shortened it to make it more bearable, but had to remain injured in the eyes of his fellow Hells Angels. Talk at church centered on the trial of J.C. Webb's killer. Tait and Marischen were afraid the Anchorage Hells Angels would bring Tait up at church for his failure to transport crank to Eureka Springs and to vent pent-up jealousies toward him. They arranged a bust code, and Marischen covered the meeting with backup in case he needed to raid the clubhouse to rescue Tait, who wouldn't be able to fight well with his arm in a cast. Tait kept a low profile during the meeting and was not brought up. The tensions were left to fester.

| HUBERT: | Okay. On this new business. We have this trial comin' up on the first of September. The murder trial of J.C. And the guy that actually did the shooting is goin' on trial the first. I'd like to send Pee Wee down |

there in case we have to get
our property back through
Lori or to have somebody
there to claim our property. Or
find out what the fuck is happenin' with our property. And
Tony said if we send somebody
from here, he can take it out of
his own expenses for himself
also. So we'll have two brothers there. Anybody object?
Does Pee Wee have the time?

PROTZMAN: I can do it. It's all right with
me. But maybe just to have
someone there from Kentucky
just to see what's goin' on too.
And this trial could be somethin' goin' on for six months.

They agreed to send someone down after the trial was
over. At the next state officers' meeting, Tait berated his
fellow Angels for not supporting him in his task of gathering guns and explosives and for not defending him
against complaints from other chapters.

McKinley, Marischen, Baltas and Bobitt met in
Oakland in August and decided to end Operation
CACUS. Tait could not see light at the end of his long
tunnel. The case just kept going on and on with drug
buys and murder-conspiracy meetings and WesCOMs
and ECOMs and churches. Tait was worn down. He was
a robot who pushed himself to work. He would not stop
until he dropped.

The agents figured they could triple the number of
arrests if they continued drug buys. McKinley and Bobitt
were all for that. But Marischen would not allow it. Tait
was his informant and he was closest to him. He
respected the fact that the other agents wanted to bust
more Hells Angels, but he realized that Tait was getting
tired. He needed to work toward an end. The murder

conspiracy was also getting out of control and the Hells Angels could very well go out and whack some Outlaws. They agreed the case would end within three months.

Sonny Barger talked to Tait in the San Jose clubhouse after the West Coast Officers' Meeting ended on Saturday, August 22.

BARGER: On U.S.A. Run I was approached. They were askin' about you in fact. And they're sayin' you're askin' for enough stuff to blow up the fuckin' world.

TAIT: I got that many pounds. I was approached by a couple of 'em who wanted to give me some. And when I went back there, they didn't have any.

BARGER: That's what they said. That you [got some] and they didn't know why you needed more.

TAIT: That ain't enough to do really very much at all with. Yes. That's enough to do one house with. I ain't gonna take on the world with nothin' like that.

Leonard Wayne (Cool Ray) Mullen pleaded guilty to the reduced charge of reckless homicide in the killing of J.C. Webb. Mullen, who had been charged with murder, had surrendered to police. Marshall H. Duncan, who was also charged, was still at large. The prosecutor offered Mullen the plea bargain because there was evidence to suggest he acted in self-defense. Lori Webb stayed in Alaska and did not testify against Mullen, even though she had witnessed the shooting. Other witnesses were drunk at the time of the shooting.

Cleveland president Kenny Yates, member Andrew Shission and a prospect rode their motorcycles to the ECOM in Minneapolis in September. They had problems with one of the bikes in Joliet, Illinois, and pulled into a gas station to work on it. Three guys with no motorcycle-gang insignia—belt buckles, T-shirts or colors—watched them. Several miles down the freeway, the bike had more problems. They pulled into another gas station. They hung their vests with Hells Angels colors on one of the bikes as they worked on the defective bike.

The three guys from the first gas station showed up.

"Give up the vests or die."

One of the Hells Angels started to walk toward the vests.

"Before you do anything stupid, you better turn around and look behind you."

Several men in a car pointed guns at the Hells Angels.

"You look like you want to do something," one of the Outlaws said to Shission. "Come a little closer."

The Outlaws shot and missed, although one bullet hit Yates in the ankle.

Tait received an emergency phone call about the shooting as he attended the ECOM in the Minneapolis clubhouse. As West Coast sergeant-at-arms, he was the man to call if shit happened. Cleveland, which had a reputation for taking care of business, would retaliate against the Outlaws. Now two plots against the Outlaws were afoot. The FBI was no longer in the driver's seat.

Tait met with his handlers on Monday, September 21, to finalize plans for a meeting with Sonny Barger that afternoon. McKinley and Baltas set up surveillance on Barger's house at 12:40 to monitor and record the conversation. Bobitt and Robert Nishiyama of BNE took up their posts two hours later.

When Tait drove up to Sonny Barger's house, he was still shaken by the beating at Oakland church the previous night of Quick Rick Bowles, who Big Al Perryman had accused of jewelry theft. As church ended, Barger said the club had some business to take care of. Perryman hammered Bowles until he was too winded to continue. He dropped Bowles to the floor, rested his

neck on the rail at the foot of the bar and lay on him and
pummelled his head.

Barger bemoaned the backwardness of East Coast
Hells Angels compared to West Coast members.

BARGER: Those guys, hell, all they do is
           talk. And they're all mouth.
           They're like, this is a bad way to
           put it, but they're like niggers.
           Whoever talks the loudest, he
           wins. They never go to battle. It's
           like out here when a nigger starts
           motherfuckin' you and you hit
           him. The guy does not know why
           you hit him. I mean honest to
           God, he does not know why you
           hit him. 'Cause all you were sup-
           posed to do is motherfuck him
           back.

TAIT: At Salem's anniversary a couple of
           months ago, I heard two members
           in a verbal argument around a
           bunch of citizens. They said
           things to each other that are
           fuckin' fightin' words. They
           motherfucker each other. They
           cocksucker each other for about
           ten or fifteen minutes until they
           got tired at yelling at each other. I
           never seen that before in the club.
           The only other place that I've
           seen something like that is in
           England. And they're ways
           behind. But they weren't that far
           behind them.

BARGER: You see, like the other things
           that's really bad about those guys
           in the east is, they have so much
           respect for guys with a lot of time

	in. Like they'd follow Big Al to death. You know Al Hogan?
TAIT:	Yeah.
BARGER:	'Cause he's got a lot of years in. And the guy's as dumb as they fuckin' come. And he uses them guys.
TAIT:	It's the same argument I hear every time about us controlling the world. The West Coast trying to control the world. Then what the fuck there to control? People are making T-shirts. Well, they're not gonna get rich makin' T-shirts. Those Eddie Arnold tapes? Yeah, he's pretty smooth, you know.
BARGER:	I buy these through Reader's Digest. They were priced between $12 and $29 a set. The thing I like about 'em, they're not just six songs on each side.

The agents who handled Operation CACUS had sheaves of assessments and evaluations of major drug traffickers within and associated with the Hells Angels. They were based on law enforcement reports and intelligence from many sources over the decades that indicated the Hells Angels had a near-stranglehold on the methamphetamine industry in California. The same names cropped up again and again. Kenny Owen's was the most frequent. Owen was a legend in the meth business. He was considered the top meth financier, manufacturer and distributor for the Hells Angels. He painstakingly learned how to cook crank and passed on the knowledge once he mastered the technique. He defied academic chemists and produced 100 percent pure crank. He was brilliant and dedicated to a life of crime.

The Bureau of Prisons once identified Owen as a

sociopath. He was quiet, low key, dressed badly, didn't spend money on flashy things. He could have been a university researcher. Instead, he was a mad professor who invented what he couldn't buy. He cruised auctions and bought in bulk things most people would consider junk. He turned it into functional laboratory equipment. He turned stainless-steel restaurant equipment bought from a hospital into a crank laboratory. He was a superb mechanic, machinist, draftsman and welder. He was a standup guy, a survivor, a self-made millionaire. Whenever he got caught, which was seldom, he did his time without a whimper. Tait and his handlers didn't fear Owen, but were realistically respectful. They could not afford to err when they dealt with Kenny Owen.

Bobitt knew the operation was about to shut down and wanted to chance a buy from Owen. Tait had circled long enough to make himself known. He let Owen see him fraternize with Barger and other Hells Angels officers. Owen was clever and sophisticated and kept law enforcement at bay. Like most other Hells Angels drug dealers, he succeeded because he only did business with people he had known since high school or had done jail time with. This made it impossible for undercover officers to make buys.

And in case his house should get raided, it was secured so heavily all evidence would have disappeared before the cops got in.

Bobitt decided Tait should approach Owen on Monday, September 28, to find out if he could provide him with crank and to set a time for the deal. At 2:15 p.m., Bobitt, McKinley and Nishiyama met Tait in Oakland to finalize plans for the operation. They decided to approach Owen at the Woodshop. The agents set up surveillance on the Woodshop at 2:44 and watched and listened as a man called Pete told Tait he could probably find Owen at home. They set up surveillance on Owen's house at 8306 Golf Links Road at 3 p.m. Tait arrived at 3:19. The operation started with his seat belt jammed.

TAIT: Any parking space. I got the same
          car here. What the fuck? Come
          on. Come on. Fuck.

To Tait's surprise, Owen fronted him a pound of crank.
Tait walked out of Owen's house and talked aloud to the
agents, who were caught off guard by Owen's offer.
Bobitt was slow out of the blocks.

TAIT: Okay. Big problems. I got the
          dope right now. I'm gonna go
          down, what the hell is that, Golf
          Link Street. Where the hell are
          ya?

Tait looked in the rearview mirror and couldn't see the
agents. Tait knew he must go by the book to ensure they
could prosecute Owen on the deal, and so he talked non-
stop to have continuity on the tape. One lapse could give
defense lawyers an opportunity to have the case thrown
out on grounds that Tait could have stopped and picked
up the crank while out of the agents' sight. The chatter
accounted for every second the agents couldn't see him.

TAIT: I'm at the stop sign, 82nd Avenue
          and Golf Links Road. I'm gonna
          make a left-hand turn here. Okay.
          MacArthur. I know where I am
          now. I'm gonna take a right on
          MacArthur.   Okay,   good,
          Panasonic's running, still on tape.
          I don't know where I should go.
          Only thing I can do is keep going
          towards the hotel.

Tait drove the car into the parking garage of the hotel,
got out, checked his tape recorder and walked to the
trunk.

TAIT: Panasonic still working. Oh, shit.
             Okay. Okay, I'm placing the evi-
             dence in a blue Converse bag,
             Converse All Star bag. I knew it.
             I'm gonna place the Panasonic
             inside of the Converse bag with
             all the evidence. Okay. Garage
             elevator works. Pressing second-
             floor elevator button. On the sec-
             ond floor. Oh, shit, shit, shit, shit,
             shit. Okay, I'm in my hotel room.
             I'm gonna take the Panasonic out.
             The evidence is out of the bag.
             The Panasonic is out of the bag
             with the evidence.

(The telephone rings.)

TAIT: Hello? Yeah. I'm sitting here with
             Panasonic on. Okay. Right. Okay.
             All right. Bye. Okay, that was Mr.
             McKinley. Let's see, how would
             you like me to read you a story?
             Let's see, "The Charge of the
             Light Brigade Into the Valley of
             Death."

Tait read until the phone rang again and Bobitt asked
him to come down and let him and Nishiyama into the
security elevator.

     Bobitt bubbled with enthusiasm as he talked to Tait
in the elevator.

BOBITT: My God, this has made my career.
TAIT: Okay. The Panasonic in the bag
             here is still running. Time is 4:46.
             I'm cutting the Panasonic off
             now.
BOBITT: Oh, uh, it's, it's still on?

TAIT:	It's on.
BOBITT:	Uh, Bobitt is with Hammer. I'm taking possession of the contraband that was furnished to him by suspect Owen. Present is Agent Nishiyama. Thank you.

Bobitt's initial enthusiasm was overshadowed by embarrassment at his boast. Yet he just couldn't hold back his joy at being the first cop to nail Kenny Owen. If Bobitt accomplished nothing else in his career, he would already have accomplished more than nearly every other narc in the state. He had the goods on the Hells Angels premier crank-cooker and possibly the world's best underground chemist.

Bobitt and Tait met at 6 p.m. to finalize plans for the payment of $10,000 to Owen. Bobitt and FBI agents Bob Barnes and Jay Colvin set up surveillance of Owen's Woodshop at 6:30. Two agents followed Tait from the Hyatt Regency Hotel to the Woodshop, where he arrived at 6:40 and gave Owen the money. The buy was over, and Owen was snagged.

Tait next told his handlers he would try to arrange to buy a pound of crank from Daly City president Jerald Caldwell. When Caldwell returned Tait's calls, he invited him to his house in Redwood City at 9 p.m. the next day, Tuesday. They looked over Caldwell's motorcycles in the garage.

"Do you have any snort?"

"Yeah."

Tait asked if he could buy a pound "to take home." Caldwell said he would have to make a phone call and "go see a guy." Caldwell left the house at 10:00 while Tait watched television. He drove to Hells Angel Robert Poulin's house in East Palo Alto, then returned home and told Tait the deal would go down at 6 p.m. the next day for $11,800. Tait arrived at Caldwell's house at 6:35 on the Wednesday and they went into his office, where Caldwell took a brown paper bag from his desk drawer.

Tait opened the bag and saw a pound of crank. Caldwell tucked the $11,800 into his pants pocket. Tait asked for something to put the package into and was handed a U.S. Department of Agriculture business envelope. The transaction was rushed because Caldwell had visitors in his kitchen. As before, Tait drove back to his hotel.

The DEA had refused to participate in CACUS when invited in 1986 by Steve Graham, head of the Presidential Organized Crime Drug Enforcement Task Force on the West Coast, which coordinates the activities of federal law enforcement agencies across the United States in major drug investigations. The agency was set up to overcome the feuding, jealousy and territoriality among agencies that had sabotaged multi-agency investigations. But even the task force cannot control rogue agencies, and the worst of those is the DEA.

Although the DEA refused to participate in CACUS, a DEA agent wanted a piece of the action. Some FBI agents thought the agent had a good shot at the record books for a lengthy investigation that had yet to be resolved. The agent found out during the summer of 1987 through someone in Steve Graham's office that the FBI had a case going with a Hells Angels informant. He wanted to know the informant's identity and asked around. He started to hit tripwires. He hit McKinley's, which is how McKinley found out about him. He also hit the Hells Angels tripwires, and talk started at Officers' Meetings about a big FBI case. Graham called the DEA agent in and told him to knock it off.

By October, CACUS agents were down to the short strokes as they prepared search and arrest warrants. The DEA agent made so much noise as he beat the bushes to find the Hells Angels informant that he threatened case security. CACUS agents decided to bring the DEA agent in, brief him and make him a partner. Marischen and Tait voted against the idea. Tait knew the DEA often tipped the Hells Angels off about raids. McKinley, Baltas and Bobitt overruled Tait and Marischen, but not without consequences. It would hurt to bring in a guy at the end of the case who didn't know spit about it and let him take credit for something he never contributed to. But they had to shut the man up.

The DEA agent and his partner were invited to the FBI Oakland residency and given copies of McKinley's affidavit to read. They were put in a room with a female agent who was confined to desk work because of an injury. The DEA agent started to mouth off to impress the woman.

"This is a bullshit investigation. Fuck the informant. I would have had this case over in six weeks." He criticized the case on and on.

The agent walked into McKinley's office and repeated the DEA agent's words. McKinley went ballistic. He called Baltas. He called Bobitt. He didn't bother to call Marischen or Tait—he knew their position. Even though angered and under heavy stress, McKinley did not breach the agreement among agents to consult before they acted. They decided to toss the DEA agent out on his ass.

The DEA agent denied he made the comments. McKinley put him up against the wall.

"You really want me to bring the female agent in here? Because if you do, I'm reporting this to the U.S. Attorney's office. Have some professional pride."

The DEA agent slunk out of the office. He was told he could get a call from the United States Attorney who would explain why he should keep his mouth shut. McKinley warned him if he opened his mouth once more about the case, he'd arrest him for obstruction of justice.

The agents pushed hard in late September to wrap up the case. They were ready to write the affidavit of the Hells Angels. They crafted situations for Tait so he could bail out and hide. They began to prepare indictments, raid plans and detention affidavits so the arrested Hells

Angels wouldn't get bail. They were under pressure because the Cleveland chapter wanted to retaliate for the shooting of Yates. The agents feared they would put the case together sloppily and fail to prevent violence they could have curbed.

The agents met with their bosses and prosecuting attorneys in the FBI's San Francisco office in early October. They said they wanted to end the case soon. The attorneys shot down the plan because it didn't leave them time to prepare the legal paperwork needed to try the cases. They demanded three to four weeks to get the legal framework in place. The agents were disappointed. Steve Graham assumed his role as leader.

"We have to do this right because we only have one chance and if we blow it and take this thing off prematurely, then a lot of people will be kicked loose because we won't be ready legally to get these people into court for trial."

Graham spoke the right words at the right time. He wielded much power, but used it only when the people he guided could not find their way themselves. His judicious use of power added weight to his counsel when he did speak. The takedown was postponed until Tuesday, November 10.

Bobitt and McKinley met Tait in Berkeley at 11 a.m. on Sunday, October 18, to make final plans for the purchase of crank from Kenny Owen. They decided that Tait should buy one pound and try to get another fronted. They also wanted Tait to get Owen to talk about his secret warehouse, which a former Hells Angel had mentioned to FBI agents who debriefed him.

Tait called Owen and asked if he could drop by at 12:30. Owen agreed. Six agents joined Tait for a briefing at 11:45 to plan surveillance of the buy. Surveillance agents were in place by 12:05. Bobitt and FBI agent Jay Colvin watched the front of the house where Tait would have to enter a gate in the cyclone fence. At 12:15, McKinley and three other agents searched Tait and his car for drugs in the fifth-floor parking garage of the

Hyatt Regency Hotel in Oakland. McKinley then gave
Tait $10,000, which the agents had photocopied to keep
track of serial numbers. They followed Tait to Owen's
house to ensure he didn't stop along the way.

After some small talk, Tait and Owen got down to
business.

TAIT:	You anticipated all right, all right. Here's 10.
OWEN:	Check it out.
TAIT:	Goddamn. Whew. Hey, could I get another one of them front for a week? 'Cause I gotta go from here, drop this, East Coast and back home, then back here. I figured a week. Would that be all right?
OWEN:	Yeah.

Owen slipped the $10,000 into the pocket of his
bathrobe. He walked to the master bedroom and
returned with another pound of crank wrapped in his
trademark brown butcher paper.

Tait walked out of Owen's house at 1:04. Bobitt
videotaped him as he placed a brown paper bag in the
trunk of his car. Tait returned to the hotel parking
garage where three agents took the crank from the trunk,
then searched Tait and his car for drugs.

For several months before he made his second drug
buy from Owen, Tait was a machine. He went non-stop.
His handlers couldn't imagine anyone else who could
maintain the pace Tait set for himself for the length of
time he did. Ken Marischen saw the signs of fatigue. He
persuaded the other agents to slow down the case. He
knew Tait wanted an end in sight. Tait in fact believed
the buy from Owen was his last operation.

"This is the last one. We're all finished."

"Almost," Baltas said.

"What's that?"

"We're going to do the thing with Ralph, the conspiracy."

Within hours, after he passed his fourth and final urinalysis, Tait would sit on Barger's front porch and implicate him in the Hells Angel plot to kill Outlaws.

By the end of summer, Tait had gathered bits and pieces of evidence that implicated Sonny Barger in the conspiracy to murder Outlaws and showed him to be the gang's national leader. But the agents wanted to prove he led the conspiracy. They didn't want snippets of conversation here and there. They would not charge Barger if they felt the charges would be dismissed or he would get acquitted. They had one last shot; they didn't want to blow it.

Bobitt and McKinley brainstormed Barger's role inside out. They needed to show he sanctioned and directed the conspiracy. Bobitt worked out of the FBI office in Oakland most of the time. He and McKinley took long walks along the trail that circled Lake Merritt. They talked about how to get evidence on Barger. McKinley was a lawyer. He knew the case law and legal issues on conspiracy. They decided they had enough evidence to prove the conspiracy itself, but they needed more on Barger.

"We need to show he is in the middle of this," Bobitt said. "We need to approach him and have Tony deliver a plan that would be approved and ask him for his help."

They looked at each other and their eyes lit up.

"We should ask him for help and arrange for an alibi so it appears that Tony has witnesses to prove he never left town," Bobitt said.

McKinley ran what he called the alibi scenario past Steve Graham to get his legal opinion. Tait would follow a precise script. He would tell Barger he would go to Florida to kill an Outlaw and feed the corpse to gators. He would then show Barger several photographs of the Outlaws clubhouse in Chicago and outline a plan to blow up the building. Tait would give Barger a telephone scrambler obtained from Monty Elliott, which the agents could list in search warrants later as something to look for and seize in Barger's house. He also would ask Barger to help secure his alibi by having someone occupy his hotel room. That would prove he was nowhere near the supposed murder scene.

Barger was shrewd. He held the power within the club, though he avoided national office because he knew that would attract law enforcement attention. He often relinquished the Oakland chapter presidency to let someone else gain experience—or to serve jail time. Barger considered consequences before he made a move.

Barger was comfortable enough with his power to allow other members to rise through the ranks. He wanted a strong succession to ensure the club survived after his death. He was a strong supporter of Ventura chapter president Gus Christie, who, like Barger, knew how to handle the media. And he liked Tait, whom he had described as the Hells Angel of the '90s—the clean-cut new breed who didn't look like an outlaw biker but acted like one.

Barger kept a letter at the clubhouse from Sacramento Hells Angel Patrick Murray McDowell, who understood the need to snow the public and elected officials with their own jargon to shelter the club from prosecution.

After reading House Concurrent Resolution 220, I feel the government is laying the foundation to close us down. In the beginning we felt that the government would try to use RICO as the means to do it. I think we have blocked them from using RICO to close us down because of our P.R. campaign.

This resolution states that outlaw motorcycle gangs have become a major criminal element within our society. If we have become a major criminal element then up until this resolution the GOVERNMENT did NOT OFFICIALLY consider outlaw motorcycle gangs as a MAJOR CRIMINAL ELEMENT.

To back up their statements, they have listed var-

ious crimes that no doubt can be tied to members
of motorcycle gangs. This resolution affects all
motorcycle clubs that are not now LEGAL ENTITIES,
meaning no records, established rules and regulations, taxes being paid, etc. As long as we remain
the way we are, and have nothing for people to
look at as our operating procedures, they can
invent whatever they want about us. Also, as soon
as we become a LEGAL ENTITY, WE WILL NO LONGER
QUALIFY AS AN OUTLAW GROUP. I feel, so as to protect
our future as a club, we must become a Non-Profit
fraternal Organization.

Tait's handlers noticed he was nervous as they briefed
him an hour after he'd bought crank from Kenny Owen.
His muscles were tense. He was less fluid. He didn't joke.
He repeated his lines to ensure he'd get them right. Tait
had to use specific language about criminal acts so there
was no doubt what he talked about. It was a language far
more graphic than codes normally used to talk about
murder. An ATF agent had taken photographs of the
Outlaws clubhouse that Tait would use as props.
He would pretend he had taken them himself when he
scouted for potential targets.

Tait's handlers took no chances for his last talk with
Barger. Four agents monitored the meeting at Barger's
house: Special Agents Jay Colvin and Bob Barnes for the
FBI, and Tim Bobitt and Robert Nishiyama for BNE.
Bobbitt was armed with his camera to document the
occasion. The agents parked near Barger's house at 4:40.
Tait arrived at 5:03. He walked up to the gate, found it
locked and yelled to Barger, "Chief!" He returned to his
rental car and talked to the agents through his transmitter.

TAIT: There's a padlock on the gate.
             Doesn't look like there's anybody
             in the house. What I'm gonna do,
             goin' right up to Lessard's, drop

the blue bag off. And when I've
done that, I'll spend 15, 20 minutes up there. I'll come back
down here and see if he's here
again. He's not here, I'll run down
the highway for a little bit and
turn around and come back. Why
don't we give him till at least five-
thirty, quarter till six, before we
blow him off. Okay? Yeah, I
thought you'd agree with me. I'm
goin' up to Lessard's now. I don't
even see the dogs in the yard or
anything.

Tait returned at 5:57.

TAIT:	Hey. Hi, Chief. Hi, Eubar.
BARGER:	Just pulled in.
TAIT:	Did ya? I was here about an hour ago. Just stopped by.
BARGER:	Yeah, we went to the races.

They sat on the porch.

SHARON:	You like something to drink?
TAIT:	A glass of water would be fine for me. This is the thing I was talkin' about, that phone scrambler. Idea is just call in, say, "How you doin'?" Turn it on like this, you clear it and—
BARGER:	Turn it on like what, now?
TAIT:	You turn it, you put it on clear, just like that. Here's all the instructions right here. If you want to turn it, the volume up or down.
BARGER:	And this works off your tele-phone?

TAIT: Yeah. You stick this on the back.
            They're about three or four hun-
            dred bucks apiece. They're better
            than nothin', but they're not fail-
            safe.

Tait pulled out photographs of the Outlaws clubhouse in Chicago.

TAIT: This is what I was talkin' to you
            about beforehand. This is at a dif-
            ferent time than the rest of these.
            This is like about five months
            beforehand I went through there.
            This is the back part of their place.
            You got cameras all around them.
BARGER: And which town is this?
TAIT: Chicago.
BARGER: Is their building the tall one?
TAIT: Yes, the brick building. Okay.
            This is the room key for that
            hotel. This is the room number.
            I'll leave the keys to the car. It's
            this white Thunderbird. It's a
            Hertz car. I'll leave them in the
            room on the table. I've prepaid
            the room for a whole week. Have
            to check out on Friday morning.
BARGER: Next Friday?
TAIT: Yeah.
BARGER: You'll be back before then?
TAIT: Yeah. I'll come in on Friday, and
            just tell 'em, just mess the bunk up
            and everything else. Like every
            day. It's on a credit card. They can
            order room service. Watch the pay
            movies and that. Have 'em watch a
            couple of movies, whatever. And
            it's on my credit card. Everything's

square away. So, put a hundred
miles. Drive to Sacramento with
the car. I'll come in on Friday,
snatch the car and turn it in and
then go straight home. To be sure,
I'll give you a ring and say, "Hi."
Even though you got this other
thing, "Hey, everything's okay.
The weather is good. Things look
good." If it doesn't look good,
"The weather's pretty shitty
around here." Okay? That other
guy that was on the loose, he just
turned himself in three days ago.

BARGER: What'd the other guy get?

TAIT: I didn't know. The person that
called me said he had bailed himself out right same time. What,
the first guy? What did he get?
He was suppose to be goin' up for
sentencing. We hadn't heard yet.
But Marshall Duncan, he just
turned himself in on Thursday
night and like bailed himself out
before. The guy who told me said
it sounded like it was preset with
a lawyer or somethin' before he
even turned himself in.

BARGER: Yeah, that would be a smart move
on his part.

TAIT: Yeah. Then the people in Midwest
there on the Great Lakes,
Cleveland? They're pretty excited
right now. I got a call out there
the other day. And they're pretty
hot. They're still snoopin' around
tryin' see what the story is. But
they don't know for sure yet. The
person that was talkin' to me—

BARGER:	This is?
TAIT:	Oh, the Broadway.
BARGER:	Oh, Broadway in Oakland.
TAIT:	Yeah. The Hyatt Regency?
BARGER:	Yeah.
TAIT:	It's right down there almost by 580. It's a big building there. And this is a security code key. So it's not the same number that's on it.
BARGER:	Okay, 1614. Is that on the sixteenth floor?
TAIT:	Yeah.
BARGER:	Where you gonna leave the car?
TAIT:	On the top deck of the fifth floor. You know the fifth floor of the parking garage there. There's a pink slip in there from the parking garage.
BARGER:	Would it be easier to do that or meet you and just take the car from you?
TAIT:	Pardon?
BARGER:	Would it be easier to do that or should we just drop you somewhere and take the car?
TAIT:	No, it would be easier for me. I can drive back there, leave it there and rent a cab tomorrow. That'll cover everything up there. I can't really think of much more. I'm figuring the way this is set, five or six and maybe more on the initial explosion. Then a secondary about maybe seven to nine seconds behind, figuring maybe kill five or six.
BARGER:	That'll be really nice after that Joliet thing.
TAIT:	Well, yeah. It's a good picture.

Okay. It's very easy to get access onto this roof right here. So I gonna leave one here, go all the way to the end of this building and leave one right there. All flush tight against the wall, to shove it in. And then come over here and if I can get up on top of this roof, to push it down and in this way. Push directional and that's after this part of it. Like I said, everything going right, should be able to kill five or six and with the main blast, then after that, just the debris.

Well, I figure that's a good three months' work. Hasn't been as productive what I like. I don't see anything else happening at the moment. It's like I said. The people in the city aren't ever gonna do nothin'. This is under my name, this room. It's under my true name.

BARGER: Which is?

TAIT: Anthony Tait. T-a-i-t. The car, everything. I figured the best way to do anything like that.

BARGER: You don't know what the license number is on the car?

TAIT: I think this is it right here. I'm just gonna leave these keys in the room. Nope, nope, don't chew on plastic.

SHARON: Stay. He's grown up, aren't you? Are you grown up?

TAIT: And other than that, I've been working my ass off. I'm beat. Did I ever show you these before?

BARGER: Which end do you speak into?

TAIT: Just like a regular telephone. It's like this right here. And you talk in. We've used them for a while. But it's better than nothin'. But we still limit what conversation is—

BARGER: Is that a spare key?

TAIT: Yeah, this is a spare key. I'll be in there tonight. And I'm just gonna leave the car there in the morning when I get ready to leave. Other than that, I'll be back on Friday. Just leave the car keys in the room. I'll grab the car Friday morning, turn it in and fly straight home. I won't even need to see you or anything. Then I'll see you 'cause I'll be down for the Halloween party.

Other than that, we got everything pretty much fixed up so Michael can go home now. Michael's been down here? Yeah. They videoed him attempting to bribe this broad [with] $45,000. He had a bunch of cash on him and it didn't work out the way he wanted it to. And so we got it cut enough to where he can go home and they probably just question him and that will be about it. Maybe he'll just have a tampering charge instead of all the rest. Jack's on the run, right. Somebody was in doin' somethin' a while ago, not us, but they brought our name up and used our name just to try to make it . . . About Jack. So his name's all over this paperwork. So you'll just know, he's kinda stickin' away from us right now. He might take an extended European vacation. But other than that, things are lookin' good . . .

BARGER: And that goes off, two out of two, huh? Give me a yell when they're really over.

TAIT: Uh-huh.

BARGER: And let me know if something happens.

TAIT: Okay.

BARGER: 'Cause they're gonna be callin' us.

TAIT: Well, I'm tryin' to steer it in another direction.

BARGER: Well, whatever happens, they're gonna think it's us because that—

TAIT: Yeah.

BARGER: —Joliet thing.

TAIT: Yeah.

BARGER: Which is good when they call. So I'll tell 'em I'm still waitin' for Taco to call me back.

Bobitt took photographs furiously as Tait and Barger played with the dogs on the front lawn. Barger walked Tait to his car. Bobitt photographed Barger as he pressed the flap on his throat to bid Tait farewell and waved to him as the car passed the surveillance van.

"So, I am finished."

Tait's car and room at the Hyatt Regency Hotel were put under visual and video surveillance at noon on Monday, the day after he spoke to Barger. At 11:19 on Tuesday, October 20, Bob Barnes and Robert Nishiyama, who watched from room 1613, saw Irish O'Farrell enter the room. He later took Tait's rental car for a spin. O'Farrell entered the room again at 10:45 on Wednesday morning and messed up the bed. He brought a woman to the room at 8:30 Thursday morning, messed up the bed and dampened towels in the bathroom before he left at 11:00. O'Farrell and the woman returned to the room at 10:30 that night and stayed until 11:00 the next morning.

The agents were surprised Barger sent O'Farrell; they expected a lesser Hells Angel to be given the task. O'Farrell thought he was a Barger clone and the second coming of Sonny. He drank too much and chased women. He made a fool of himself when drunk, fought too much and had been shot and stabbed. Despite his failings, he carried a lot of juice in the club.

When Tait had walked out of Sonny Barger's house that Sunday, he thought he had come in from the cold. He was placed in a secure office in Austin, where he worked with FBI agents to finalize the paperwork for the November 10 raids that would end the covert phase of Operation CACUS.

Marischen learned that the Cleveland Hells Angels planned to retaliate for the shooting of Hells Angel Kenny Yates. They were going to stage a drive-by shooting with automatic weapons at the Outlaws' Pumpkin Run in Joliet, Illinois, on Halloween. The FBI wasn't ready to take down CACUS but would have to if the shooting couldn't be prevented. Marischen had Tait call Cleveland Hells Angels from Austin to forestall the shooting.

Tait called Kenny Yates and Gary Alan Wolf on Tuesday, October 20, and Wednesday on the safe phone they had previously agreed to talk on. They told him a plan was afoot to bomb the Outlaws and they expected to have the "groceries" in two weeks.

"Hey, I'm on the road. I don't need anybody pulling the cork here and putting me in danger. Can't you guys hold off a little while? I'm riding out down south looking to take care of business and you guys are talking about going out and popping a cork."

After much soul-searching, Marischen asked Tait on short notice to fly to Cleveland to persuade them to postpone the retaliation. Tait had been away from the club for nearly two weeks and there may have been leaks about his involvement with the FBI. There were certainly enough Hells Angels who questioned why he wanted so many weapons and explosives. Tait left Austin in such a hurry he didn't have time to pack a gun in his stowaway baggage as was his practice. He was nervous going into Cleveland unarmed. Marischen slipped him a gun.

Tait talked with Yates and Wolf on Wednesday, October 28. Yates said he arrived from Oakland the previous day and they intended to hit the Outlaws on Halloween. They said Donnie Mahovlic was en route to Cleveland from Oakland with explosives and bombs to use in the attack.

Tait asked them to postpone their attack until Friday, November 13. He said he realized their situation was unrelated to the J.C. Webb shooting and they had every right to seek vengeance. But his plans had long been in the works and he had a responsibility to his chapter to carry them out. He asked Cleveland to wait until he had killed the Outlaws he planned to kill. They agreed.

FBI agents wracked their brains to find a way to ensure the Cleveland Hells Angels didn't breach their word to Tait and attack the Outlaws. Someone ran their names through police computers and saw Gary Wolf had outstanding traffic violations. A police officer shot out Wolf's brake light with a pellet gun to justify a traffic stop. He was arrested that Friday and spent Halloween weekend in jail.

Tait called Ed Hubert in Anchorage that day.

HUBERT:	Where are you?
TAIT:	Oh, I'm a long ways away. You doin' anything for the next ten minutes?
HUBERT:	Well, not really. Why?
TAIT:	Okay. Could you go across the street to the Quick Stop? And stand over there by the phone?
HUBERT:	You gonna call me?
TAIT:	Yep.

Hubert picked up the ringing pay phone at the Quick Stop.

HUBERT:	What's goin' on?
TAIT:	Ahhh, not too much. Hey, listen, I took care of one of them problems that we had. You understand what I mean?
HUBERT:	I think so.
TAIT:	Okay. One of them guys that did that thing—
HUBERT:	Yeah.
TAIT:	—was hidin' out with somebody and I managed to run 'em down. And, and I went and visited him.
HUBERT:	Oh.
TAIT:	Okay.
HUBERT:	I always thought he turned himself in.
TAIT:	Oh, he turned himself in. But he was stayin' somewhere.
HUBERT:	Oh.
TAIT:	Okay?
HUBERT:	Yeah.
TAIT:	All right. Now, them guys that wanted to see me in the Midwest?
HUBERT:	Yeah?
TAIT:	Well, I went and saw them. They're rockin' and rollin' tomorrow night.
HUBERT:	Yeah?
TAIT:	They're goin' to a party tomorrow night in the same place they lost that property. I'm kickin' off somethin' else somewhere else, another singular thing. So it's in conjunction with their party.
HUBERT:	Yeah.
TAIT:	Okay?

HUBERT:	Okay. Did the other singular thing have to do with the same thing . . .
TAIT:	Yeah. It had to do with the same thing and it worked out fine.
HUBERT:	Good.
TAIT:	There was no problem whatsoever. (He chuckles.) To me it was a gimme.
HUBERT:	Sounds good.
TAIT:	But I'm pressin' on with this thing tomorrow night and I'm pretty sure this'll be a gimme too. I'll let you know, probably Sunday afternoon. I'll call you back on the next one that you're beside.

San Francisco Hells Angel Jack Dee (Patch) Myers, who sold a pound of cocaine to Tait in August, was stabbed to death in Daly City on Saturday, October 31. Hells Angel J.R. Serrano told detectives he would turn in the murderer but would not vouch for his condition "after we're through with him."

Operation CACUS had been run on a need-to-know basis since January 1985. Agents suffered mind-numbing fatigue through overwork rather than share the burden and broaden the circle of those in the know. Only hand-picked, trusted law enforcement officials, such as Sacramento police officer Bert Sousa, were brought in when extra hands and eyes were needed. The agents pulled off a next to impossible feat: they defeated the indomitable intelligence-gathering juggernaut of the Hells Angels. Whatever vibes the Hells Angels picked up about an FBI investigation melted into the general paranoia under which the club and all drug dealers operate. They see a narc behind every phone pole. But once you chase down every possible narc, you realize you spend more time doing that than selling dope. So security gets lax. After 23 months of unparalleled secrecy, it was inevitable someone would screw up.

A cleaning lady walked into U.S. Attorney Crandon Randell's Anchorage office the week before the scheduled raid. She was a longtime Alaska resident and knew a lot of people in Anchorage. On workdays, she made small talk with the city's high-powered prosecutors, their secretaries and clerks. On her days off, she socialized with the Hells Angels, to whom she felt she must communicate any information she came across that affected them. She didn't consider herself part of an underworld intelligence network; she just believed she owed the Hells Angels because she belonged to the biker subculture.

Since she did most of her work after everyone left the office, the cleaning lady read the papers on Randell's desk at her leisure. She became nervous as she read the first page of an indictment against the Hells Angels Randell had left lying about. She leafed through the document, which detailed the entire case: Anchorage Hells Angel Anthony Tait was an FBI informant who helped the bureau build a national case against the Angels, who were accused of selling drugs, guns and explosives and of conspiring to murder. Some of the Hells Angels named in the indictment were her friends. They were to be arrested during simultaneous raids on Tuesday, November 10, in their homes and clubhouses and businesses in Alaska, California, Kentucky and North and South Carolina.

One week before the raids, an Anchorage cleaning lady knew more than the nearly 600 police officers who were to conduct them.

The paperwork was completed the first week of November. Warrants and affidavits were sworn and indictments were handed down. The U.S. Attorney's office would indict more than 40 high-ranking officers and members of the Hells Angels Motorcycle Club for a lengthy list of criminal acts. The crimes included use of

an organization in furtherance of criminal conspiracies
and racketeering; conspiracy to commit murder; conspiracy to commit arson; manufacturing and distribution of
unlawful firearms, destructive devices, explosives and
weapons; theft of United States government property;
interstate transportation of stolen property, firearms,
weapons, destructive devices and explosives; manufacturing and distribution of controlled substances; conspiracy to manufacture and distribute controlled substances
and interstate transportation of controlled substances.

The cleaning lady's life became very complicated.
She placed the document back on the desk and wrestled
with her conscience. She would lose her job and probably go to jail if she warned the Hells Angels. Yet she
feared they would be angry with her if they found out
she didn't share the information. She never considered
that no one would be the wiser if she kept her mouth
shut.

Marischen and supervisor Tony Hodge flew to Fairbanks
two days before the scheduled raids to brief team leaders.
They gave them information packages to make their jobs
easier and minimize the risk of injury or death. The
packages contained addresses of buildings to be raided,
with details such as floor plans, what doors were secure,
which buildings had metal doors, which Hells Angels
were armed and where drugs, guns and explosives were
cached.

Their work done, the FBI agents drove to the airport
and waited on the tarmac for passengers to disembark
from the plane just arrived from Anchorage so they
could embark and return south. Marischen watched five
Anchorage Hells Angels walk off the plane. They were
slated for arrest in two days. The operation would foul
up if they were in Fairbanks at the time.

The Hells Angels had flown to Fairbanks to kick ass.
They had stated Alaska was a one-patch state and had
forcibly stripped many gangs of their colors over the

years. The Vietnam Veterans Motorcycle Club organized in Fairbanks despite warnings from the Hells Angels. They didn't wear patches, but they rode the streets. The Angels decided to take care of business. Tait was in hiding and Marischen had no idea what the Hells Angels were up to. The FBI no longer had eyes and ears in the club.

Hodge held the plane. Marischen got off and hung around the Hells Angels as they rented a car. They didn't recognize him. As they drove off, Marischen showed his badge to the woman behind the counter and asked how long they had rented the car for—one day. He checked airline reservations to confirm they would return to Anchorage that day. Then he ran to the plane.

The Vietnam Veterans members never showed up at the Angels' Fairbanks compound for the confrontation.

The cleaning lady spent anxious days and nights as she tried to think her way out of her dilemma. She may have suspected Anthony Tait would die if she talked. Or booby traps would be set for police officers on November 10. Or everyone would lie low and all evidence would disappear. She thought so hard she forgot to warn the Hells Angels.

BNE Special Agent Tim Bobitt had organized the raids. In California alone, more than 400 law enforcement officers were needed to execute search warrants. BNE was experienced in drug busts and searches and the safety issues they involved. The agency made available all its agents in the state, except for a handful on emergency duty.

Hand-picked team leaders were briefed in the Bay Area on Sunday, November 8. They were given information packages to brief their teams.

WSIN's Karen Sanderson prepared documents and charts for use during the raids. She compiled all pertinent information about every building to be raided. Every raid team received an officer-safety printout that listed whether the house was secured and protected by electronic warning devices, how many guard dogs were present, whether occupants had a history of violence, whether there were guns on the premises. Another print-out listed places in each building where Tait had seen drugs hidden in secret rooms, behind secret panels and even in oven mitts hung in the kitchen.

Sanderson also prepared a chart for the press conference later on raid day to show the scope of the operation. She would later sift through seized material to look for evidence against the Hells Angels. She would also prepare charts for trials to help everyone keep track of the chronology of events.

Bobitt told team leaders to assemble their teams on Monday and scout the area they were to raid. Surveillance was established early Tuesday morning on the major players such as Kenny Owen, Sonny Barger and Chico Manganiello.

Unlike previous raids, the Hells Angels were caught off guard in the early hours of November 10. In the past, they greeted police freshly showered, in pressed pants or starched jeans. Fireplaces contained burned records. On November 10, they looked like shit because they were dragged out of bed in their pyjamas. Police found guns, drugs and records of deals in their houses.

Agents took no chances for the raid on Kenny Owen's house. He was known as a violent and vicious convicted felon; his house was fortified and protected by sophisticated electronic surveillance equipment—every room contained speakers that broadcast sounds from the front of the house and driveway and he had three Doberman pinschers. An FBI SWAT team was assigned to secure the house and arrest Owen. A cunning scheme was used to lure him out. ATF Special Agent Jim Flanigan had spent the previous week returning to Hells Angels in Oakland private property such as telephone directories and photographs seized in prior raids. Word spread that he was making the rounds. Flanigan knew Owen from earlier investigations and had returned seized property to him before.

A SWAT team stood poised behind the tall cyclone

fence that surrounded Owen's property as Flanigan stood outside the gate and called to Owen. Owen opened the front door and asked the agent what he wanted. Flanigan said he had property to return. Owen said he didn't want it. Then he told Flanigan to wait and walked out of the house toward the gate.

"You know, Flanigan, you're not my most favorite person."

As Owen neared the gate, Flanigan said he had a warrant for his arrest. He opened the lock with the combination Tait had given him and the SWAT team rushed into the yard. Owen was speechless. He did something he had never done during a raid: he turned purple.

The FBI agent told Owen they would search the house. Owen gave them his keys and the guard dogs were herded into the garage. A police dog sniffed out several spots where crank was hidden. The agents heard a strange sound from the back of the house. They approached cautiously and peered into a bedroom. A money-counting machine shuffled through a wad of $100 bills. Owen had been so busy counting money he'd mislabeled a wad of $100 bills as twenties. The money-counter was surrounded by a shredder, a photocopier, several computer terminals, radio scanning and electronic equipment, and a viewing screen for a video camera that monitored the front of the house. Owen's computer was booted up to Andrew Tobias's *Managing Your Money*. Two red steel foot-lockers contained $1.5-million cash. More money was found in a large safe. The dog found 15 pounds of crank in a footlocker in the garage.

Agents for the FBI, ATF and BNE, along with uniformed Oakland Police Department officers, raided Kenny Owen's secret warehouse at 811 54th Avenue in Oakland at 10 a.m. They parked away from the beige stucco multi-unit warehouse and approached on foot. They announced three times they were FBI agents with a search warrant. When no one answered, they smashed in the door with a sledgehammer. The agents called in a locksmith after they found several safes. One six-foot safe contained nine pounds of crank in clear plastic bags and $975,000 in cash. They also found chemicals and clandestine lab equipment.

The Woodshop also yielded crank and money. The money appeared to be Owen's weekly income.

Agents who knocked at the door of the Hells Angels Oakland clubhouse at 4019 Foothill Boulevard were greeted by Don Dinehart and Alan White. White was arrested on an outstanding traffic warrant, as was James Elrite, who was found in the business office with Mouldy Marvin Gilbert. The agents seized $350,000 in cash and $100,000 in gold and silver coins from a safe.

Within hours, 38 Hells Angels across the U.S., mostly club officers, were behind bars.

"It had to be Tony from Alaska, right?" Hells Angel Raoul Villasenor asked police.

EPILOGUE

HELLS ANGELS ARRESTED in Operation CACUS were tried in courts across the United States. The FBI paid Anthony Tait's salary while he testified. The FBI also gave him a $250,000 cash bonus, of which the IRS took $104,000. The 1988 murder-conspiracy trial in Kentucky was the largest, longest and most wracking. The judge appeared to favor the defendants and allowed their lawyers a leeway rarely seen in courts. One defense lawyer badgered Special Agent Tim McKinley during cross-examination with an outrageous memo he had supposedly written. The FBI agent was confused. He hadn't penned the memo, yet here was the lawyer waving it in his face. He finally figured out the document had been cut and pasted from three original memos to create a fictitious document that made McKinley look ridiculous.

Hells Angels lawyer Tony Serra called the prosecutor a "lying dog." The prosecutor objected.

"Well, Your Honor, what I meant was supine canine," Serra explained.

He got away with it.

Defense lawyers were allowed to subpoena Hells Angels who would never testify and paid their travel and living expenses with public money. These bikers sat in court to provide security and support for Angels on trial. The court made taxpayers foot the bill for wives and girlfriends that defense lawyers hired as paralegals.

A Hells Angel girlfriend showed up in court with a T-shirt that read "Tony Tait said what?" The Hells Angels had bookmarks and notepads printed with the query, which was illustrated with a laughing cartoon character. The Hells Angels had a lot of money to toss around.

With the exception of two members, the Hells Angels in court proved to be whining punks unsuited for membership in a motorcycle gang. They cried government harassment. Sonny Barger was sniveler supreme. Yet he demonstrated for the Kentucky jury that he ran the Hells Angels. He interrupted the dozen defense-counsel members when he wanted a question asked. He wrote notes, walked to the defense-counsel lectern and placed them in front of lawyers. They dropped their own questions and adopted Barger's queries, though they were often ridiculous and had nothing to do with cross-examination of the witness. If Barger didn't like the answer or the way the question was asked, he stood beside the lawyer and scribbled furiously. Barger also participated in many sidebar discussions with the judge. Everyone in the courtroom knew he called the shots.

The only two Hells Angels who proved to be standup guys were Oakland member Mike Lessard and Daly City member Robert Poulin. They kept their mouths shut and took their lumps while others groveled and showed the world the club was as spineless as the punks who sought power in its numbers. Mike Lessard refused to tell a judge where he got the explosives he sold Tait. The judge threatened to hold him in contempt.

"With all due respect, Your Honor, I wouldn't be a man."

Chief Judge Edward H. Johnstone of the United States District Court heard the conspiracy case against the Hells Angels in Louisville. He supported Sonny Barger after the jury found him guilty of shipping a stolen government document and conspiracy to murder. Johnstone issued this memorandum and order in 1989 after Barger asked for a letter of reference to support his request for transfer from prison in Arizona to California, where he would be closer to home and the Hells Angels.

Ralph Hubert Barger Jr. has moved the court to recommend that his sentence imposed by this court be served at Pleasanton, California. The United States vigorously opposes the motion . . .

[But] throughout the long proceedings before this court the conduct of Mr. Barger and his co-defendants was exemplary. Each defendant showed respect for the court and its orders. Mr. Barger was enlarged on bond during most of the trial. He obeyed each condition imposed by the enlargement order. His appearances were punctual. At no time did he display any tendency of violence. Neither Mr. Barger nor the remaining co-defendants did anything during the entire proceedings to disrupt the court or create any disturbance. Indeed, the defendants showed more respect for the court than did some of the prosecution witnesses.

The court heard testimony concerning allegations that threats against others were made by Mr. Barger and Mr. O'Farrell while they were incarcerated. After several hearings these allegations were rejected. The confidential informants supplying the basis of the allegations were found to be highly unbelievable. It was the view of this court that Mr. Barger represented no threat or danger to the community nor, based upon conduct observed by the court since the return of the indictment, constituted a security risk.

Having disclosed the court's observations made

during the trial, this matter is concluded with the hope that past animosity between the prosecution and defense can be put to rest.

It is therefore ordered that a copy of this memorandum shall be forwarded to the Bureau of Prisons and made a part of their file maintained for Mr. Barger.

The Hells Angels and Outlaws struck a deal during the Kentucky trial to present a unified front for the media. They denied animosity between the clubs. The Hells Angels promised not to retaliate for the shootings of J.C. Webb and Kenny Yates, and in turn the Outlaws promised not to retaliate for the shooting of their members after the Yates incident.

Cleveland Hells Angels had taken care of business, but killed an innocent man in the process. Hells Angels prospects John Ray Bonds and Mark S. Verdi and chapter security officer Steven Wayne Yee mistook Sandusky record store clerk David Hartlaub for the president of the Outlaws Sandusky chapter and shot him to death on February 27, 1988. Bonds waited in the back of Hartlaub's van and fired 14 rounds from a MAC-10 into him as he sat down. One bullet ricocheted off the dashboard and struck Bonds in the hand. He dropped his mask and gloves in the van so as not to be caught with them. In doing so, he left behind samples of his blood and hair. The Hells Angels spent a small fortune in 1990 trying to persuade the court that DNA "genetic fingerprinting" tests were not credible and could not be admitted as evidence in the case. They hoped to have the two-year-old procedure—used in hundreds of homicide, rape and paternity cases—ruled unreliable. Prosecutors said the tests were foolproof because each person's genetic material is unique. Tests showed blood taken from Bonds matched blood found in the victim's van and in Yee's car. Bonds was found guilty. Yee pleaded guilty. Bonds and Verdi got their patches after the killing.

The Hells Angels were more successful with two

other hits. Two Hells Angels walked into a Joliet tattoo parlor and shot the president of the Joliet chapter of the Outlaws in the eye with a .45-caliber pistol. They bound another Outlaw's wrists and feet, shot him in the back of the head and left the corpse by a railway track near an Outlaws hangout.

The two clubs allegedly struck a deal in Sturgis, South Dakota, in 1990 that allowed Outlaws to kill a Hells Angel in Quebec without fear of retribution. The Hells Angels gave up one of their own to maintain peace.

Operation CACUS could have gone on for years had the murder conspiracy not forced agents to shut down the case. Tait could have bought drugs from every Hells Angel dealer and decimated the club. Although CACUS sent two of the club's main cookers—Chico Manganiello and Kenny Owen—behind bars, many more are free.

Many persons convicted in connection with Operation CACUS received their longest-ever sentences. Here is a partial list:

- Ralph Hubert (Sonny) Barger: conspiracy to violate federal law (conspiracy to commit murder) and conversion of government property—three and a half years in custody.
- Charles Daniel (Chico) Manganiello: distribution of methamphetamine—$300,000 fine, special parole for life, forfeiture of real and personal property.
- Kenneth Jay (K.O.) Owen: distribution and possession of methamphetamine—41 years in custody, $2.1-million fine, 20 years special parole, forfeiture of $2,411,996 and real and personal property.
- Raoul G. (Rudy) Villasenor: distribution of cocaine—10 years custody, four years special parole, forfeiture of real and personal property.
- Werner Franz (Krusi) Sohm: distribution of methamphetamine—five years in custody, three years parole, likely deportation.
- Jerald Emmett Caldwell: distribution of cocaine— five years in custody.

- James Frank (Guinea) Colucci: possession of methamphetamine—one year in custody, $14,665 fine and costs.
- John Robert Curry: possession of firearm by a felon, disposing of stolen military explosives, improper storage of explosives, conversion of stolen U.S. government property—three years in custody.
- Mark William Davis: manufacture of methamphetamine, attempt to manufacture, conspiracy to manufacture—18 years in custody.
- Arthur Kent (Fishhead) Carasis: possession of methamphetamine—15 years in custody.
- Montgomery David (Monty) Elliott: distribution of cocaine—four and a half years in custody, three years special parole, $10,000 fine.
- Jeffrey Lynn Esley: possession of an unregistered destructive device—one and a half years in custody.
- Richard Allen Fabel: alteration of a serial number, possession of an unregistered machine gun—three years in custody, four years probation.
- Lawrence Russell (Russ) Hagel: conversion of property—one year in custody (suspended). Possession of an unregistered firearm, a sawed-off shotgun—10 years in custody, two years probation.
- Lawrence Herrera: possession of methamphetamine—15 years in custody.
- Edwin Floyd (Eddie) Hubert: distribution of cocaine—two years in custody, six years supervised release. Felon in possession of a firearm—five months in custody, $3,000 fine. Conversion of government property—probation.
- Christopher A. Livesay: possession of an unregistered machine gun—six months in custody, three years probation, $550 restitution.
- Daniel D. (Ma) McIntosh: possession of an unregistered destructive device, possession of an unregistered silencer, transfer of an unregistered silencer—six years in custody.

- Michael Vincent (Irish) O'Farrell: conspiracy to violate federal law (conspiracy to commit murder), conversion of government property— three and a half years in custody.
- Dennis E. (Bigfoot) Pailing: possession of cocaine, distribution of cocaine, possession of an unregistered machine gun—one and three-quarter years in custody, three years probation.
- Gerald Michael (Pee Wee) Protzman: conversion of government property—probation.
- Richard Allen (Sleazy Ric) Rickleman: possession of a firearm by a felon—one year in custody, $3,000 fine.
- Carl James (J.R.) Serrano: distribution of cocaine, possession of a firearm by a felon—five years in custody.
- Thomas Deszo Vinczen: possession of an unregistered machine gun—three years in custody.
- John Makoto (Fuki) Fukushima: possession of an unregistered firearm (machine gun)—one and a half years in custody, special parole with a non-association clause, $25,000 in fines in addition to $32,000 already seized.

Oakland Hells Angel Werner Sohm couldn't understand why he was busted for selling crank to Tait. "But it was only a pound," he told arresting officers on November 19, 1987. "Why are you picking on me? It was only a pound."

He did his prison time and fled to Europe when released on parole. He wrote authorities and told them not to look for him because he wouldn't be back.

Operation CACUS took 34 1/2 pounds of explosives off the streets: 20 pounds of C-4, 10 pounds of commercial high explosives, two pounds of Tovex commercial explosive, two pounds of dynamite and half a pound of TNT; plus 25 blasting caps, both electric and non-electric.

Tait and the Charleston, South Carolina, Hells Angels dug in vain for explosives and LAWs rockets in the summer of 1987. One of the Hells Angels who buried them had moved them without telling anybody, then died.

Bureaucracy added insult to injury in Mike Lessard's explosives case. Federal officials billed him upon his release from jail for failing to pay the $200 transfer tax for each sale of explosives to Tait. He was also assessed a penalty for tardy payment and billed more than $2,000. (Lessard's conviction was overturned in February 1994.)

Ken Marischen testified at Lessard's trial and made arrangements to meet Ted Baltas at a bar afterwards, to which Baltas gave him directions. Marischen walked into the dark room, glanced around quickly, sat at the bar and ordered a beer.

The female bartender approached him sheepishly. "I've got a drink for you. Some people bought you a drink."

Marischen looked around. His eyes still had not adjusted to the darkness. He didn't recognize anybody.

"That group back in the corner. I'm sorry, but I have to give you this."

"Sure, no problem."

She set down a Shirley Temple.

"Who in the shit . . . " Marischen turned on his stool. He thought some of the guys, maybe Baltas, had set him up. "Who in the hell sent that?"

He looked to the corner and recognized Pee Wee Protzman and a group of Hells Angels in colors.

"Hi, Shirley. Hi, Shirley," they called out in their best falsettos.

"Thanks, guys, but no thanks."

Marischen took a long time to finish his beer because he didn't want them to think they ran him out. He returned to the office and called Baltas. "Where the hell are you sending me to?"

"No, it's the other bar."

Every day until the end of the trial, the Hells Angels greeted Marischen in the court building. "Hi, Shirley."

"Hi, guys."

Tim McKinley proved that Kenny Owen bought a metric ton of monomethylamine gas 18 months before he was busted and cooked 2,200 pounds of crank. He made about $30-million if he sold each pound for the low price of $12,000. By the time that crank hit the street, $127-million to $140-million was spent on it. The FBI seized $2.4-million and 30 pounds of crank from Owen. They have no idea where the remaining $27-million he made in the 18 months before his arrest went. Police officers found an item on Owen's computer that listed the net worth of four individuals: A, B, C and D. Each was worth $1-million. Owen was A and they have a good idea who B and C are.

Oakland Hells Angel Irish O'Farrell, a registered sex-offender with convictions for robbery, rape, sodomy, grand theft, burglary, assault and other charges, never made it to jail. He was shot and stabbed to death on the outdoor patio behind the Halfway Club in San Leandro two weeks before he was to report to a federal prison in Atlanta to begin his sentence. O'Farrell and Barger were convicted in October 1988 of conspiracy to transport and receive in interstate commerce explosives with the intent to kill.

O'Farrell drank in a San Leandro bar where a member of the prison-based Aryan Brotherhood recognized him as the Hells Angel who tried to collect a drug debt from him two months earlier. He feared he would be beaten again. He jumped O'Farrell from behind in the parking lot, stabbed him five times in the back, once in the neck and once in the chest. He then shot him four times from behind with a .25-caliber pistol to show disrespect for the dying Hells Angel. Then he shot Angel Michael Musick in the shoulder. The wounded Angel ran away.

Hells Angel Odis (Buck) Garrett, one of the club's drug kingpins, escaped the clutches of Operation CACUS, but was done by a subsequent investigation. In 1992, he was sentenced at age 49 to life in prison without parole for the manufacture and distribution of hundreds of pounds of crank in the 1980s. He was convicted on a panoply of charges that included leading a continuing criminal enterprise, money laundering and arranging money transactions to evade the IRS. Garrett, a former president of the Nomads chapter in California, made millions of dollars cooking and trafficking crank. He used the club as his network to distribute the drug outside the state.

The Sacramento Clandestine Laboratory Task Force arrested Garrett, associates Carl H. Dulinsky, D.L. Braddock and Harris B. Shimel in 1989 after lab raiders searched a cabin on the 1,400-acre Yankee Jim Ranch in the northeast corner of California. They found the makings of a large speed lab and enough chemicals to make $600,000 worth of methamphetamine. Dulinsky and Braddock were indicted with Garrett. Dulinsky pleaded guilty to helping Garrett make the meth and testified against him in return for a promise by prosecutors to get his 22-year sentence shortened. U.S. Attorney General Edward L. Knapp said it would cost about $25,000 to clean chemical-contaminated soil in a drainage ditch near the cabin that housed Garrett's lab.

Garrett was further charged in 1990 with organizing and operating a large-scale methamphetamine distribution ring with clandestine laboratories in San Bernardino, Butte and Modoc counties. The 36-count indictment sought forfeiture of more than $2-million in property from Garrett, including three ranches, a house in Shingle Springs, a Rockwell Aero Commander airplane, 43 head of cattle, a cutting horse called Bucky Badger O'Lena, two GMC pickup trucks, a backhoe tractor, a bulldozer and a 10-horse trailer, all bought with drug money.

Garrett supervised five people who manufactured and distributed more than 30 kilograms of speed from 1985 to 1989 at the Gold Valley Ranch near Essex in San Bernardino County, at the Crystal Clear Ranch in Oroville in Butte County and at the Yankee Jim Ranch near Alturas in Modoc County. He used money from the sale of that speed to buy a 77-acre ranch in Ione and the Yankee Jim Ranch.

The only benefit of being sentenced to life for Garrett was that prosecutors in Oregon decided not to pursue one of the state's longest-standing murder cases against him. Garrett and Robert (Bugeyed Bob) McClure were accused of murder in March 1991 in the execution of Margo Compton, her twin daughters and Gary Selsar on August 7, 1977. Garrett was secretary-treasurer of the Hells Angels Oakland chapter in 1977 when Compton testified against him in a San Francisco prostitution case.

Brenda Fowler couldn't be gotten rid of and she popped up unexpectedly to inconvenience everyone. Marischen had to deal with her continually, even after she was supposed to be out of Tait's life. She called regularly. Brenda nurtured the notion that Tait would get a lot of money from the case and she would get a share of it. Tait encouraged her with his frequent promises that they would be together when the case ended.

Brenda called Marischen from Colorado a week after the CACUS raids and told him Anchorage Hells Angel Rick Fabel had called and asked her to return to Alaska to help the Angels defend themselves against CACUS charges. She told Fabel she had split with Tait and didn't know where he was. She said she was sorry for what he did to them and she didn't agree with it. Fabel asked Brenda to return to Anchorage to talk to his lawyer and to testify against Tait.

"I can't do that. I'm afraid you're going to kill me."

The next day, Marischen conducted a second raid on Pee Wee Protzman's house. A police officer had noted, but didn't seize, during the November 10 raid a concealed derringer holster. Marischen found Brenda's name and Colorado phone number on a slip of paper underneath the gun. He realized Brenda had called Rick Fabel after the raid to distance herself from Tait and had given him her phone number. Fabel gave the number to other Hells Angels.

Brenda called Marischen in a panic a few days later. She said she'd got several hang-up phone calls. She saw Sons of Silence, the fifth most-powerful outlaw motorcycle gang in the United States, at the restaurant across from her apartment. Marischen had to assume she told the truth. He called the FBI's Denver Division and asked what they could do to protect her. They sent a unit to the restaurant and arrested one of the bikers on drug charges. The bikers were there coincidentally.

Phil Benson, Rick Fabel's lawyer, called Brenda that week and asked her to return to Alaska to help the Hells Angels. He guaranteed she wouldn't be harmed and offered his personal protection. She said she didn't know anything and did not want to get involved.

Marischen requested money to relocate Brenda immediately. He felt there was enough of a threat against her now the Hells Angels had her phone number. The FBI authorized $12,000 with the caveat that she must keep secret her new location—the bureau would not relocate her again. The FBI moved Brenda to the Warwick Hotel in Denver temporarily in December until the money arrived from Washington. She entertained friends and ran up an $1,800 bill in two weeks.

After Brenda got her FBI money, she briefly travelled to Phoenix to look for a job as a dancer. She bought a Lincoln Continental, a couch, a chair and a loveseat. She returned to Aurora, Colorado, where her mother lived. Then she moved to Denver.

Brenda's aunt in Colorado received a large envelope from the San Francisco private investigation firm run by Paul and Jack Palladino after Christmas 1987; they asked that the 10 pages of legal documents be given to Brenda. In April or May 1988, Brenda's aunt received a phone call from Paul Palladino, who swore bitterly against Tait and said he must talk to Brenda. He dropped his bait in the middle of the rant: he said Tait would probably be paid $750,000 for his work as an informant. He left his San Francisco telephone number.

Palladino then sent the aunt another envelope with

newspaper clippings on the case. She gave the envelope to Brenda. Several weeks later, Palladino told Brenda she could get $300,000 from Tait because as his wife she had rights to half his money. He offered to help her get a divorce later.

Brenda's situation got dirtier by the day. She was busted twice for prostitution in Aurora. She used the name Roxanne Hamilton and had a Colorado driver's license under that name—one of several false licenses. She couldn't keep a lid on her secret: she told police she was a protected witness who worked for the FBI. In September 1988, she called Denver police and had her boyfriend arrested for wrecking her place. It seemed to police she staged the incident. Brenda's life was in turmoil. She was on coke and pills. She moved in with Aurora police Sergeant Bruce Smith, who didn't know her background. He found out from the FBI when they looked for her to testify at trials.

The FBI undermined Marischen's attempts to hide the fact that Brenda Fowler was his informant. Marischen had been informant coordinator of the Anchorage Division since 1982 and knew how to hide someone in paperwork. When Hells Angels lawyers demanded all FBI informant files related to the Hells Angels, bureaucrats handed everything over. All they excised was the definition of a TE, or top echelon informant. Anyone could figure out who the informant was from reading dates and information given by the FBI.

The documents that identified Brenda came from the budgetary side of the bureau. Brenda's case showed how easy it was to unmask an FBI informant. FBI number-crunchers required all expenses be justified and that documents specify who got the money. Brenda's true name was never used, but her self-chosen codename—and stage name—was Honie. Anyone who read the documents and the explanations for making the payments could figure out who she was. One explanation for a payment read: "The source provides the extraordinary opportunity to monitor the activities and corroborate the information given by the TE." Another said that "the source traveled with TE to . . ." The FBI also left in informant identification numbers. Brenda was AN 466-OC; AN meant she was from Anchorage, OC meant she was an organized-crime informant. None of this material was excised from the documents obtained by Hells Angels lawyers. The cumulative reading of the paperwork pointed the finger at Brenda once the reader knew Tait was the top-echelon informant. And after November 10, 1987, that was no longer a secret.

The FBI made other mistakes, and Brenda took advantage of the bureau's and its agents' weaknesses. Brenda took care of Brenda.

McKinley was in his office at the start of the Kenny Owen trial in early 1988 when Brenda, whom he had never met, called in tears. She said the Hells Angels found her and she couldn't get hold of Marischen or Tait. She said the Hells Angels asked about her in bars and one bartender gave her up. "They found me. The Hells Angels are going to kill me."

McKinley did not know she had already received $12,000 from the bureau to relocate. He called a bureau supervisor in Washington and related the story. Then he did something he had never done in 17 years as an FBI agent: he proposed the bureau immediately give her $5,000 to relocate. He said the recommendation was based on his knowledge of the intimate facts of the case and that they were dealing with stone killers with a history of making witnesses disappear.

In an unusual move, the supervisor orally authorized McKinley's proposal. McKinley did not know he was being scammed; he did not check to verify that the Hells Angels had found her; he never followed up to see if she moved; he just took her word and gave her $5,000. McKinley next heard of Brenda Fowler when she testified on behalf of the Hells Angels in the Kentucky trial in the fall of 1988 and in Chico Manganiello's trial.

She testified that Tait had called her girlfriend and asked her to pass on the message there was an emergency, could she please call. Brenda returned the call to the FBI office in Kentucky. Tait told her that, as his wife, if she got a subpoena, she could refuse to testify against him. Tait said he was going to write a book about his life and make a movie in which Molly Ringwald would play Brenda. "A big fat nigger" would play Ed Hubert. Then he asked if she would sign an annulment when the trial was over.

Brenda testified that McKinley paid her $5,000 to keep the Hells Angels from finding her for fear she could testify against Tait and hurt his credibility. In court she lied to save the Hells Angels, but she was poorly briefed by defense lawyers and she lied badly. She told the court that Tait took drugs to Manganiello's house and never bought from him. She faltered when she described the wrong house and gave wrong dates. Brenda disappeared before the prosecution could cross-examine her. Her testimony was so unbelievable that the judge ruled it inadmissible. She returned to Colorado.

On another legal front, the Anchorage Hells Angels won and then lost their discrimination lawsuit against the Crazy Horse Saloon. A 1987 Superior Court ruling against Crazy Horse owner Jeanette Johnson concluded the Death's Head insignia was a constitutionally protected form of free expression that could not be banned from a public place. But, in 1988, the Alaska Supreme Court unanimously disagreed, saying Johnson did not violate the Hells Angels' free-speech rights when she banned their colors from her bar. "The proprietor of a small establishment such as the Crazy Horse may validly refuse to serve anyone for any reason not prohibited by statute." The Crazy Horse banned drunks, prostitutes, pimps, cameras, minors, weapons and club colors to cut down on bar fights that jeopardized its liquor license, not to mention the safety of patrons.

*   *   *

Though preoccupied with legal battles, the Hells Angels continued to party. They liked the Sturgis Run in South Dakota so much they bought 120 acres north of the town as a campground. Oakland Hells Angel Edward J. (Deacon) Proudfoot, who had performed Tait and Brenda's sham marriage at the U.S.A. Run in 1984, bought the plot in 1990 for $100,000. The Hells Angels christened it the Bent Shoe Ranch.

The Angels were so weakened by Operations Roughrider and CACUS they sought ways to entice new blood into the club in January 1991. Charleston, South Carolina, Hells Angel James (Oats) Oldfield wrote to David (OB) Harbridge, editor of the *World B.H.C. (Big House Crew) Newsletter* for incarcerated Hells Angels. He mentioned a letter from Sonny Barger in which the Chief complained the club lost more members than it gained. Mitch from Rochester suggested to Oldfield in another letter that Hells Angels write to thousands of U.S. servicemen in Saudi Arabia to show they had support back home. This would attract to the Hells Angels a new crop of servicemen, not unlike those who founded the club in 1948—footloose and on the lookout for action. Oldfield asked Hells Angels to keep their eyes open for a mailing list with soldiers' names.

Meanwhile, civilization crept up on the gang. New York City Hells Angels decried the gentrification of East 3rd Street as yuppies moved into the neighborhood and renovated in the late 1980s. The Angels got so nasty that police began in late 1990 to strictly enforce laws in the neighborhood where the Hells Angels had reigned all-mighty since 1969. Riot cops stood guard as city workers painted over—while Hells Angels swore at them—the yellow lines of the parking grid the Hells Angels had mapped out in the street in front of their clubhouse. Hells Angels would not allow anyone else to park in their designated parking area, although it was on a public street.

"The lines have been there for many years," said Deputy Inspector Michael Julian. "They symbolize their control over the block. Because of their outrageous behavior and violence, we're taking back the block. They're terrorizing the residents. If somebody's bumper crosses those lines they destroy the car and beat up the operator. There's been gay-bashing, homeless men hit, a black construction worker hit with a hammer and a wrench. The people are afraid to prosecute. We find out when we take people to the hospital for stitches. Well, we're not waiting for that any more."

New York City chapter president Bob Maganza sniveled to the media. "Just because one or two people on the block complain they come down with a cop. It used to be you'd get into an argument with a guy, have a fight and that was the end of it. Now every time you get in a fight with a guy he brings back a cop."

Sonny Barger served his time and now runs Sonny Barger's Oakland Custom Cycle at 4010 Foothill Boulevard, Kenny Owen's old Woodshop. The business is owned by Barger, James (Guinea) Colucci and a man called Steve who financed the operation. Barger gets his third of the profits for lending his name to the business. While the building is legally in Linda Hill Walton's name, she isn't expected to claim it or ask for rent.

The FBI bureaucracy that hounded and haunted Tim McKinley and Ken Marischen during the case kept after them as late as 1993, when Marischen received administrative questions from supervisors in Washington who didn't even work for the bureau during Operation CACUS yet second-guessed decisions taken six to eight years earlier. The rules changed several times after CACUS went overt, and they wrote Marischen to point out he should have followed 1993 procedures in the mid-1980s. They asked for memos that explained why he had not done so.

Trials and appeals generated by Operation CACUS dragged on into 1994. All but one of the agents involved in the case remained on the job.

Ken Marischen retired from the FBI in 1993.

Tim Bobitt was promoted to supervisor in the California Bureau of Narcotic Enforcement and is hard-pressed to find time to fish.

Ted Baltas finally finished the house he left semi-renovated during the CACUS trials. His understanding wife tolerated for months a kitchen sheathed only in plastic and without floorboards.

Tim McKinley has a happy third marriage and continues his zealous pursuit of bad guys.

Karen Sanderson is supervisor at the Western States Information Network. Her husband, Bill, succumbed to cancer, leaving her to raise two talented and well-mannered children. She re-married in 1995.

Steve Graham is a Marin County court judge in California, where he exposes his optimism in human nature with tolerant sentences.

Bert Sousa continues to hound bad guys on the ground and from the air for the Sacramento Police Department.

The Hells Angels have been known to write to dictionary companies and ask them to remove the words *Hells Angels* from dictionaries. They sued this author, before the Death's Head and the name Hells Angels were registered in Canada, for the publisher's use of a drawing of the Death's Head on the first-edition cover of the 1987 book *Hells Angels: Taking Care of Business*. The English-language publisher declared bankruptcy to get out of the suit. The French-language publisher in Quebec settled out of court and promised to never again publish a book about the Hells Angels. The publisher said he didn't want to spend money to defend the charge even though it was groundless. The Hells Angels said they wanted to get the book off the shelves. They used legal terrorism to do so.

The Hells Angels sued Marvel Comics for calling a female superhero Hell's Angel. They claimed in the lawsuit to be an "organization of motorcycle enthusiasts" and accused Marvel of "getting a free ride" on the bikers' "powerful evocative" image. In their lawsuit, the Hells Angels accused Marvel of unfair competition and damaging the club's "goodwill" by deceiving the public into thinking the bikers endorsed the comic book. "Through publicity, fact and fiction, the name Hells Angels has acquired very widespread public recognition . . . and evokes strong and immediate reactions whenever it is uttered." The lawsuit added that the comic book Hell's Angel had spawned "public confusion."

The publisher countered: "Marvel's fantasy heroine with super powers doing battle with Satan to save souls could not logically be confused with a violent motorcycle gang that has been recognized as one of the largest illegal drug-manufacturers in the world."

Marvel changed the comic book's title to *Dark Angel*.

Life continued violently for those supposedly left untouched by Operation CACUS.

Linda Hill Walton, who remained a Hells Angel associate after her husband, Sergey, informed on the club and went into the Witness Protection Program in 1980, took up with Hells Angel associate Blair Guthrie, a partner of Kenny Owen. She stunned many people when she married Guthrie, a homely fellow with a big wallet. Linda owned the building at 4010 Foothill Boulevard that Kenny Owen called his Woodshop.

The CACUS raids spooked Guthrie. He thought he was going to get done, so he loaded up his car with a huge amount of cash and ran with Walton. They hid at a Berkeley motel, where the car and money were stolen. Walton fled to Texas in 1988. She feared Guthrie stalked her and planned to kill her. She went to the DEA, which built a case against Guthrie based on Walton's offer to testify against him. The DEA raided Guthrie's house and found weapons and $1-million in a plastic pipe buried under the front lawn. Guthrie went to jail on a weapons conviction.

A man delivered flowers to Walton's Texas house in the summer of 1992. He shot her four times as she opened the door. She will be paralyzed for life. Guthrie got out of prison and became a prospect, then member, of the Hells Angels Oakland chapter.

Blair Guthrie was lucky he didn't get done by Operation CACUS. He and Tait crossed paths a few times but were going in different directions. Tait hung around members and didn't fraternize with associates. Ted Baltas of the Bureau of Alcohol, Tobacco and Firearms would describe Guthrie as the devil in human clothing. He had been shot, stabbed and beaten. If he were a cat, he'd have used up nine and a half lives. Guthrie was shrewd, knew his business and appeared low-key and easygoing until someone got on his bad side. Then he took care of business.

Ted Baltas left the federal building one night and crossed the street to Harrington's to have a beer with a fellow ATF agent. He wasn't in the bar long when Guthrie walked in. Harrington's was a common watering hole for the Hells Angels and law enforcement during the 1979–1981 RICO trials. Guthrie recognized Baltas, sat with him and talked for two hours. He felt the ATF was about to do him.

"We have nothing on you at all right now," Baltas said. "You could pack up all your shit and get out of here and you'd never have another problem in your life. Take your money and go live happily ever after somewhere."

"Where am I going to go?"

"What do you like to do?"

"I like motorcycles." Guthrie was like a little kid. He was flustered. He didn't want to leave Oakland. "I don't want to do that. I like this place."

"Blair, you got lucky."

"I've got 10 machine guns. You're never going to find them."

Baltas used this information when he testified against Guthrie in the DEA case that sent him to jail on weapons charges. But that night at Harrington's, Guthrie got the best of Baltas.

"How's your brother doing back on the East Coast?"

Baltas was caught off guard. Guthrie had checked into his background and located his family. The Angel laughed as Baltas tried to compose himself.

"Hey, you know all about me, there's no reason why I shouldn't know all about you."

Baltas struck back. "How are your twin daughters doing, going to that private Catholic school?"

Ted Baltas called Tait in early May 1995. He said he found six photographs of Tait during a raid on Kenny Owen's 120-acre ranch. Agents found a boxed methamphetamine laboratory covered with Blair Guthrie's fingerprints. They also found stolen cars, forklifts, jet-skis, a buried Browning M2 50-caliber machine gun and an M79 grenade launcher with grenades all soaked in cosmoline and paraffin wax for long-term storage.

Baltas told Tait the photographs belonged to Blair Guthrie, who avoided arrest when Owen's wife, Laufey, was taken into custody.

"I thought Blair was smarter than this," Tait joked. "He shouldn't be trying to play catch me, fuck me."

Tait visited the author in Canada at the end of May and talked about Guthrie's unhealthy interest in Tait's health.

In the early hours of July 4, 1995, police found a burning Ford Bronco beside a highway in Sacramento County. The body behind the wheel was 80 percent burned. There was a bullet hole in the temple and a bullet hole in the abdomen and a bullet exit hole in the neck. The person was shot lying down and his corpse was placed in the truck and torched. What goes round had come round for Blair Guthrie.

Tait, who was once more in Canada in mid-July to visit the author, chuckled when told of Guthrie's death.

"Shit happens when you party naked and do not post a guard," he said.

Oakland chapter vice-president Mark Perry moved to San Francisco where he assumed the same role in that city's Hells Angels chapter. The 37-year-old powerlifter and killer with a four-page criminal record lost control of his motorcycle on Interstate 580 west of the Market Street ramp on Monday, May 22, 1995 and rammed the back of a van. Two cars ran over his corpse.

Oakland Hells Angel James Ezekiel (Jim Jim) Brandes, the club's mad bomber, made it his goal in life to kill Special Agent Ted Baltas of the Bureau of Alcohol, Tobacco and Firearms after Operation CACUS was over. Although he left the gang, Brandes made repeated threats on Baltas's life. He was stopped with bomb manuals and Baltas's home address in his car. Brandes hanged himself in jail in 1995. He left a suicide note that said he would not allow the judge who sentenced him to 10 years in jail the satisfaction of knowing he had served the term.

Anthony Tait has a price on his life and must forever remain security-conscious. The Hells Angels started to track him the day they learned he turned on them. Three Hells Angels put a $675,000 contract on his life. Any one who kills Anthony Tait will be a legend among the Hells Angels. He will also die, because the Hells Angels don't pay.

A Hells Angels lawyer told McKinley the club spent $350,000 for background checks on Tait. McKinley believed the private investigators who did the work screwed the Hells Angels by overbilling for readily available information.

Tait went into the U.S. Marshals Witness Protection Program in the summer of 1989 and signed out in March 1990. He knew the program was designed to help convicted felons who cannot think for themselves. He didn't like being told what to do, especially by marshals who repeatedly exposed his new identity. A banker told Tait he couldn't open an account for him because his social security number—part of the new identity arranged by the marshals—was false. A marshal walked into the bank manager's office and said the number must be legitimate because Tait was a protected witness. Tait took the marshal into the hallway and threatened to beat him to a pulp for exposing his new identity.

"You can trust him. He's a banker," the marshal said.

Defense lawyers had interviewed Tait before the trial. He didn't have to answer, but they had a right to ask questions. Because of threats against his life, the session was held in the Oakland FBI office. An FBI SWAT team stood poised at the other end of the room. The defense lawyers were professional. Then two San Francisco private investigators who have worked for the Hells Angels for decades—Jack and Paul Palladino—sat across the table from Tait. They were hired by Hells Angels defense attorney Tony Serra and were there to interview Tait on behalf of lawyers for Kenny Owen and Werner Sohm. Jack Palladino, dressed in a shiny sharkskin suit, spoke first with a sing-song Italian-mobster accent reminiscent of a B-grade movie.

"Tony . . . we're not here to ask you questions . . . We're here to bring you news . . . from Haines . . . Alaska . . . a little town of 900 people . . . where your momma's living . . . for now. Hahaha."

Tait blanched. He rose two inches in his chair before he regained his composure. Steve Graham cautioned Palladino that he was there to ask questions and if he continued to make threats, he would have to leave. The Palladinos adopted a Mutt and Jeff style of questioning designed to rattle and intimidate Tait rather than elicit answers. One brother asked a question, then the other, with no time for Tait to respond. They threw innuendo and fiction at Tait and even accused him of murdering his younger drug-addict sister, Minto Kathleen, who disappeared in 1982.

"Have you received psychiatric care?"

"Have you abused women?"

"Will you answer questions about being tested for AIDS because of anal intercourse?"

Paul Palladino dug up information for Phil Benson, lawyer for Anchorage Hells Angel Rick Fabel. Benson arranged to visit the Anchorage FBI office to copy documents and photographs to be used in the case against his client. Palladino accompanied him. At one point he turned to Marischen.

"I hope you have Anthony in a safe place."

Marischen was surprised Palladino would make such a threat, however veiled. "Could you repeat what you just said to me?"

The private eye lamely said that witnesses who would testify against Tait feared him.

Hells Angels also tried to intimidate Tait when he testified. They extended their index fingers, cocked their thumbs and pretended to shoot him. Tait stared back and adjusted his shoulder holster.

After Operation Roughrider, Hells Angels had talked on tapped phones about skinning FBI agent Tim McKinley and torturing him to find out about informants. Operation CACUS pushed them over the edge.

Chico Manganiello told a U.S. marshal during his trial: "You tell McKinley he's taken this thing way too personally." Hells Angels etiquette before they kill a cop is to warn him to back off because he's taking things too personally. Manganiello's warning was in the past tense.

An Angel walked up to McKinley when Kenny Owen was convicted and said, "You're dead, motherfucker."

The Hells Angels used private investigators and their contacts in the airline industry to check passenger lists to track and stalk Tait and his handlers. They couldn't find Tait, who traveled under assumed names with heavily armed bodyguards. Marischen traveled under his name once between trials: he flew from San Francisco to an Ontario airport with plans to drive to Los Angeles. His girlfriend waited for him in the airport bar. A contingent of San Bernardino Hells Angels also waited in the bar, and they chatted up the woman. She heard them say they were "waiting for a tall, bald cop to come down

from San Francisco." Marischen's girlfriend was terrified.
She grew tense as the flight's arrival time neared. The
Hells Angels watched to see who would meet Marischen,
but when the plane arrived no bald cop walked off. They
waited a while and then left. Marischen had missed his
flight and booked on a later plane. His girlfriend was still
there when he arrived at another gate.

Tait's former girlfriend, Tina Thrasher, and their
daughter Crystal lived in Coeur d'Alene, Idaho, when
CACUS went overt. She had moved there with her
Fairbanks boyfriend. The Hells Angels had someone in
the phone company pull her mother's phone records to
see where she regularly called. They checked to see
under whose name the most frequently called number
was listed and recognized the man as Thrasher's
boyfriend. Thrasher was away the weekend the Hells
Angels broke into her house. They trashed the place and
mutilated one of Crystal's dolls. Mother and daughter
entered the Witness Protection Program.

"It's typical," Tait said of the mutilated doll. "And
the thing that is so ridiculous is that these people know
me. And they know what would happen if they did
something to my family. My mother, my sisters and
brother, they had nothing to do with this. My daughter
had nothing to do with this. This is me. Just me,
nobody else. If they're going to hurt my family, I know
where every one of those Hells Angels live and I have
the skill level and the expertise to take every single one
of them out. And that is exactly what would happen. I
would hate to be like Henry Lee Lucas, traveling
around the U.S. killing every Hells Angel that I ran
into, but that is exactly what would happen. It would
do society a lot of good. But I'd hate to become like
them."

Hells Angels attacks on Tait took another tack on
July 28, 1989, in a letter to Tim McKinley from John P.
Sutton, partner in the San Francisco patent, trademark
and copyright firm of Limbach, Limbach & Sutton.

We represent Hells Angels Motorcyle Corporation in trademark matters. Our client has valuable trademark rights in the words HELLS ANGELS, DEATH HEAD design, and other trademarks that are protected by federal registrations on the trademarks . . .

The registrations related to membership in the collective licensed by the corporation as well as to certain items of merchandise worn by members of the organization. One of the former members of the organization is Anthony Tait, known to you to be an informant against the members of our client in a variety of criminal investigations.

It is my understanding that Mr. Tait had unlawfully kept many items bearing the registered trademarks which were provided to him solely as a member of a chapter of the corporation. He is no longer a member of any chapter, and indeed acts contrary to the interests of the trademark owner. Accordingly, we seek the return of the items bearing the trademarks which are either in your possession or in the possession of Mr. Tait, your protégé under the Witness Protection Program.

Specifically, we understand that Mr. Tait or you have a vest bearing the Hells Angels patch as registered in U.S. Registration No. 1,301,050. We understand that you have two items of ivory bearing both the front view of the death head and the side view of the death head as shown in Registration Nos. 1,213,647 and 1,243,951. We understand that there is a enameled Frisco death head and a small gold side view death head. We also understand there are four belt buckles bearing the trademark, a ring indicating membership in the Anchorage chapter of the corporation, a knife with the side view death head on it, a banner bearing the "Hells Angels" mark, a rubber stamp with the words "Hells Angels," and two jackets bearing the words "Hells Angels." Finally, we understand that he absconded with approximately 25 to 30 Hells

Angels T-shirts and various "Hells Angels" hats, pictures and posters.

Use of these items is likely to cause confusion, to cause mistake, or to deceive in conjunction with your operation or the activities of Mr. Tait who is no longer a member of the organization. We understand that your organization has Mr. Tait attend law enforcement seminars while wearing the various trademarks of our client. In particular, such a seminar was held in Sacramento on June 7, 1989, at the Radisson Hotel. Such use of the trademarks is a violation of our client's federal rights and we hold you responsible, as the relevant official in the Witness Protection Program, for the infringement of our client's trademarks. We understand that there will be similar law enforcement seminars in Oregon and elsewhere.

We ask that you surrender up the items bearing the trademark to us so that this problem can be resolved. Otherwise, we will seek the assistance of a United States District Court to have these items "delivered up and destroyed" . . .

McKinley, a lawyer, replied on July 31, 1989.

Because of the haste with which Mr. Tait had to assume a hidden identity, much of his personal property is not, and has not been, in his possession or under his control. He does not, for example, know precisely how many T-shirts he may possess bearing a facsimile of a form or insignia generally associated with the Hells Angels Motorcycle Club.

Mr. Tait advised that he acquired all items bearing insignia generally associated with the Hells Angels Motorcycle Club either by purchasing these items with his own funds or with government funds or was given same by individuals purporting to be members of the Hells Angels Motorcycle

Club, and as such, considers these items to be his personal property with the exception of those few items purchased with government funds which he, in turn, gave as gifts to members of the Hells Angels Motorcycle Club, and no longer enjoys an ownership interest in.

Regarding the belt buckles, jackets bearing insignia and so on, Mr. Tait has surrendered ownership interest of those items to the U.S. government as evidence in its continuing criminal trials against members of the Hells Angels Motorcycle Club, and as training aids at the conclusion of the government's inquiries into the criminal activities of members of the Hells Angels Motorcycle Club and criminal use of the organization itself.

Neither Mr. Tait nor the U.S. government intends to use any registered trademark associated with the Hells Angels Motorcycle Club for commercial purposes or gain with the possible exception that Mr. Tait may at some time seek to exercise his rights under the First Amendment of the Constitution to publish in written, filmed or video medium a non-fiction work dealing with the criminal activities of the Hells Angels Motorcycle Club and its members. In such an event, photographic facsimile of insignia generally associated with the Hells Angels Motorcycle Club would logically be employed. No doubt, at such time, your office would be contacted for its feelings . . .

Your assertion that the trademark laws apply to property sold or conveyed by the Hells Angels Motorcycle Club would be akin to the Coca Cola Bottling Company seeking the compelled return of its empty bottles because they bore a facsimile of the Coca Cola trademark. If the Hells Angels Motorcycle Club wishes to assert such a position, then it would appear it should provide each member with club insignia and should have its members execute a contract or written memorandum of understanding that title to the property remains with the Hells Angels Motorcycle Club.

As you may be aware, at the present time, many members of the Hells Angels Motorcycle Club fabricate without license and convey without license, either through sale or gift, many items bearing insignia associated with the Hells Angels Motorcycle Club, including, but not limited to, keyrings, rings, pins, T-shirts, lighters, lighter holders, decals and emblems. Consensually tape recorded conversations of meetings of the West Coast Officers of the Hells Angels Motorcycle Club evidence this problem.

Likewise, many members of the Hells Angels Motorcycle Club engage in a pattern of racketeering and robbery when they kidnap, assault, beat and, in some instances, maim non-members of the Hells Angels Motorcycle Club who have come into possession of a tattoo or article of clothing or item of jewelry bearing a facsimile of an image generally associated with the Hells Angels Motorcycle Club. Consensually tape recorded conversations of meetings of the West Coast Officers of the Hells Angels Motorcycle Club evidence this problem.

Thus, on one hand you have an organization which does not demonstrate due diligence in protecting its trademark interests, while on the other hand frequently engaging in gross criminal misconduct in stealing property of another which bears a facsimile of an image which may or may not be confused with a true trademark of the Hells Angels Motorcycle Club.

Additionally, your assertion . . . that Mr. Tait is presently (or has been since November 10, 1987, when the investigation reached an overt phase) holding himself out to be a member of the Hells Angels Motorcycle Club is not correct. Mr. Tait realized that two of the written by-laws of the Hells Angels (No cops; no snitches) would likely be invoked to end his formal membership in the organization.

The June 7, 1989, conference which you mentioned in your letter was a training and information sharing conference presented by the Western States Information Network for narcotics officers from the five western states. Both Mr. Tait and I spoke at the conference, and I assure you that Mr. Tait did not hold himself out to be a member of the Hells Angels Motorcycle Club. The information discussed at the conference was for law enforcement use only in pursuit of violators of applicable local, state and federal criminal laws.

The fact that the Hells Angels Motorcycle Club became aware of Mr. Tait's presentation at the . . . conference speaks loudly for the efforts of the Hells Angels Motorcycle Club as a criminal organization in avoiding prosecution; the fact that you received an inaccurate recitation of what occurred at that conference speaks, I suppose, about the reporting quality, or lack thereof, of a corrupt law enforcement officer while reporting back to his criminal masters . . .

McKinley wrote to Karen Sanderson at WSIN to alert her about Sutton's letter. He recapped his response to the trademark issue, then discussed the issue of security and law enforcement corruption.

Sutton's letter is simply another example of the many conduits of law enforcement information available to the Hells Angels Motorcycle Club. In the instance raised by Sutton, it is merely amusing as the information reported to the Hells Angels Motorcycle Club was only historical in nature and non-critical. Had such information been more pro-active, i.e., advance information that Tait would be speaking at the Western States Information Network conference, then the impact would have been tragic and resulted in the death of Tait.

This should be viewed as yet another reminder of the need to be diligent in protecting critical information with the application of a need-to-know sharing of information. In regard to the Western States Information Network conference only those persons with a critical need to be aware of Tait's presence at the conference were so advised until Tait spoke at the conference.

Anthony Tait is now an agent for a foreign service. He works from Africa to Afghanistan and enjoys himself thoroughly trying to make the world a better place.

Law enforcement realized too late that the Hells Angels and other outlaw motorcycle gangs are organized-crime syndicates. Then they hit them too softly. There were 1,000 Hells Angels in 67 chapters worldwide when Operation CACUS went overt in 1987. Today there are more than 1,200 members in 85 chapters in 17 countries. British Hells Angels, for example, have evolved from uncouth mopes into international drug barons since Tait first met them in 1985. At that time, their greatest pleasure was derived from urinating on each other. Their main source of income was public welfare, supplemented with the proceeds of the theft of televisions, video equipment and jewelry. Under the tutelage of American and Swiss Hells Angels, they have become underworld businessmen with members who are accountants and lawyers.

British Hells Angels have bought a fleet of merchant ships to transport tons of cocaine bought from the Colombian Cali Cartel. British police have determined the Hells Angels have set up at least 15 Swiss bank accounts worth $13-million. Their worldwide real-estate holdings include a dairy farm, 40 apartment blocks and dozens of businesses.

British police seized two of the Hells Angels unregistered trawlers, which are named after boats that were lost at sea in the early 1980s. They used a mini-sub to recover three tons of jettisoned cocaine that had been packed in drainage pipes on the decks. The Hells Angels sank another trawler that carried two tons of cocaine in 9,000 feet of water.

The British Angels also use advanced technology to store their drugs. A trawler drops a container of drugs attached to an electronic receiver and beacon to the bottom of the ocean. A weight anchors the drugs and instruments to the bottom. A buoy keeps them off the sand. A recovery ship tracks the beacon's signals and electronically triggers a release that snaps the anchor cable. The buoy floats the drugs to the surface where they are recovered.

Most people still get suckered by the Toys for Tots runs and believe outlaw bikers who donate teddy bears to kids must be good guys. Criminals over the centuries have bought public goodwill with magnanimous gestures. Remarkably, the world is still populated with persons loath to think, who accept the fabricated rather than ferret out the truth. The abyss in the mind fosters the abyss of the soul. And there is no shortage of sociopaths to occupy that realm.

Acknowledgments

I thank the individuals who, with the consent of their agencies, answered my questions about the minutiae of Operation CACUS. I am grateful for their time, assistance and trust. Some of these people I have known for years. The others, I hope to know for years to come.

Thanks to Special Agent Timothy McKinley of the Federal Bureau of Investigation for his honesty and candor; to retired FBI Special Agent Kenneth Marischen for his professionalism under adverse conditions; to Special Agent Theodore Baltas of the U.S. Bureau of Alcohol, Tobacco and Firearms for his insights and humor; to Supervisor Tim Bobitt of the California Bureau of Narcotic Enforcement for his openness and wit; to Supervisor Karen Sanderson of the Western States Intelligence Network for her understanding, patience and caring; to Judge Steve Graham for his judicious account of interagency politics.

Special thanks to Bert Sousa, a true gentleman, for his support, encouragement and hospitality.

And thanks to Anthony Tait for the challenge.

Acknowledgments

I was appalled by the ease with which the gang manipulated the justice system and media, tampered with witnesses, perjured themselves with no action taken by the liberal courts even when presented with evidence.

Hells Angels leader Ralph Barger told me, "If we can keep our public-relations campaign, we will soon have someone on every jury."

The gang has repeatedly made threats to kill me, having observed them for years through telephoto lenses, video cameras and rifle scopes. They are out of their league. The world is my jungle.

My heartfelt thanks goes out to the core investigators who, along with me, made sacrifices that were needed to bring the case to conclusion. There were so many people involved in Operation CACUS that I can't thank each one personally. I do thank Judge J.S. Graham for his wisdom and guidance, S.A. Ted Baltas, S.A. Tim McKinley, S.A. Jay Colvin, S.A. Bob Barnes, S.A. Tim Bobitt for all the assistance, backup, support through the rough times and good times and their friendship.

To S.A. Ken Marischen, for being there when I needed him to believe in me and the cause.

-ANTHONY TAIT